Computer graph design:
Robertino Tănase

Literary adviser:
Ahmet Aki (Physics teacher)

Computer make-up:
Carmen Raduna
Robertino Tănase

Translation:
Vanina Şerban
Diana Ceauşu
Mădălina Mitruţ

Original title of the book:

Probleme de Fizică
Pentru liceu
Mecanică

ISBN-13: 978-1502811691
ISBN-10: 1502811693

PHYSICS PROBLEMS WITH SOLUTIONS

For Olympiads and Contests

(MECHANICS)

OCTAVIAN RADU

I dedicate this book to the
memory of my father,
Marin Radu,
and also to those who were
Teacher Liviu Cristian Tăutu
Engineer George Radu

INTRODUCTION

This selection of mechanics problems was mainly prepared for high school students, both for those in the first year and for those who want to study for admission in faculties or for the Physics Olympiad. The selection is also useful for the high school Physics teachers.

I consider that this selection of problems covers a large area which is significant for all students who are willing not only to gain a thorough knowledge in Physics, but also to achieve a high standard of performance in this domain.

This work includes 120 mechanics problems, most of them being highly original. Apart from the author's contribution in highlighting some new aspects in the field of mechanics studied in high school and in introducing them into problems, I must underline that most of the subjects of the problems have a technical background, many of the problems focusing on aspects that students observe (or can observe) in everyday life. The solutions given involve a high degree of accuracy and I must admit that the author finds solutions which are accessible to the majority of students.

This work represents a selection of applications (problems) meant to test and improve the entire knowledge of mechanics acquired by first-year high school students in Romania. That is why this work is very appropriate both for final reviews in class and for the training of students who are preparing for Physics Olympiads.

The author of the book, physicist OCTAVIAN RADU, is one of the most active and talented teachers in Bucharest, his students (among the best in Bucharest, either within high school or within Physics seminars) obtaining remarkable results in National and International Olympiads every year.

The interesting theme, the inspired selection of problems, doubled by the originality of many of the subjects proposed, the accuracy of the solutions given, which are accessible to most students, as well as the pragmatic approach guarantee its well-deserved success in education.

Univ. Prof. Dr. Phys. DAN IORDACHE
Polytechnic University in Bucharest

FOREWORD

OCTAVIAN RADU's selection of physics problems contains 120 mechanics problems followed by their complete solutions. This work offers high school teachers and students a basic material necessary in the process of understanding and going deeply into mechanics.

I consider that this book improves the skill of coping with the difficulties usually encountered when trying to solve physics problems similar to the ones frequently presented in high school textbooks.

This selection is an asset, given the wide variety of problems included, whose similarity in style to the problems proposed within scholar competitions transforms them into an auxiliary material, which successfully comes as a completion to the textbook. In other words, their wide theoretical coverage and applicability in everyday life contribute fundamentally to the thorough understanding of the most complicated chapters in mechanics.

The solutions given to the problems are based on the theory provided in the high school physics curriculum, the explanatory solutions containing both the description of the physical phenomenon, and all the mathematical formulae necessary in order to reach the correct final results.

I am convinced that the way in which this selection of physics problems was elaborated will ensure a major contribution not only in the training of students, but also in the development of their rational thinking in accordance with the requirements of the scientific accuracy. This way, the students interested in the advanced study of physics will find in the present book an enjoyable background to help them successfully approach other chapters of physics, based as well on the principles of mechanics.

Prof. LIVIA DINICA
Physics Method School Inspector for Bucharest

AUTHOR'S WORD FOR THE SECOND EDITION

In the time interval between the two editions I had the possibility to analyze "the impact" of this book on the public-students and teachers interested in Physics. So, I could improve the presentation of the solutions where it was necessary. And I performed these modifications following their presentation to students to be solved. Many of these students got excellent results at the National Physics Olympiads and the International Physics Olympiad.

Among these students I want to remind Marius Cauţun., Alexandru Hening, Sergiu Ungureanu, the winning awards of the International Physics Olympiad and of the International Olympiads held Yakutsya every year. In the present they are students at Bremen University in Germany.

With the present edition, written in English I benefited, with the translation and adapting to the Physics international education requirements, from valuable and extraordinary support, given with a special generosity by my good friend and also colleague, teacher Ahmet Aki from Turkey, who is in the present permanent teacher at The International Computer High School Bucharest-Romania. His experience in the field weighed very much in the making of the decisions concerning the presentation in the English final shape of many ideas enounced in the texts or solutions of the problems.

I also want to remind the logistic support given by the principal of this high school, the teacher Fatih Göktaş, who was by my side me during the whole work..

In the first phase the translation was made by the translator Vanina Şerban and the student Diana Ceauşu; the verification of it was made by the teacher Madalina Mitrut from the Bilingual High School "Decebal".

Also here at this High School where as a matter of fact I work, the teacher Carmen Raduna began the computer writing of the mathematical equations, which was continued and also finalized with the graphics design by the Physics technician Robertino Tănase from the International Computer High School of Bucharest.

Also, former student Bogdan Patraşcoiu was of a great help for me.

I am sincerely thankful towards all the people mentioned.

All these thanks are added to those expressed in the first edition to Univ.Prof.Dr.Phys.Dan Iordache from Polytechnic University in Bucharest, and to the Physics Method School Inspector for Bucharest Livia Dinică for the significant valuations made for this book.

In the end, I want to thank my wife Adriana for the help and the understanding without which this edition may not have existed.

Octavian Radu,
Bucharest, Romania

THEORY

For the best results while solving the problems in this book, you should consider the following theoretical matters:

Dynamics-Newton's Laws

I. First Law

An object at rest remains at rest, and an object in motion continues in motion with constant velocity (that is, constant speed in a straight line), unless it experiences a net external force.

II. Second Law

$\vec{F} = m \cdot \vec{a}$

F = force	(N)
m = mass	(Kg)
a = acceleration	(m/s^2)

III. Third Law

If a body exerts on another body a force called action, the latter exerts on the former a force which is equal in magnitude but opposite in direction, called reaction.

The principle of superposition of forces

If several forces act simultaneously on a particle, each force produces its own acceleration, regardless of the presence of the other forces; the resultant acceleration is the vector sum of the individual accelerations.

Force of friction

Laws of friction

- The force of friction between two bodies during sliding does not depend on the surface area of contact between two bodies.
- The force of friction during sliding is proportional to the normal pressing force acting on the contact surface. $F_f = \mu N$, where F_f = force of friction, μ = coefficient of friction, N = normal pressing force.

NOTE: the statement above is valid only for the motion of a body that is in contact with another body.

In the stationary situation ($\vartheta = 0$), the magnitude of the force of friction is equal to the projection of the resultant of the external forces along the contact plane, being situated in opposite direction.

Uniform rectilinear motion

Motion law:

$$x = x_o + \vartheta\,(t - t_o) \qquad (\vec{\vartheta} = const.)$$

x = final position
x_o = initial position
ϑ = velocity
t = final time
t_o = initial time

One-dimensional motion with constant acceleration

$$(\vec{a} = \frac{\vec{F}}{m} = const.)$$

Velocity as a function of time

$\vartheta = \vartheta_0 + a\,(t - t_o)$
ϑ = final velocity
ϑ_0 = initial velocity
a = acceleration
t = final time
t_o = initial time

Displacement as a function of time

$$x = x_o + \vartheta_0\,(t - t_o) + \frac{a}{2}\,(t - t_o)^2$$

Velocity as a function of displacement

$$\vartheta^2 = \vartheta_0^2 + 2a(x - x_0)$$

Motion of a body under the influence of gravity

Considering that motion takes place vertically upwards, we can rewrite the laws above, considering that $a = -g$.

Therefore

$$\vartheta = \vartheta_0 - g\,(t - t_o)$$

$$y = y_o + \vartheta_0\,(t - t_o) - \frac{g}{2}\,(t - t_o)^2$$

$$\vartheta^2 = \vartheta_0^2 + 2g(y - y_0)$$

By imposing the condition to stop ($\vartheta = 0$) at the maximum height ($y = y_{max}$), we obtain

$t = t_r = \dfrac{\vartheta_0}{g}$ = time necessary to rise to the maximum height

and $y_{max} = h_{max} = \dfrac{\vartheta_o^2}{2g}$

and the descending time is given by the expressions

$t_d = \sqrt{\dfrac{2h}{g}}$ or $t_d = \sqrt{\dfrac{2\vartheta_0^2}{2g \cdot g}}$, that is to say $t_d = \dfrac{\vartheta_0}{g}$, hence $t_d = t_r$

The total time $t_t = t_r + t_d = 2\,t_r = 2\,t_d = 2\,\dfrac{\vartheta_0}{g}$.

In case of projectile motion (the initial velocity makes an angle $\alpha > 0$ with the horizontal), we can express various physical quantities that characterize this phenomenon depending on the initial velocity ϑ_0, the gravitational acceleration g, and the angle α.

If we analyze the figure below, we can write

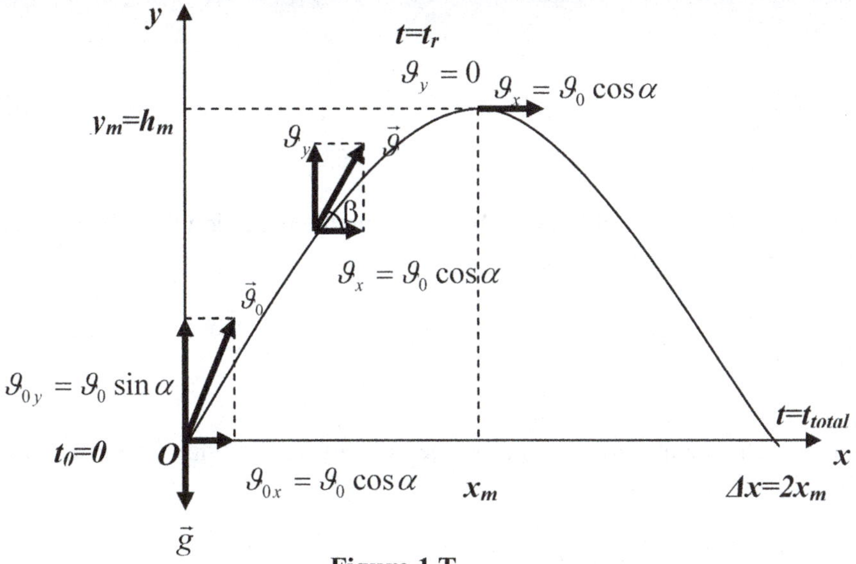

Figure 1.T

$$Ox: \begin{cases} \vartheta_x = \vartheta_{0x} = \vartheta_0 \cos\alpha \\ x = \vartheta_0 \cos\alpha \cdot t \end{cases} \qquad Oy: \begin{cases} \vartheta_y = \vartheta_0 \sin\alpha - g \cdot t \\ y = \vartheta_0 \sin\alpha t - \frac{g}{2} \cdot t^2 \end{cases}$$

By eliminating time from the equation of x and by substituting it into y, we obtain

$y = x\, tg\, \alpha - \frac{1}{2} \cdot \frac{g}{\vartheta_0^2 \cos^2 \alpha_0} \cdot x^2$, which gives the equation of the trajectory.

By imposing the condition to stop in the vertical ($\vartheta_y = 0$), we obtain the rising time as $t_c = \frac{\vartheta_0 \sin\alpha}{g}$, and the maximum height becomes $y_m = h = \frac{\vartheta_0^2 \sin^2 \alpha}{2g}$.

We can also find out that the displacement covered horizontally during the flight

$\Delta x = \vartheta_x \cdot t_{flight} = 2\ \vartheta_0 \cos\alpha \cdot t_c = 2\ \frac{\vartheta_0^2}{g} \sin\alpha \cos\alpha$

then

$$\Delta x = \frac{\vartheta_0^2}{g} \sin 2\alpha .$$

We can find the maximum range by imposing the condition that sin2α = max, that is $sin 2\alpha = 1$ where $\alpha = 45^o$.

Therefore $\Delta x_m = \frac{\vartheta_0^2}{g}$.

The angle made at a given time by the velocity vector with the horizontal is given by the expression:

$$tg\beta = \frac{\vartheta_y}{\vartheta_x} = \frac{\vartheta_0 \sin\alpha - g \cdot t}{\vartheta_0 \cos\alpha} \text{ then } tg\beta = tg\alpha - \frac{g}{\vartheta_0 \cos\alpha} \cdot t$$

Uniform circular motion

$$|\vec{\vartheta}| = \text{Constant}$$

Characteristic expressions:

$s_f = s_o + \vartheta\ (t - t_o)$

where s_f = final position

s_o = initial position

ϑ =tangential speed

$\omega = \frac{\Delta\theta}{\Delta t}$, ω=angular speed$(\frac{rad}{s})$

$\Delta\theta$ = the angle swept out

by vector $\vec{R}$.(*rad)*

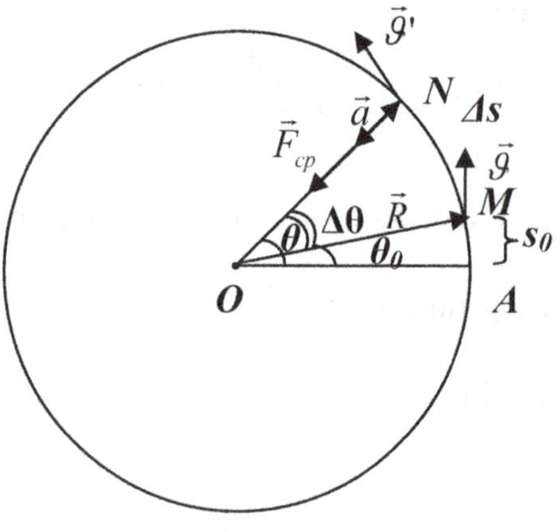

Figure 2.T

$\vartheta = \omega \cdot R$

$\omega = \frac{2\pi}{T}$, where T is the period and represents the time necessary for a complete rotation. *(second, s)*

$\nu = \frac{1}{T}$, where ν is the frequency and represents the number of rotations performed per unit time. ($\frac{1}{s} = s^{-1}$)

The centripetal acceleration is given by one of the following expressions:

$$a_{cp} = \frac{\vartheta^2}{R};\ a_{cp} = \omega \cdot \vartheta;\ a_{cp} = \omega^2 \cdot R;\ a_{cp} = 4\pi^2 \cdot \frac{R}{T^2}$$

The centripetal force is the force that keeps a body on circular path, thus

$$\vec{F}_{cp} = m \cdot \vec{a}_{cp} \qquad \vec{F}_{cp} = m \cdot \omega^2 \cdot \vec{r}$$

The force is directed towards the center of the circle.

The centrifugal force is taken from the system of the body that moves (non-inertial system) and is equal in the magnitude and opposite in direction to centripetal force.

The deformation of solids

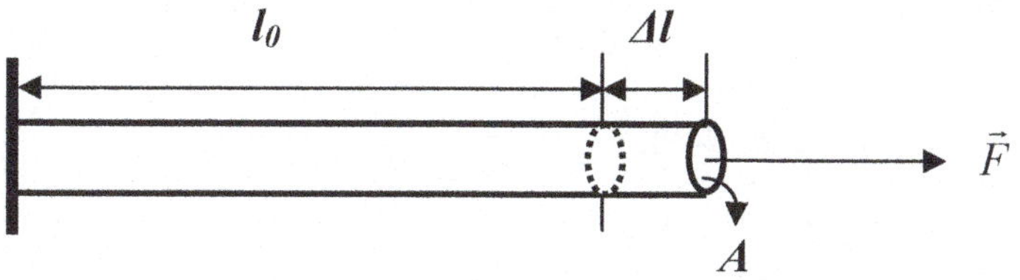

Figure 3.T

$$\frac{F}{A} = E \cdot \frac{\Delta l}{l_0}$$

F = deforming force (N)
A = cross-sectional area (m^2)
E = Young's modulus ($\frac{N}{m^2}$)
Δl = linear deformation (m)
l_0 = initial length before deformation (m)

Notations:

$$\sigma = \frac{F}{A} = \text{tensile stress } (\frac{N}{m^2})$$

$$\varepsilon = \frac{\Delta l}{l_0} = \text{tensile strain}$$

The elastic force is the reaction force of the elastic body to external actions.

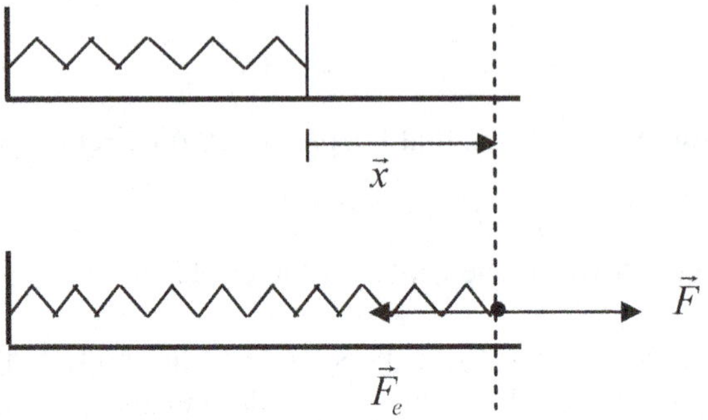

Figure 4.T

$$\vec{F}_e + \vec{F} = 0$$

$$\vec{F} = k\vec{x}$$

$$\vec{F}_e = -k\vec{x}$$ <u>*Hooke's Law*</u>

k = spring constant $(\frac{N}{m})$

Since $F = \frac{AE\Delta l}{l_0}$, we deduce that: $k = \frac{AE}{l_0}$

Oscillatory motion

This is the motion of a body or material system that repeats at equal time intervals and takes place symmetrically with respect to a point called equilibrium position. A restoring force always acts on the body toward this position.

Characteristic physical quantities:

The period of the oscillatory motion T is the time necessary to perform a complete oscillation.

The frequency ν of motion is the number of oscillations performed per unit time.

$$\nu = \frac{1}{T}$$

We deduce that $\nu T = 1$.

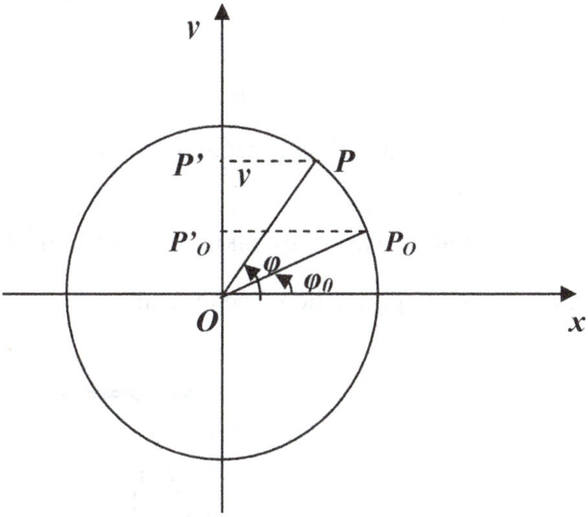

Figure 5.T

The equation of motion (y) is the displacement of the oscillator relative to the equilibrium position.
The amplitude A is the maximum displacement which the oscillator can have during oscillation.

An object can perform a harmonic motion if it moves under the action of a force of the following form: $F = - ky$.

The time-dependence of displacement is

$$y = A \sin (\omega t + \varphi_0) \qquad (\omega t + \varphi_0 = \varphi)$$

where ω is the angular frequency of the oscillatory motion

t = corresponding time moment

φ_0 = initial phase of motion

φ = (total) phase of motion

velocity in simple harmonic motion is

$$\vartheta = \omega A \cos(\omega t + \varphi_0)$$

And the acceleration has the following expression:

$a = -\omega^2 A\, sin(\omega t+ \varphi_o)$ or

$a = - \omega^2 \cdot y$

Since $F = m \cdot a$ and $F = - ky$, we deduce that $k= m \cdot \omega^2$.

Then from $\omega = \frac{2\pi}{T}$, we obtain the period of the simple harmonic motion of mass-spring system as

$$T = 2\pi\sqrt{\frac{m}{k}}.$$

In the case of the gravitational pendulum, the force restoring to the equilibrium position is

$F = - mg\sin\theta = -mg\frac{x}{l}$, by taking into account that $a = - \omega^2 \cdot x$, we deduce the period of the gravitational pendulum as

$$T = 2\pi\sqrt{\frac{l}{g}}.$$

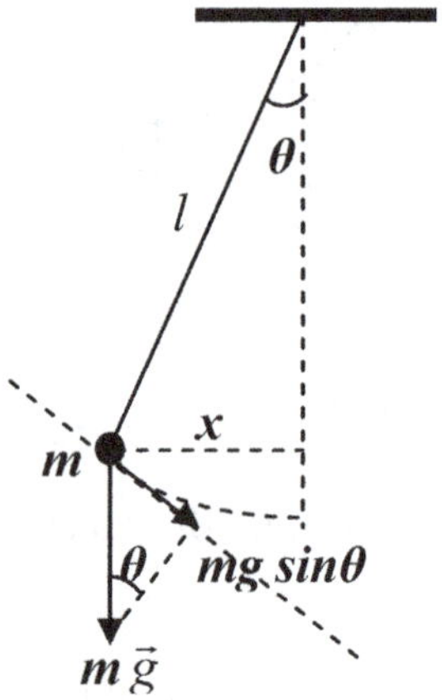

Figure 6.T

Law of universal attraction

The force between two particles with masses m_1 and m_2 separated by a distance r, is a force of attraction, acting along the line that connects the particles and has the following expression:

$$F = G\frac{m_1 \cdot m_2}{r^2}$$

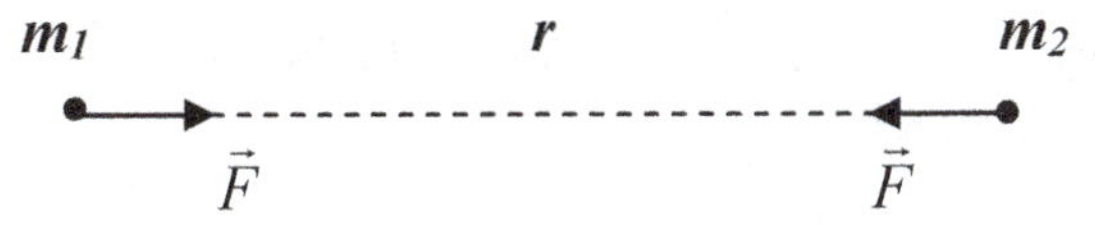

Figure 7.T

where G is the constant of universal gravitation and has the value $G = 6.673 \cdot 10^{-11}\ \mathrm{Nm^2/kg^2}$.

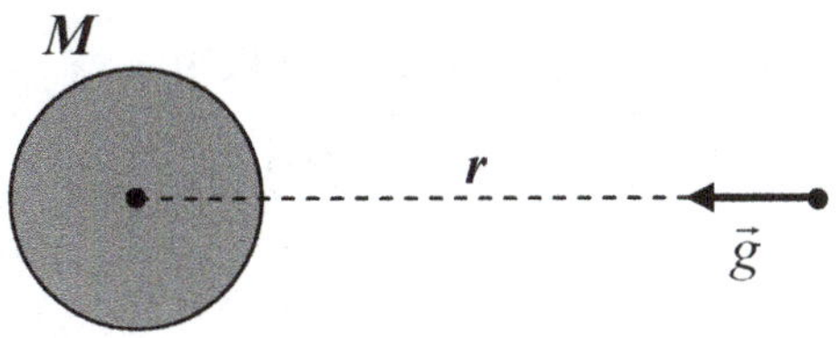

Figure 8.T

The intensity of the gravitational field at a distance r from the center of a body of mass M is

$$g = \frac{GM}{r^2} \quad \left(\frac{m}{s^2}\right)$$

It represents the acceleration imparted to a body (called "test body") that could be situated in the considered point.

Work and Energy

The work done during the motion of a particle in a field is

$$W = \vec{F} \cdot \vec{x} = F \cdot x \cos\alpha$$

(J (Joule) =N · m)

$\vec{F}$ = force

$\vec{x}$ = displacement vector

α = angle between the orientation of the force and that of the motion

The average power, within a time interval Δt is equal to the ratio of the work done to the time necessary to produce this work

$$P = \frac{W}{\Delta t} \qquad (\text{w (watt)} = \frac{J}{s})$$

The kinetic energy of an object in motion is the half of product of its mass and the square of its velocity.

$$KE = \frac{1}{2} \cdot m\ \vartheta^2 \quad \text{(Joule)}$$

The work-kinetic energy theorem is

$W_{net} = \Delta KE$

W_{net} = the net work done by the external forces on the object during motion

ΔKE = change in kinetic energy of the object

The potential energy of an object in a gravitational field is

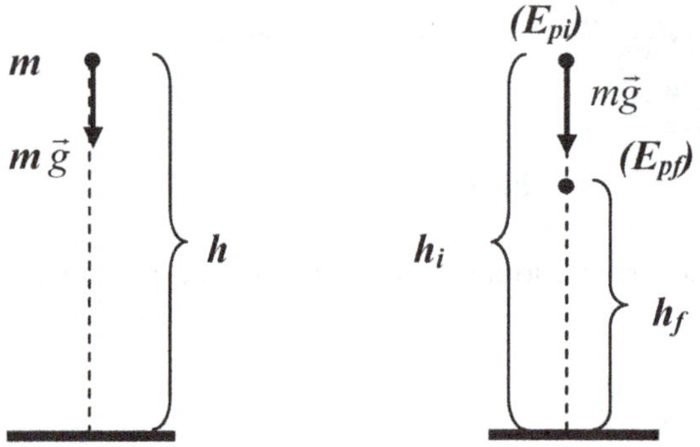

Figure 9.T

$PE = m\,g\,h$ (Joule)

m = mass of the object (kg)

h = height of the object relative to a reference level (meter)

If the body moves under the action of weight, then

$W = -\Delta PE_g$

Spring potential energy

$$PE_e = \frac{k}{2} x^2 \quad \text{(Joule)}$$

PE_e = spring potential energy

k = spring constant

x = displacement from equilibrium position

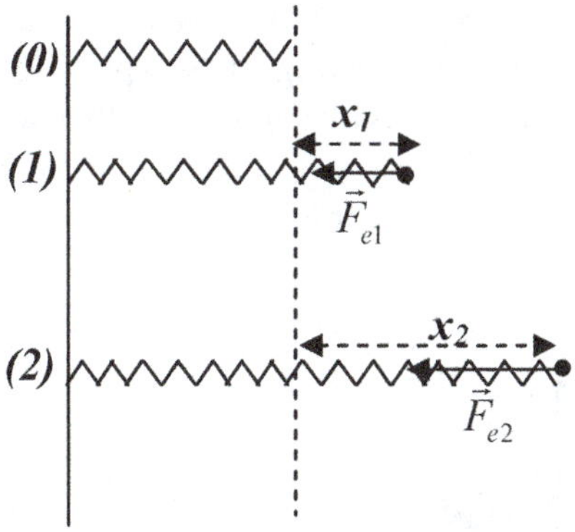

Figure 10.T

The work done by the **spring** force has the following expression:

$$W = -\Delta PE_e = -(\frac{k}{2}x_2^2 - \frac{k}{2}x_1^2)$$

The total (mechanical) energy of an isolated system represents the sum of the kinetic energy and the potential energy.

If the motion of such a system takes place without the action of a non-conservative force, then the total energy is conserved.

$$E_t = KE + PE = const.$$

Momentum and Collisions

$$\vec{p} = m \cdot \vec{\vartheta} \qquad [p] = \text{kg}\,\frac{m}{s} = \text{N} \cdot \text{s}$$

$\vec{p}$ = momentum of the body

m = mass of the body

$\vec{\vartheta}$ = velocity of the body

$\vec{F}\Delta t = \Delta \vec{p}$ - the impulse-momentum theorem

$\vec{I} = \vec{F} \cdot \Delta t$ - impulse of the force

The center of mass of a system consisting of two particles is a point on the segment separating them, which it divides into two other segments, so that

$$\frac{m_1}{d_2} = \frac{m_2}{d_1}$$

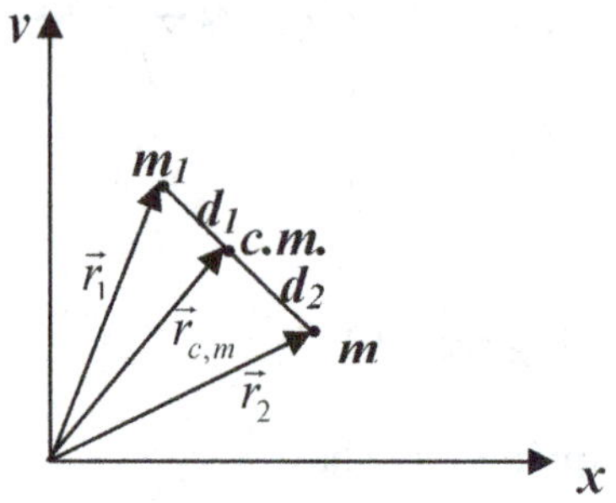

Figure 11.T

The position of the center of mass is given by the following expression:

$$\vec{r}_{cm} = \frac{m_1 \vec{r}_1 + m_2 \vec{r}_2}{m_1 + m_2}$$

and the velocity by the expression

$$\vec{\vartheta}_{cm} = \frac{m_1 \vec{\vartheta}_1 + m_2 \vec{\vartheta}_2}{m_1 + m_2}$$

For the acceleration, we can write

$\vec{a}_{cm} = \frac{\vec{R}}{m_t}$, where $\vec{R}$ is the resultant of the external forces acting on the system, and m_t is total mass in the system.

Also, $\vec{a}_{cm} = \frac{m_1 \vec{a}_1 + m_2 \vec{a}_2}{m_1 + m_2}$

The inelastic collision (one-dimensional) of two bodies

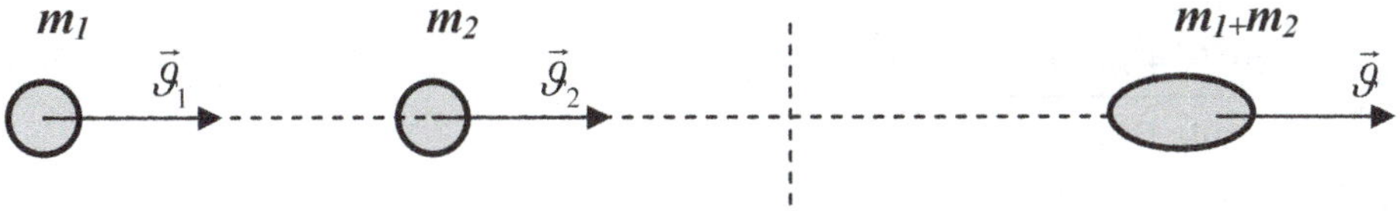

Figure 12.T

Since the momentum of the system is conserved, we can write

$$m_1\, \vartheta_1 + m_1\, \vartheta_2 = (m_1 + v_2)\, \vartheta$$

or

$$\vartheta = \frac{m_1\vartheta_1 + m_2\vartheta_2}{m_1 + m_2}$$

where ϑ is the common velocity of the bodies after collision.

We also witness a loss of kinetic energy, after the impact, which is usually retrieved in the form of heat.

From the conservation of energy: $KE_{1i}+KE_{2i} = KE_f + Q$, we deduce

$$Q = -\Delta KE = \frac{1}{2}\cdot\frac{m_1 m_2}{m_1 + m_2}(\vartheta_1 - \vartheta_2)^2 .$$

In the case of elastic collisions (in which the objects get separated after collision) we witness the conservations of the momentum, and also the kinetic energy.

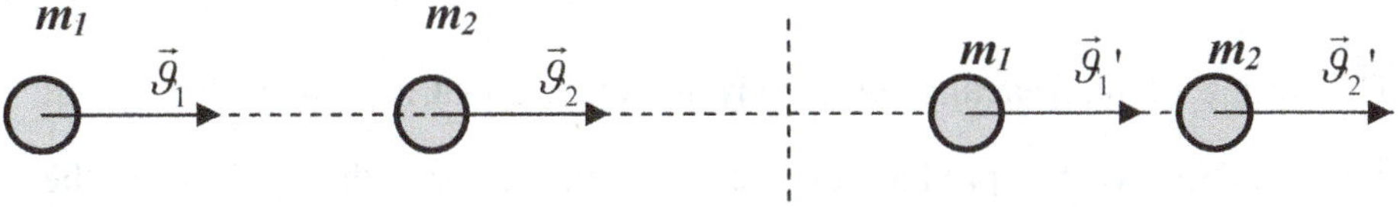

Figure 13.T

From the equations

$$\begin{cases} m_1\vartheta_1 + m_2\vartheta_2 = m_1\vartheta_1' + m_2\vartheta_2' \\ \frac{1}{2}m_1\vartheta_1^2 + \frac{1}{2}m_2\vartheta_2^2 = \frac{1}{2}m_1\vartheta'^2_1 + \frac{1}{2}m_2\vartheta'^2_2 \end{cases}$$

we deduce that

$$\vartheta_1^{'} = 2\frac{m_1\vartheta_1 + m_2\vartheta_2}{m_1 + m_2} - \vartheta_1$$

and

$$\vartheta_2^{'} = 2\frac{m_1\vartheta_1 + m_2\vartheta_2}{m_1 + m_2} - \vartheta_2$$

Particular situations in elastic collisions:

I. The collided body (of mass m_2) is initially stationary ($\vartheta_2 = 0$).

$$\vartheta_1^{'} = \frac{m_1 - m_2}{m_1 + m_2} \cdot \vartheta_1$$

$$\vartheta_2^{'} = 2\frac{m_1}{m_1 + m_2} \cdot \vartheta_1$$

II. Collision with a mobile wall (the mobile wall has the mass $m_2 >> m_1$)

$$\vartheta_1^{'} = 2\vartheta_2 - \vartheta_1$$

$$\vartheta_2^{'} = \vartheta_2$$

If the wall is stationary:

$$\vartheta_2 = 0,$$

$$\vartheta_1' = -\vartheta_1$$

$$\vartheta_2^{'} = 0$$

Torque

The torque of force acting on a body to rotate about a point called "pivot point" is the vector product of the position vector $\vec{r}$ that points in the application point of the force and the force.

$$\vec{\tau} = \vec{r} \times \vec{F} \qquad \tau = r\,F\,\sin\alpha$$

If we change the position of the force $\vec{F}$ on its line of action, its torque does not change with respect to the same point, and if we note b as the smallest position vector, also called the arm of the force, we obtain $\tau = b \cdot F$

$$|\vec{\tau}| = bF = rF\sin\alpha$$

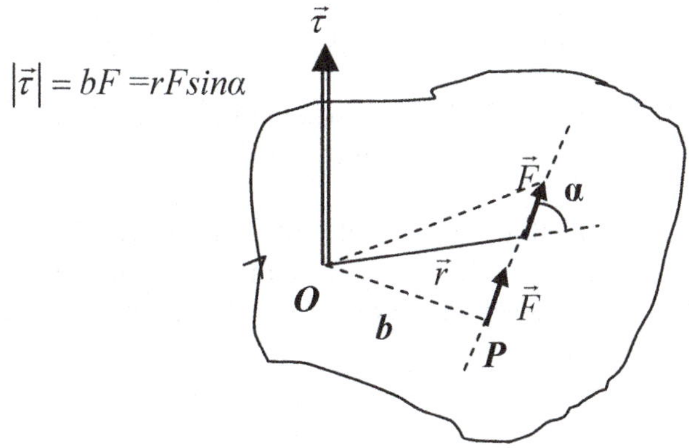

Figure 14.T

The angular momentum of a particle

Similarly to the torque of a force about a pivot point, we can also define the angular momentum of a particle as

$\vec{L} = \vec{r} \times \vec{p} = \vec{r} \times m\vec{\vartheta}$ where $\vec{r}$ is the position vector relative to a given point and $\vec{p}$ is momentum vector

The theorem relating torque to angular momentum:

The torque of a force relative to a pivot point is equal to the change in the angular momentum per unit time, relative to the same pivot point.

$$\vec{\tau} = \vec{r} \times \vec{F} = \frac{\Delta \vec{L}}{\Delta t}$$

The mechanical equilibrium

a) The condition for translational equilibrium

The necessary and sufficient condition for a particle or a rigid body to be in equilibrium is that the resultant of the forces acting on it is zero.

$$\vec{F}_R = \sum_{i=1}^{u} \vec{F}_i = 0$$

b) The condition for rotational equilibrium (only for rigid body)

The rigid body is the body with finite dimensions which, if submitted to external actions, does not change its form or dimensions.

For a system of forces applied to a rigid body to keep it in equilibrium, there is a necessary and sufficient condition that the sum of the components of the forces on two lines perpendicular to each other and the resultant torque of the system relative to a certain point is zero.

$$\vec{\tau}_R = \sum_{i=1}^{u} \vec{\tau}_i = 0$$

The center of weight of a rigid body is the point of application of the weight of the rigid body.
The necessary condition for a rigid body placed in a gravitational field in order not to overturn is that the vertical line passing through the center of weight passes inside the support base.

Fluid mechanics

Fluid statics

The pressure is the ratio of the force, F that acts perpendicularly to a surface with the area A.

$$p = \frac{F}{A} \qquad \left(\text{Pa (Pascal)} = \frac{N}{m^2}\right)$$

The fundamental principle of hydrostatics:

The pressure difference between two points inside a liquid in equilibrium is the ratio of the magnitude of the weight of a column of that liquid to the horizontal base area of the column:

$$p_2 - p_1 = \frac{W}{A} \quad or \quad p_2 - p_1 = \rho g h$$

Pascal's law

The pressure exerted on a certain surface of a stationary liquid is transmitted in all directions, with the same intensity in all the liquid, as well as towards the walls of the containing vessel.

Archimedes' law

An object completely or partially submerged in a stationary fluid is pushed upwards by a vertical force equal to the weight of the fluid displaced by the object. This force is called Archimedes'force (F_A) (This force is also called buoyant force).

Particular situations:

a) When $W>F_A$, the body sinks. Its apparent weight in the fluid is $W_a = W - F_A = mg\left(1-\frac{\rho_f}{\rho_o}\right)$

If released freely, the object descends with an acceleration $a_d = g\,(1-\frac{\rho_f}{\rho_O})$.

When
b) $W = F_A$, the object remains stationary inside the fluid.
If the object is homogenous
$\rho_f = \rho_o$
When
c) $W< F_A$, the resultant force acting on the object is directed upward (toward the surface of fluid). And it is $F_R=F_A-W$.

If released from rest, the body climbs with the following acceleration:

$$a_c = g\,(\frac{\rho_f}{\rho_0}-1)$$

Dynamics of fluids

Flow of mass:

$$Q_m = \frac{\Delta m}{\Delta t} \quad (\frac{kg}{s})$$

Flow of volume:

$$Q_v = \frac{\Delta V}{\Delta t} \quad (\frac{m^3}{s})$$

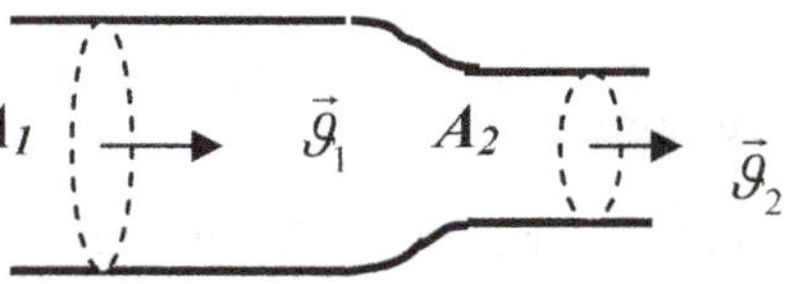

Figure 15.T

The equation of continuity:

$$Q_v = A_1\,\vartheta_1 = A_2\,\vartheta_2 = A \cdot \vartheta = constant$$

Bernoulli's Equation

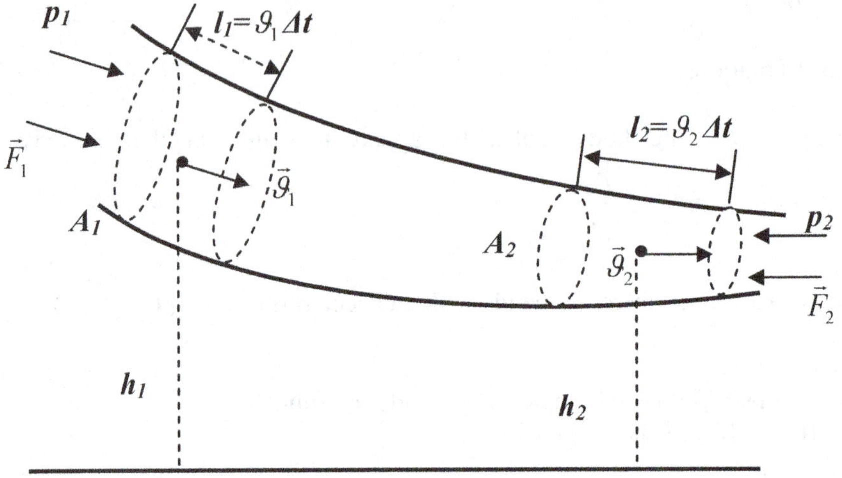

Figure 16.T

For a fluid in motion, its total pressure is expressed by three terms and it is the same wherever it is measured.

Thus:

$$p_1 + \rho g h_1 + \frac{\rho \vartheta_1^2}{2} = p_2 + \rho g h_2 + \frac{\rho \vartheta_2^2}{2}$$

or

$$p + \rho g h + \frac{\rho \vartheta^2}{2} = const \quad \text{(Bernoulli's Equation)}$$

where

p = static pressure

$\frac{1}{2}\rho\vartheta^2$ = kinetic energy per unit volume

$\rho g z$ = potential energy per unit volume

PROBLEMS

1. Calculate the minimum distance necessary for a locomotive of length l to reach the same line again, but having a direction opposite the initial one, if the configuration of the switch yard where the operation is performed looks like the one in Figure 5. The radii, R, of the circular arcs on which the movement takes place are known.

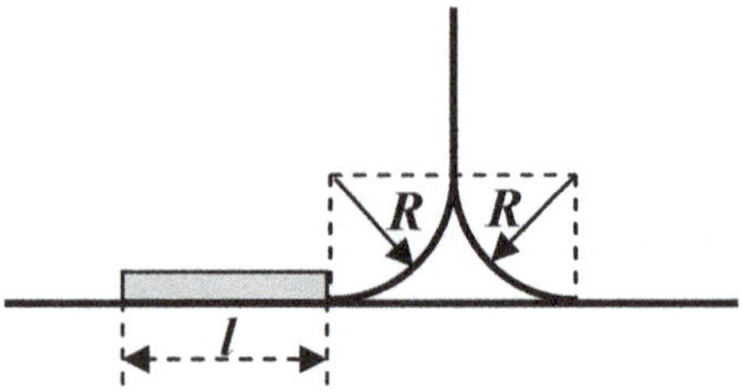

Figure 1

2. A sportsman having the mass m climbs on a cable (of negligible mass) passing over a pulley attached to the ceiling of a sports hall. A body of mass M is suspended from the other end of the cable.

What force must the sportsman exert on the cable to remain still with respect to the ground? What is the acceleration that the body of mass M will have?

The gravitational acceleration g is known.

Numerical application: m=70 kg; M=40 kg; g=10 m/s^2.

3. A force F directed with an angle β above the horizontal, is exerted on a body of mass m in order to put it into motion in the vertical plane.

Knowing the gravitational acceleration g, find the angle α with the horizontal, which is made by the velocity that the body gains just after the force stops acting.

4. Two identical cylinders, each of small radius and mass m, are "wrapped" with an inelastic and perfectly flexible conveyor of negligible mass. The distance between the cylinders is maintained constant by means a light rigid rod. The coefficient of friction between the conveyor and the ground is μ.

A man of mass M standing on the conveyor (see Figure 4) starts moving with a constant acceleration with suitable shoes that do not allow him to slide on the conveyor.

What is the maximum acceleration with which he can move relative to the ground, if he does not slide?

Consider that the interaction between the conveyor and the cylinders is so perfect that it does not let them slide.

The gravitational acceleration g is known.

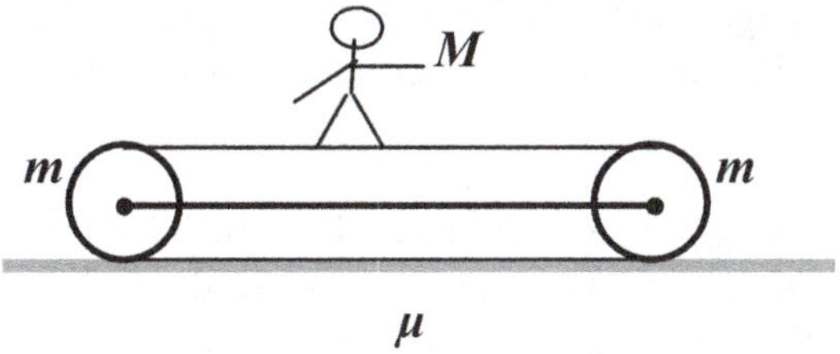

Figure 4

5. When reading the chronometer display, a passenger who is in a subway station notices that the time interval between the last train that has passed and his train is Δt_1 and in the following station this time interval becomes Δt_2 ($\Delta t_2 < \Delta t_1$). The distance between the two subway stations is l.

Knowing that in order to go through the entire line of length L the first train needs a time τ, calculate the average velocity of the second train as well as its average velocity with respect to the first train.

6. Two runners participating in a competition are running on two parallel tracks located at a certain distance one from the other.

The second runner starts running from a point which is symmetrical to a beacon illuminating the sports ground, relative to the first track and he has a distance s as an advance. (Both runners start running at the same time) Knowing that the first of them runs with a constant velocity ϑ_1, find the constant velocity of the other runner considering he will get in the shadow of the first one when the first runner has covered the distance equal to ns.

7. Two particles start moving simultaneously in the same direction and have motions on the same coordinate axis, as follows: the first leaves from the origin of the axis with an initial velocity ϑ_{01} and an acceleration a_1; the other one has an initial velocity ϑ_{02} and an acceleration a_2.

Find the initial coordinate of the second one knowing that the two particles in motion meet when their velocities are equal.

Numerical application: ϑ_{01} =5 m/s ; a_1=2 m/s^2 ; ϑ_{02} =3 m/s ; a_2=3 m/s^2.

8. From the top of a smooth inclined plane of an angle α and a height H, a body is released to slide freely.

At a given moment during sliding, the body meets a breach and makes collision with it and loses the velocity it had acquired and then falls down vertically.

Find the height at which the breach is situated, knowing that the body reaches the ground at the same moment as if it had continued its way on the inclined plane.

9. From the top of a frictionless inclined plane of an angle α and a height h, a body is thrown along the plane towards its bottom. Knowing that the descending time is equal to the time necessary for a body thrown vertically upwards with the same initial velocity as in the first case from the same height h to reach the ground, determine the value of this velocity.

10. A body is thrown from the top of a frictionless inclined plane of an angle α and a height h.

Determine the initial velocity imparted to it, knowing that the time interval during which the motion takes place is identical to the time necessary for a body to fall freely from rest from the same height h.

The gravitational acceleration g is known.

Numerical application: h=2 m; α=30°; g=10 m/s^2.

11. The ice formed on the surface of a lake can be broken by a metallic ball falling freely from rest from a height h.

We throw the same ball from the edge of the lake by imparting it an initial velocity ϑ_0. Determine the maximum distance measured from the launching place to the place where the ball can still break the ice by falling.

Numerical application: $h = 2$ m; $\vartheta_0 = 7$ m/s; g=10 m/s^2.

12. A glass ball released from rest over a horizontal plane is broken if the height from which it is released is greater than h.

The same ball is thrown horizontally from the highest point of a plane inclined at an angle α. Find the minimum initial velocity that must be imparted to it so that the ball is broken when it hits the inclined plane.

Numerical application: h=1.25 m; α=30°; g=10 m/s^2.

13. Two bodies thrown from the ground from the same point, with different angles, and the same initial velocities, fall at the same point.

Calculate how much the distance covered by the bodies in the horizontal is bigger than the difference between their maximum heights. We know that the angle with which the first body makes with the horizontal line at the instant it is thrown, $\alpha < 45°$

14. A body thrown from the ground with an angle α returns to the ground after covering a horizontal distance b. Then this body is thrown with the same velocity and with the same angle α above the horizontal from a tower having a height h_1 and returns to the ground after covering a horizontal distance s.

Calculate the height h_2 from which the body must be thrown from another level of the same tower with the same initial velocity at the angle $\alpha' = -\alpha$ (below the horizontal) so that it will fall on the ground at the same distance s from the tower base.

Numerical application: s=3 m; b=1 m; h_1=3 m.

15. A body fired from the ground covers a horizontal distance b. If it is thrown from the tower having a height $h=b$ with the same velocity and the same angle as in the first case, after it covers a horizontal distance s, it hits the ground.

Find the point where the body might fall in the case it is thrown horizontally, from a height H and with the same initial velocity.

Numerical application: b=2 m; s=3 m; H=4 m.

16. A body is thrown horizontally from a height with a velocity ϑ, and covers a horizontal distance d until it reaches the ground. Afterwards, a balloon in equilibrium in the air is launched from the same point in the direction assigned by the launching point and the ground contact point of the first body.

Find the velocity that must be given to the balloon, knowing that the time interval necessary for each motion is the same.

The air resistance encountered by the two bodies will be neglected. The gravitational acceleration g is known.

Numerical application: d=3 m ; ϑ=2 m/s ; g=10 m/s^2.

17. A body is thrown horizontally with a velocity ϑ from a height. Find out the distance that the body covers horizontally when it vertically covers the kth level difference which is equal to h.

The gravitational acceleration g is known.

18. A ball is launched with a horizontal velocity ϑ from the top of a narrow stairs. The steps of the stairs have identical heights, equal to h. The ball makes a perfectly elastic collision with the horizontal edge of each step. Find the length of the nth step (counted from the top of the stairs).

The gravitational acceleration g is known.

19. Each of the wheels in Figure 19 has four circular orifices, each situated symmetrically at equal distances from the center. Each pair of orifices belonging to the wheels is placed in the same vertical. The wheels rotate with the same constant frequency ν and the distance between them (measured in the vertical) is H.

A ball is released from rest from a height h above the upper wheel and it passes through orifice 1 on the upper wheel. After it covers the distance H between the wheels it passes through orifice 2' on the lower wheel. The ball passes through these orifices of the wheels in the same rotation of the wheels.

Find the height h.

Numerical application: $\nu=1\ s^{-1}$; $H=1$ m; $g=10\frac{m}{s^2}$.

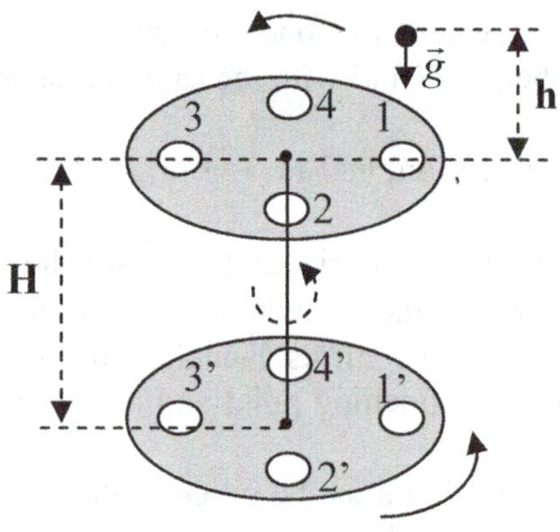

Figure 19

20. The semicircular pipe in Figure 20 is suspended from the ceiling by a spring, a ball having a mass m and a velocity ϑ (with an initial direction vertically upward) is thrown into the pipe. We suppose that this velocity is constant in magnitude during the motion inside the pipe and that the horizontal displacements of the entire system during this process are neglected.

Find the total mass M of the pipe and the strings connected to the spring so that the tension force of it decreases n times at most relative to the previous situation (while the ball is inside the pipe). We know the pipe radius R and the gravitational acceleration g.

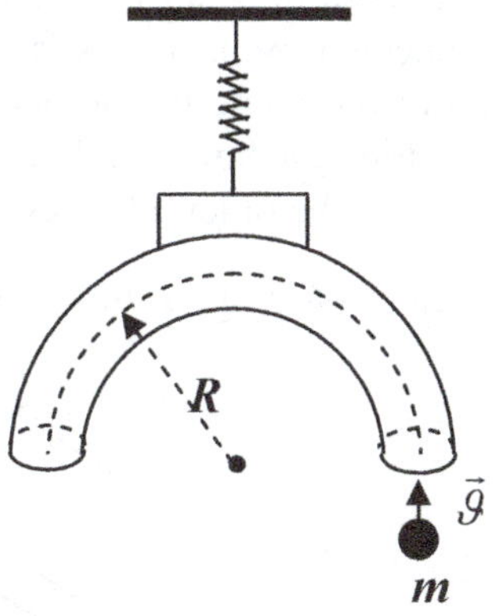

Figure 20

21. A rod of length l and negligible mass whose ends are attached to two identical rectangular parallelepiped bodies slides down from the top of a toboggan having a height H.

The motion takes place without friction and the rod is perpendicular to the direction of motion. In front of the end of the bottom which is horizontal, the toboggan surface is divided into two paths of equal widths. These paths make the angles α_1 and α_2 (where $\alpha_1 = -\alpha_2$) with the horizontal and their lengths are d (see Figure 21).

Calculate the coefficient of friction between the path inclined at the angle $\alpha_2<0$ and the body moving on it so that when the rod is at the end of the toboggan, the bodies at its ends have equal velocities.

What must be the height h of the bottom of the toboggan so that after making only one full rotation in the vertical plane, the rod must have a horizontal position when it reaches the ground?

Its position will be considered as horizontal at the moment it leaves the toboggan.

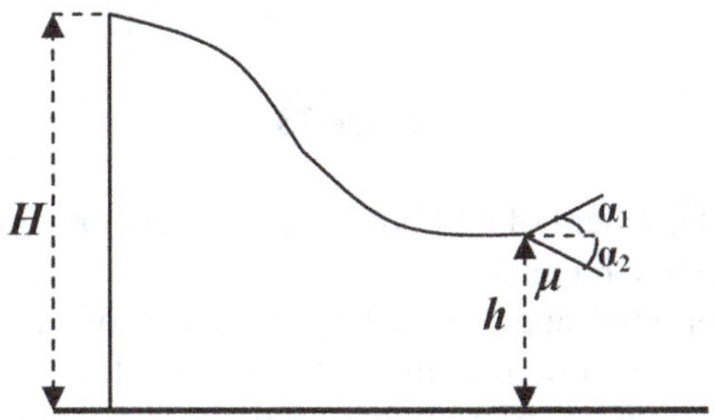

Figure 21

22. Consider the system in Figure 22. The body of mass M leans against wall P placed at the bottom of an inclined plane of an angle α and a length s. This body is connected by an inelastic string passed over an ideal pulley mounted at the top of the plane to another body of mass m placed at the same height as the first. Find the horizontal velocity that must be imparted to the body with mass m so that the other one may detach from the wall.

Numerical application: M=2 kg; α=60°; s=3 m; m=1 kg; $g=10\frac{m}{s^2}$.

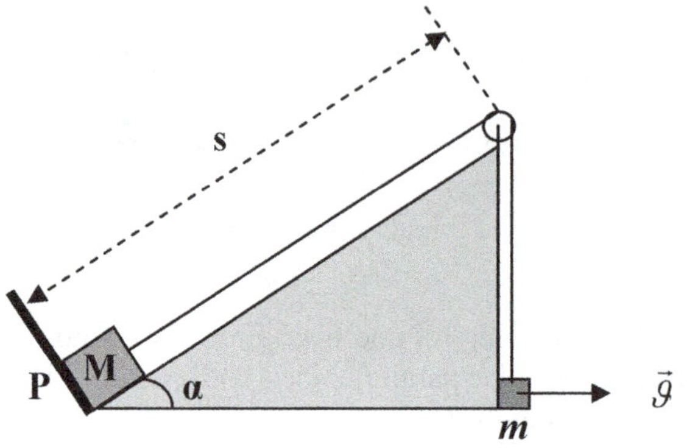

Figure 22

23. Consider the system in Figure 23. If the known values are m_1 and m_2 as the masses of the bodies and the coefficient of friction **μ** between the body of mass m_1 and the horizontal plane, find the interval of values of the mass of the third body so that the system remains still.

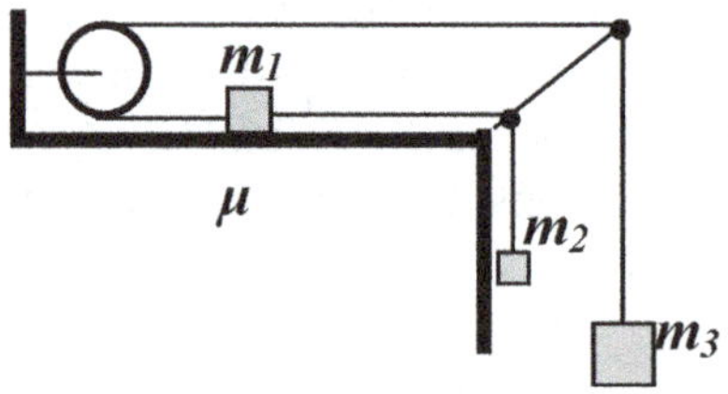

Figure 23

24. In the basement of a building there is a car repair shop where only all-wheel drive cars are repaired.

Find the optimal angle α that the way out of the workshop should make relative to the horizontal, so that the exit is made as quick as possible.

The coefficient of friction between the tires and the asphalt μ is known, and we presume that car engines are very strong and that the climbing is performed without an initial velocity.

25. What is the maximum acceleration with which a stairway can be climbed if it has an inclination α with the horizontal and its steps are horizontal? The coefficient of friction between the shoe sole and the steps is μ.

The gravitational acceleration g is known.

Numerical application: $\alpha = 45^\circ$; $\mu=0.5$; $g=10$ m/s^2.

26. A cyclist trying to climb a hill starts from its bottom and notices that the rear wheel begins to rotate by skidding on the ground as soon as he begins climbing.

Taking a run, he covers a distance s_1 on the horizontal plane with the maximum acceleration and succeeds to climb a fraction f of the entire slope (by pedaling during the entire motion).

Calculate the minimum distance that must be initially covered on the horizontal line in order to climb the entire hill. Consider that the entire weight of the cyclist is concentrated on the back wheel.

27. On a vehicle practice ground, a car must move with a constant velocity to cover a complete circular path during a time interval t.

Knowing the coefficient of friction between the wheels and the asphalt μ, determine the maximum radius of the circular path it can cover.

We presume that the car can reach a very high velocity.

28. The coefficient of friction between the wheels of a car and an inclined road allows the car (an all-wheel drive car with a powerful engine) to climb on the road with a maximum acceleration a_c.

Find the maximum acceleration that the car can have in the case of descending, knowing that the angle made by the road with the horizontal line is α.

The gravitational acceleration g is known.

29. A stuntman intends to use his car in order to perform successive jumps between two ramps of equal heights. The angles made by the ramps with the horizontal are $\alpha_1=\alpha_2=\alpha$, and the distance between them is l (see Figure 29).

The car is an all-wheel-drive and is considered to be very powerful. The coefficient of friction between the wheels and the ground is μ.

Supposing that the ramps are very long, find the minimum time interval necessary to make two successive jumps, measured from the moment the car is started until it is stopped, after the second jump (the time necessary to turn the car round is neglected).

The gravitational acceleration g is known.

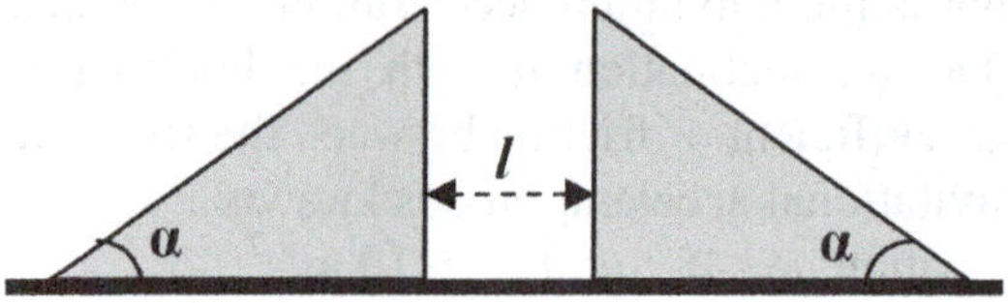

Figure 29

30. A body placed on a horizontal plane is driven by a force which makes an angle α above the horizontal.

Determine the maximum acceleration of the body while moving on the horizontal plane.

The gravitational acceleration g is known.

31. Consider the system in Figure 31. The coefficient of friction between body 1 and the ground is μ. Body 1 is bound with an inelastic string of negligible mass to body 2, which is on a frictionless circular path whose center is on pillar *AB*.

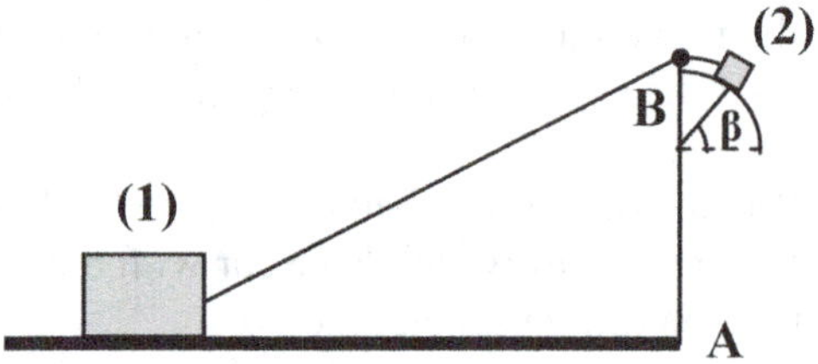

Figure 31

The line joining body 2 and center of circular path makes an angle β above the horizontal. The system was initially blocked.

Calculate the acceleration of body 1 if the system is released from rest.

The masses of the bodies are known, namely m_1 and m_2, as well as the gravitational acceleration g.

Neglect the contact effect of the part of string existing between the pulley and body 2 with the surface on which body 2 is placed.

32. Two relaxed springs with the lengths l_{01} and l_{02} and spring constants k_1 and k_2 respectively are attached to two nails one-to-one on a horizontal plane. In this case the distance between the fixed ends of the springs is l. If the free ends are joined by stretching the springs, find the extension of each spring and the tension in them.

Numerical application: k_1=5 N/m; k_2=8 N/m; l_{01}=2m; l_{02}=3m; l=8m.

33. An elastic cable having a length L has a cross-sectional area A which is square in shape. The cable is cut into n equal parts along its cross-sectional area as shown in Figure 33a. Then these parts are stuck together in a way that forms a rectangular parallelepiped body (Figure 33b).

By applying stresses to the new body thus formed as shown in Figure 33b, find the ratio of the elastic constant characterizing it to the elastic constant of the cable.

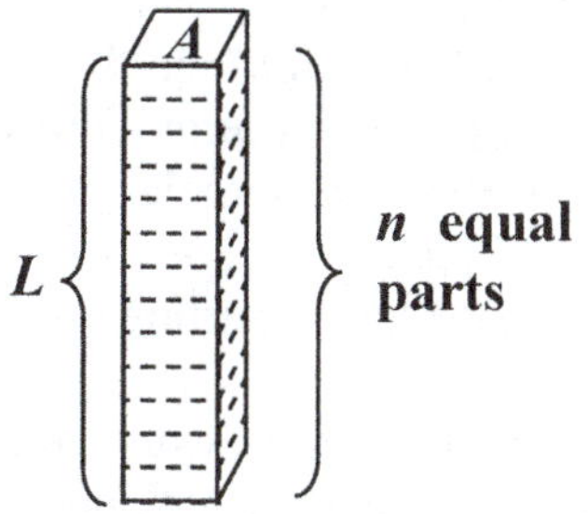

(a)

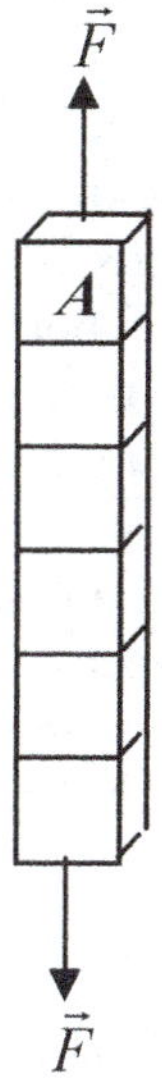

(b)

Figure 33

34. If the body in the previous problem undergoes tension as shown in Figure 34 show that the ratio required does not depend on the number n.

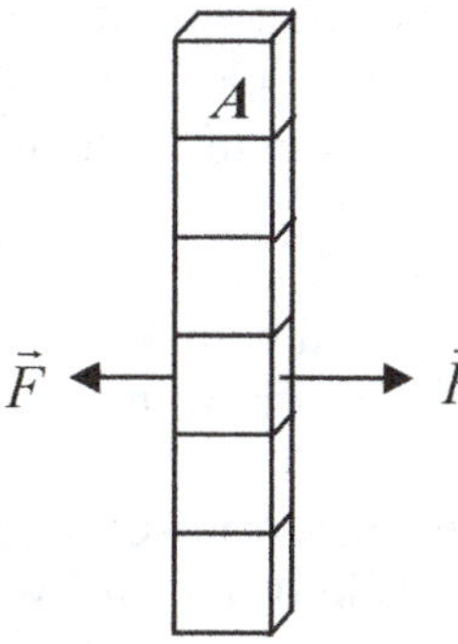

Figure 34

35. An elastic string resists against a breaking tension so that the ratio of this tension to its cross-sectional area is φ.

If the cross-sectional area is diminished n times on a part of the string representing a fraction f of its total length, calculate the relative extension of the string when stretched until breaking. We know Young's elasticity modulus as E.

36. A flexible, inelastic, cylindrical body of length l and cross-sectional area A is made up of a substance of very low density. Its tensile stress is σ.

By making a uniform hole along the axis of the cylinder, we obtain a tube whose wall thickness is a. The tube is filled with a liquid of density ρ, and afterwards its ends are stuck to each other through a certain procedure.

The circular body thus formed is set into circular motion with acceleration around its center in the horizontal plane

Find the frequency of the system when the liquid starts spurting out.

37. On a certain planet, the weight of a body represents the geometric mean of its weight measured at the surfaces of another two planets of known radii R_2 and R_3. Knowing that the density of the first planet represents the geometric mean of the densities of the other two, find its radius.

38. The masses of two celestial bodies are M_1 and M_2, and the density of the second body is ρ_2.

Find the distance between them knowing that the intensity of the gravitational field is cancelled at a point positioned on the surface of the second body.

39. For a storehouse located at a height from the road an inclined platform is built to carry the containers to the storehouse by dragging them.

Calculate the value of the efficiency of this process, knowing that if a container is pushed downwards on the platform and then left free, it continues its motion until it reaches the base with the same initial velocity that had been imparted to it.

40. In what situation is a maximum power needed in order to lift certain materials on an inclined platform with a constant velocity?

41. At the top of an inclined plane of a height h, making an angle α with the horizontal, there is a chain of length l which, if released from rest, descends until it reaches the base of the plane (see Figure 41). When it stops, a fraction f of its length remains on the horizontal plane which continues the inclined one.

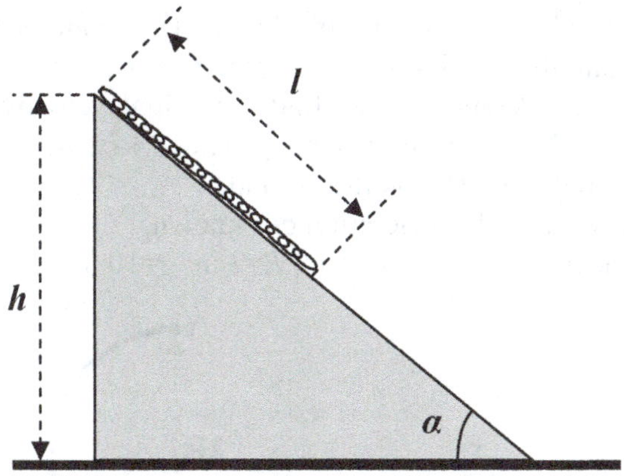

Figure 41

Knowing the coefficient of friction between the chain and the inclined plane μ_1 and the coefficient of friction between the chain and the horizontal plane μ_2, determine the height h of the inclined plane.

42. Next to the fence in the back of a yard of length S=10m there is a stake to which a dog is tied down with an elastic string. The length of the string in unstretched state is l_0=4m.

The dog can go at a distance l=5m far from the stake, afterwards it can remain in stationary position.

Supposing that the dog is very strong, find out if one can enter the yard.

43. A very strong dog is tied down to its cage with an elastic string whose length in unstretched state is l_0=4m. The cage is not fixed on the ground and the dog can go at a distance l=5m far from it, afterwards it can remain in stationary position.

Supposing that the coefficients of friction of cage-ground and dog-ground are the same, find the minimum ratio of their masses, so that the dog can never move the cage. The cage is in the back of a yard and the dog cannot move in more than one direction.

44. A locomotive of mass m with an initial velocity ϑ can stop in a minimum time interval Δt after its wheels are blocked.

If it moves uniformly with the magnitude of velocity ϑ on a curved path of radius R, find the power that the locomotive has to get from the engine.

It is assumed that the rails are situated in the same horizontal plane. The gravitational acceleration g is known.

45. Consider the system in Figure 45. From point C a body is launched horizontally, and it does not experience frictional force on plane CB. Knowing that $AB=2R$ and $CB=L$, find the initial velocity with which the body was launched, so that after leaving path BA (which is semicircular) it returns to the initial point (C) on the ground.

The gravitational acceleration g is known.

Numerical application: $L=5$ m; $R=2$ m; $g=10$ m/s^2.

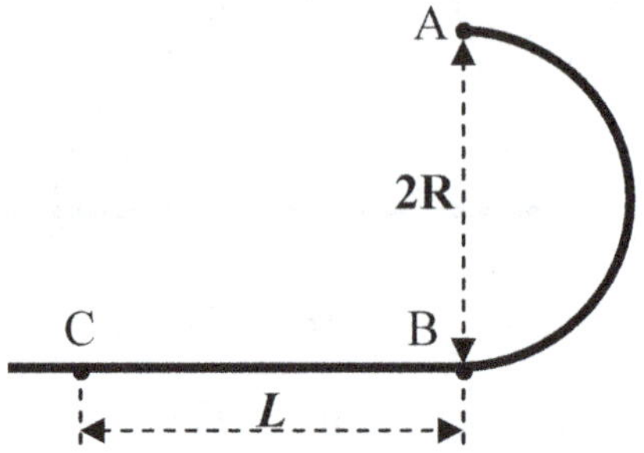

Figure 45

46. A motorcyclist trying to make circular motion with radius R in vertical plane (see Figure 46) manages to maintain his velocity constant until he reaches the height h relative to the horizontal plane where he started his motion; at this point he stops the engine.

Determine the coefficient of friction between the wheels and the road so that a complete revolution can be performed successfully. Consider that the motorcycle is powerful and that the entire weight of the motorcyclist is concentrated on the driving wheel.

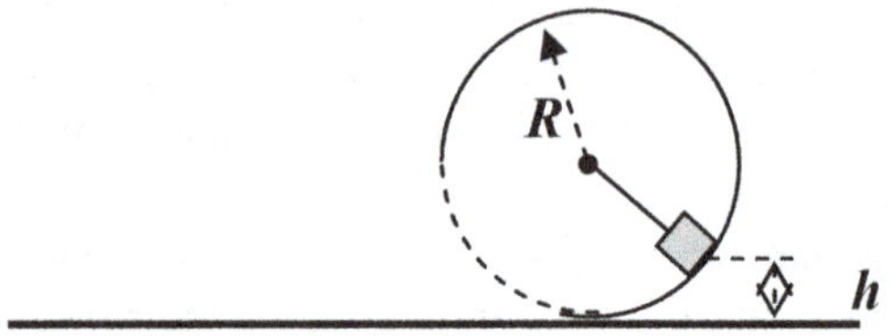

Figure 46

47. Consider a frictionless inclined plane (see Figure 47) of height h and angle α. One end of an elastic string is connected to point B, the other end is passed through an orifice at point D on the plane and connected to a body of mass m initially stationary at point A. This body comes to rest at point C at the bottom of the inclined plane. The line drawn from point B to point D is perpendicular to side AC.

Knowing that the length of the string in unstretched state is equal to the length of segment *BD*, determine its elastic constant. The gravitational acceleration *g* is known.

Numerical application: m=2 kg ; α=30° ; h=2 m ; $g=10\frac{m}{s^2}$.

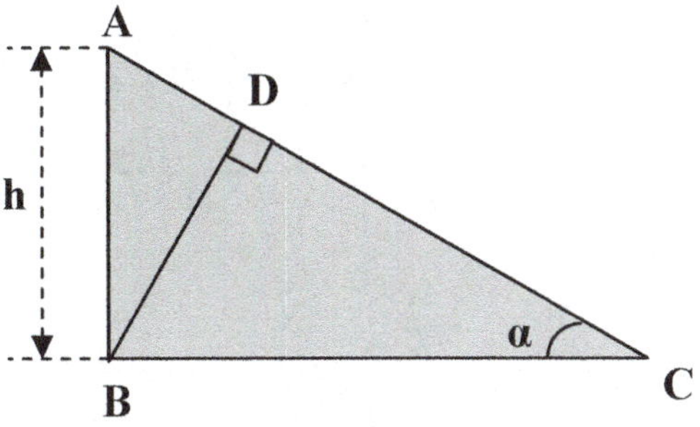

Figure 47

48. Two rods of length *l* and negligible masses are attached to each other by an articulation. The free end of one of the rods is hinged at a fixed point. A body is connected to the free end of the second rod (see Figure 48)

If this system is released from rest, calculate the velocity of the body at the moment when the angle made by the two rods is *α*.

The gravitational acceleration *g* is known. All frictions are neglected.

Numerical application: l=1 m; α=60°; $g=10\frac{m}{s^2}$.

Figure 48

49. The body of mass *M* shown in Figure 49 is placed on a horizontal plane. By means of a spring an inelastic string passing over a frictionless pulley, the body is connected to a pan of negligible mass. A body is released from rest from height h and makes inelastic collision with the pan. Knowing the gravitational acceleration as g, find its minimum mass that can remove the contact of body M with the plane.

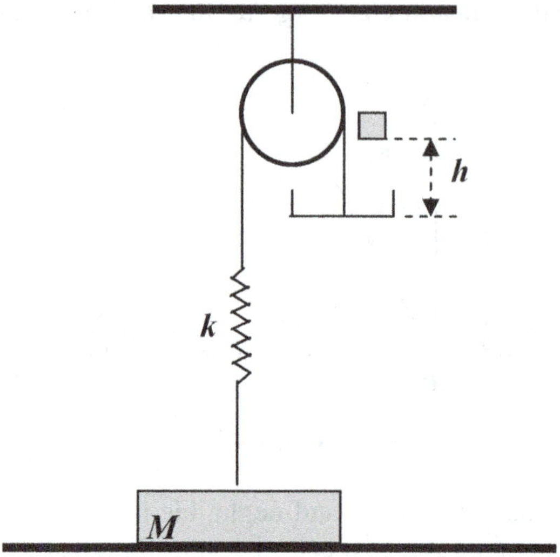

Figure 49

50. Consider the system in Figure 50. We know: the mass m of the body initially placed on the horizontal plane, the mass M of the incline with the angle α, the coefficient of friction μ between the incline and the horizontal plane, the spring constant k of the spring and the distance s between the free end of the spring and the base of the incline. The body of mass m can move everywhere without friction. Determine the initial velocity ϑ_0 that should be imparted to it so that the incline may move on the horizontal plane.

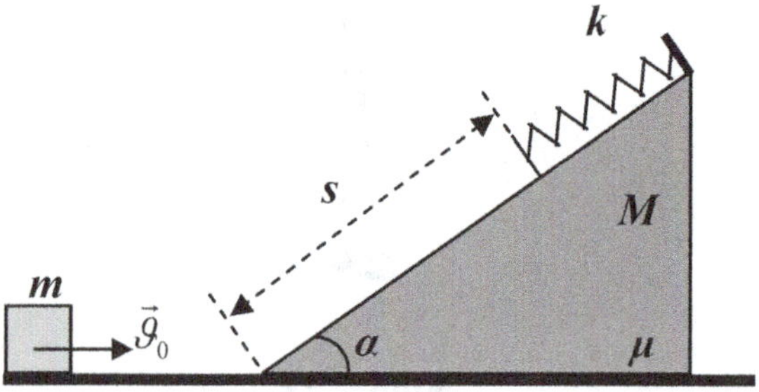

Figure 50

51. A body of unknown mass is attached to a fixed point O by an elastic string having elastic constant k and length r in unstretched state (see

Figure 51). When released to slide down on path AB whose shape is a quarter of circle with a radius equal to the length of the string, the body continues its motion on plane BC. Paths are frictionless.

Find the mass of the body if you know the extension Δl of the string at the moment when the body loses the contact with plane BC.

The gravitational acceleration g is known.

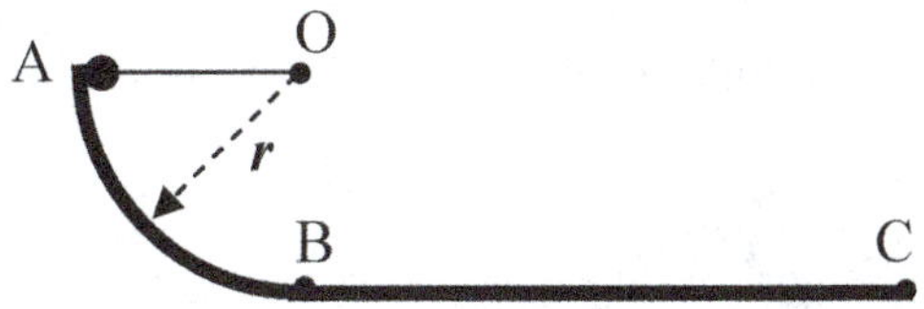

Figure 51

52. Consider the system of bodies in Figure 52, their masses are specified in the figure, as well as the length of the string connecting bodies 2 and 3, which are at rest at the same height.

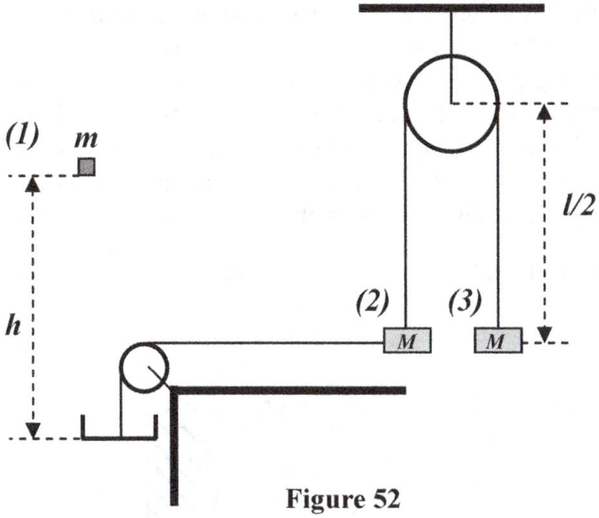

Figure 52

Determine the acceleration of body 3, just after body 1 which is released from rest at a height h makes an inelastic collision with the balance pan. Both strings are considered to be inelastic. The gravitational acceleration g is known (the mass of the balance pan will be neglected)

Numerical application: m=2 kg; M=3 kg; h=5 m; l=4 m; $g=10\frac{m}{s^2}$.

53. One end of a very long cable whose linear density is γ is placed at the bottom of a body having the shape of an inclined plane of angle α and mass M. This body undergoes an inelastic collision with another body of mass m and the velocity ϑ before the collision (see Figure 53).

The coefficient of friction between the body of mass M and the horizontal plane is μ, while the frictions between this body and the cable, as well as between the body of mass m and the plane are neglected.

Determine the length of the cable part on the inclined plane at the moment when the bodies stop (assuming that the body of mass M has such a length that the cable "climbing" on it will not reach its maximum height).

Figure 53

54. The body of mass m shown in Figure 54 can move on two parallel frictionless metallic bars A and B which are on the horizontal. Above it there is another body of mass M so that their inclined surfaces come into contact. The body of mass M is also in contact with wall P.

Knowing that the line $ED=l$, as well as the angle α made by this line with the horizontal plane and neglecting frictions, find the velocities of bodies M and m at the moment when they lose contact (we assume that the vertical motion of body M takes place between bars A and B, and its thickness is smaller than the distance between them).

Numerical application: l=0.5 m; α=60°; $g=10\frac{m}{s^2}$; M=10 kg; m=15 kg.

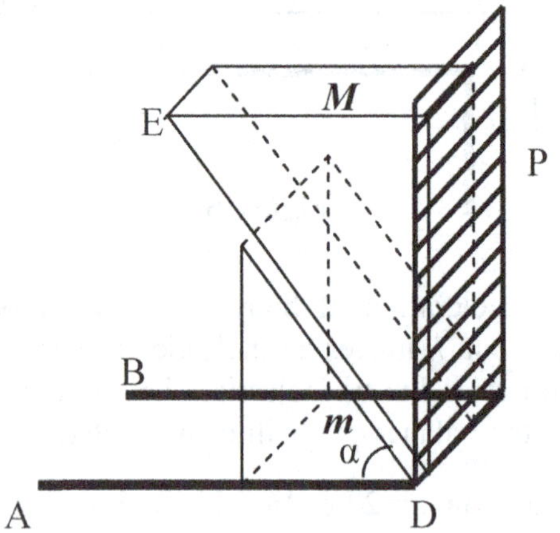

Figure 54

55. One of the ends 1 of a dumbbell (each of them of mass m) leans against the upper end of a circular arc placed as shown in Figure 55.

The other end 2 is placed on a horizontal plane following the circular arc. Then the dumbbell is released from rest.

Determine the minimum force that should be exerted horizontally on end 2, in the opposite direction to the circular arc at the moment when the dumbbell reaches the horizontal position so that it has an accelerated motion.

It is assumed that end 1 that performs the displacement on the concave part of the circular arc has not reached the horizontal plane yet. The motion is frictionless. The gravitational acceleration g is known.

Numerical application: m=2 kg; α=30°; $g=10\frac{m}{s^2}$.

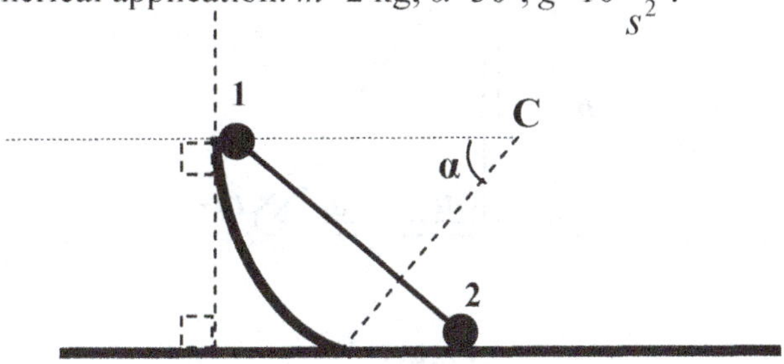

Figure 55

56. Consider the system of bodies in Figure 56. The body of mass M_0 moves with a velocity ϑ, on a frictionless horizontal plane. The bodies of mass m and M are initially attached to the body of mass M_0. When they are released, the body of mass M descends covering the entire height l, and at the moment when the body M_0 stops, it reaches the ground.

Determine the height l.

The gravitational acceleration g is known.

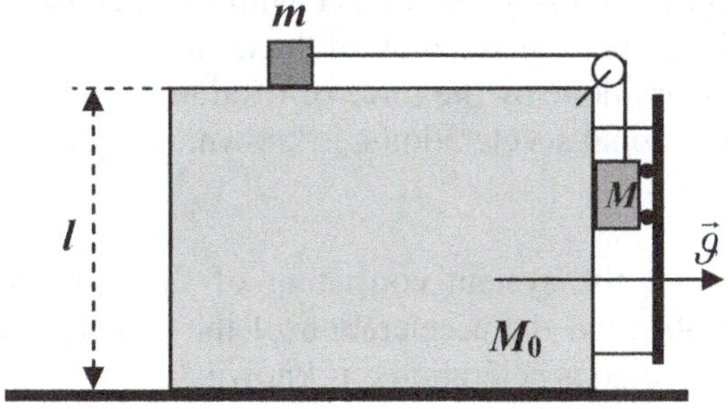

Figure 56

57. Three identical cylinders of mass m each and negligible radii are "wrapped" with an inelastic and perfectly flexible, conveyor of negligible mass (see Figure 57). A point form body of mass M is attached to the conveyor at the highest point (A), and then it is released from rest

Find the maximum velocity of the body relative to the ground.

All interactions are so perfect that they don't let any part of the system slide.

The gravitational acceleration g is known.

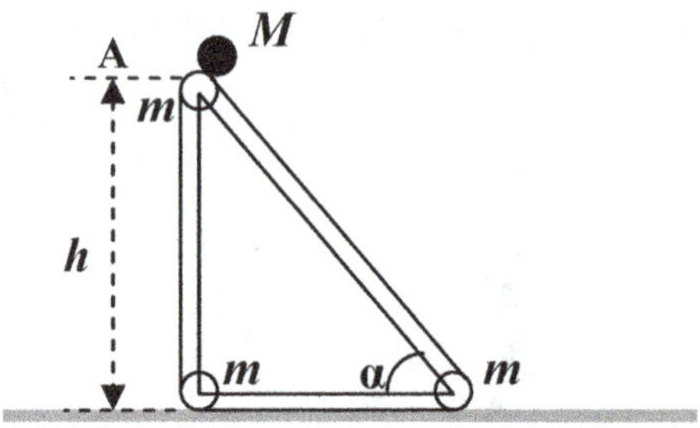

Figure 57

58. An inelastic, flexible, homogenous string of length l is twisted and placed on a horizontal plane of height $h<l$ above the floor. By pulling very slowly one of its ends, it starts descending. During its motion it follows a vertical straight line path.

Within which time interval will the entire string reach the floor?

The gravitational acceleration g is known.

59. A body of mass m that is released to slide from rest at the top of a hemisphere of radius R loses its contact with the hemisphere after having covered a level difference equal to half of the radius.

Find the work done by the force of friction acting on the body during motion. The gravitational acceleration g is known.

60. Consider the system consisting of the pulleys and masses as shown in Figure 60. Find the acceleration of the center of mass of the two bodies. The gravitational acceleration g is known.

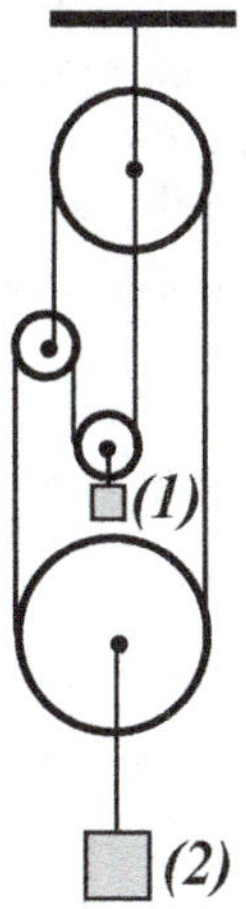

Figure 60

61. Two identical bodies are placed one next to the other on a frictionless horizontal plane and connected by an inelastic string of length l.

A force parallel to the horizontal plane is exerted on one of the bodies in a time interval, t_1, measured from the moment the force begins exerting until the string becomes tight.

Calculate the distance Δx that the bodies cover together, under the action of the same force during the time interval t_2, starting just after the moment when the string becomes tight.

Numerical application: l=1 m; t_1=3 s; t_2=6 s.

62. Two bodies of masses m_1 and m_2 are placed on a frictionless horizontal plane. They are connected by an inextensible string of negligible mass. Initially, the distance between the bodies is smaller than the length of the string (see Figure 62).

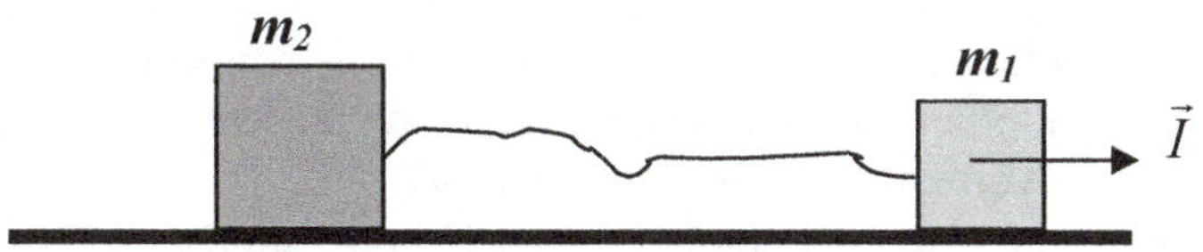

Figure 62

If an impulse I is imparted to the mass m_1 as shown in the figure, determine the heat released after the second body starts to move.

Numerical application: I=4 N s; m_1=1 kg; m_2=2 kg.

63. Imagine a dumbbell on the edge of a table, having an end outside the table. A velocity ϑ is suddenly imparted to the end which is outside the table, vertically downward. (See Figure 63)

Knowing the distance between this end and the edge of the table as a fraction f of the total length of the dumbbell, find the maximum height to which the dumbbell reaches.

The gravitational acceleration g is known.

Numerical application: f=0.1; υ=4 m/s; g=10 m/s^2.

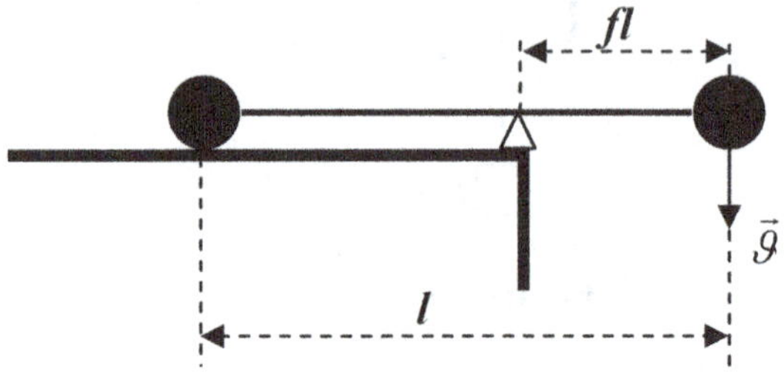

Figure 63

64. Imagine a dumbbell on the edge of a table so that a fraction f of its length is outside the table. A velocity is suddenly imparted to the body placed at the end of this fraction, vertically downward. Just after the dumbbell loses the contact with the table, the table is moved very quickly so that the dumbbell may move freely.

Calculate the maximum ratio of the magnitude of the displacement vector to the length l of the dumbbell, so that it may touch its horizontal surface while falling, regardless of the position at the time it returns to the table. Is it possible for the dumbbell to return to the table in vertical position after only a quarter of rotation?

65. Two identical dumbbells of length l are connected by an axle situated at the midpoint of their lengths and are placed on a frictionless horizontal plane in vertical position (see Figure 65).

A small impulse is imparted to each body at the bottom in the opposite directions so that both dumbbells will rotate vertically and reach the horizontal position.

Determine the velocities of the bodies which are initially at the top, relative to the ones on the plane at the moment when the dumbbells reach the horizontal position.

The gravitational acceleration g is known.

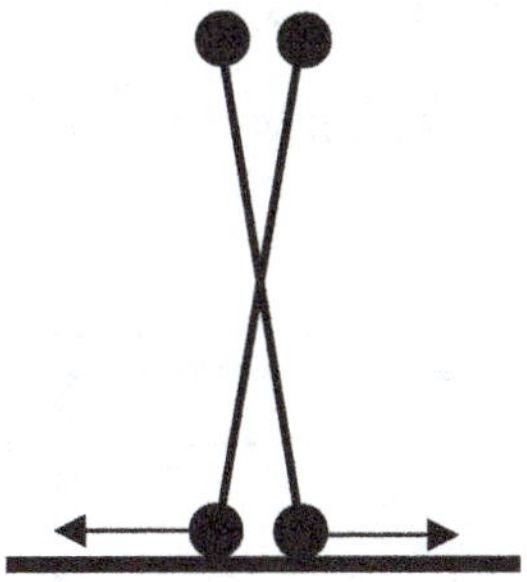

Figure 65

66. In the previous problem, we assume that friction exists between the plane and the bodies of the dumbbells.

Determine the angle made by dumbbells relative to the horizontal in the case the system can start moving by itself. The coefficient of friction μ is known.

67. A homogenous rod leans on a frictionless horizontal plane making the angle α with the horizontal (see Figure 67). If released from rest it will fall and its end which is in contact with the plane at the beginning will move along the plane until the other end reaches the plane.

Determine the ratio of the length of the rod to the distance covered by the end on the plane at the beginning. .

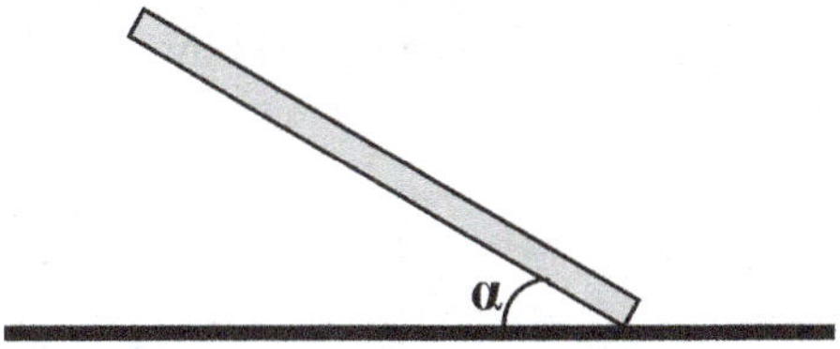

Figure 67

68. Two identical balls are connected by an inextensible string of length l and of negligible mass, passed over a pulley placed at the edge of a table (see Figure 68).

When the system is released, ball 2 begins to move vertically downwards. Considering the interaction between ball 1 and the pulley (P) as insignificant, determine the velocities ϑ_1 and ϑ_2 of the balls as soon as the ball 1 has left the table. All frictions are neglected.

The gravitational acceleration g is known.

Numerical application: l=0.7 m; $g=10\frac{m}{s^2}$.

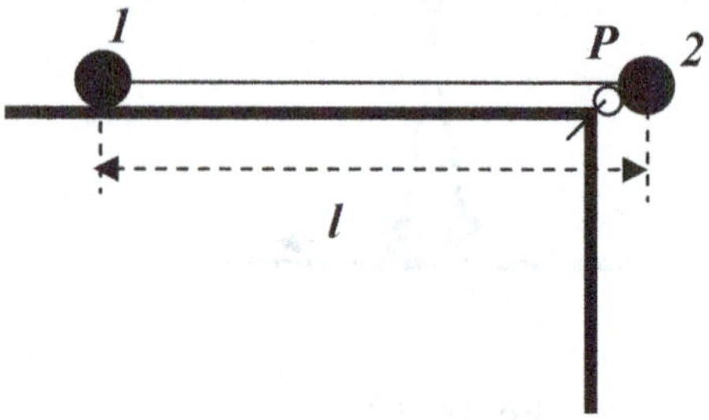

Figure 68

69. Two rigid, light rods of lengths l_1 and l_2 are welded together, making a right angle. Two identical bodies of small dimensions are attached to their free ends.

The system thus formed is placed on a horizontal surface and it is held in the vertical plane. The rods make equal angles with the horizontal line: $\alpha = \frac{\pi}{4}$ (see Figure 69).

On the left of the point of contact with the ground there is a small hump that does not allow the system move towards this part.

The system is released from rest and body 2 undergoes an inelastic collision with the ground. Supposing that the system stays in the vertical plane during the entire motion, find its velocity after the collision.

The gravitational acceleration g is known.

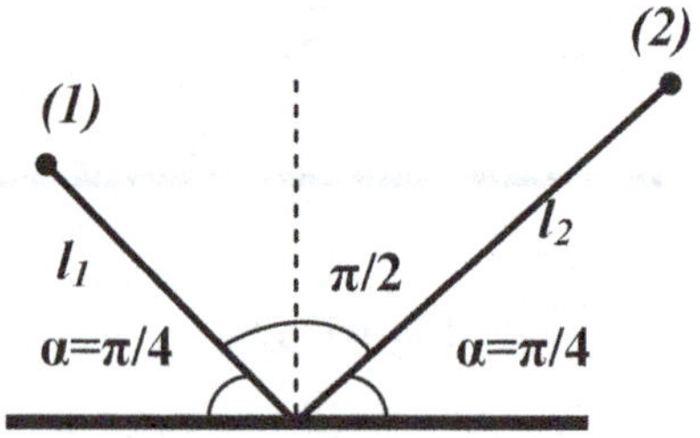

Figure 69

70. A swing is suspended by inelastic strings of the length l each and negligible masses. The chair of the swing has a mass m_1 and it is very close to the ground when it is in equilibrium position.

A monkey of mass m_2 standing on the chair in the equilibrium position jumps out of it. During its motion in the air, it reaches the maximum height h and covers a horizontal distance b from the initial position.

Find the maximum angle of inclination of the swing after the monkey has jumped out of it.

71. Two bodies are thrown horizontally from a height h, with velocity ϑ. The first body undergoes an inelastic collision with the ground, and then it continues its motion by experiencing friction until it stops. The vertical component of the velocity of the other body decreases by a fraction f when it makes collision with the ground, and finally when it returns to the ground it stops at the same point where the first body stopped.
Find the coefficient of friction between first body and the ground. The influence of the change in momentum at the normal in the stopping process during the collision will be neglected.

72. A body of length l and width a is launched as shown in Figure 72. The initial velocity imparted to it is equal to the velocity gained at the ground level by the body falling from rest from a height which is equal to half of its length l. Consider that the collision undergone with the horizontal plane is inelastic.

Find the relation between l and a so that the body doesn't overturn when it meets a small nail at point C. The plane is frictionless.

Assume that during the fall, the body does not make rotation.

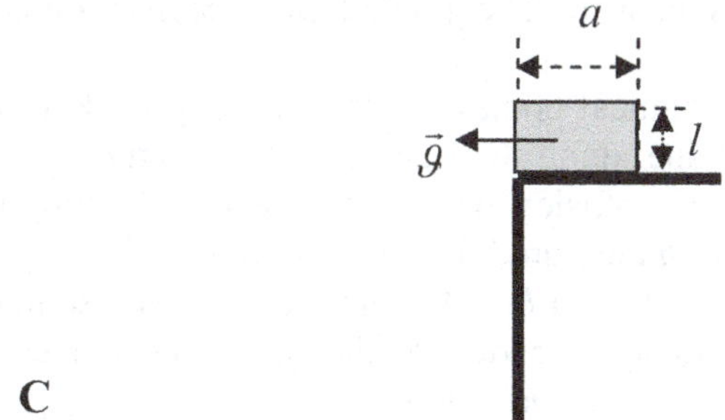

Figure 72

73. A perfectly flexible and inextensible cable is placed on an inclined plane of length l and angle α<<1 with the horizontal (see Figure 73). The length of the cable is equal to the length of the plane. The friction between them, as well as between the inclined plane and the horizontal plane are to be neglected.

The cable is released from rest. Find the velocity of the inclined plane when the cable leaves it. We know the mass of the cable m and the mass of the inclined plane M, as well as the gravitational acceleration g.

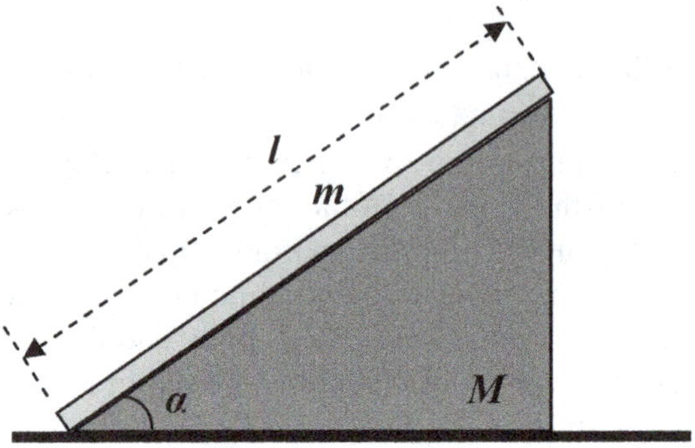

Figure 73

74. A dumbbell of length l=1m is placed along a frictionless inclined plane that makes an angle α=30° with the horizontal.

Consider that one of its ends is at the bottom of the incline which is followed by a frictionless horizontal plane. If the dumbbell is released from rest, calculate its velocity after leaving the inclined plane.

Also assume that the collision between the dumbbell and the horizontal plane is inelastic. The gravitational acceleration is g=10m/s^2.

75. Two identical bodies are launched upwards from the bases of a double inclined plane along their surfaces (see Figure 75) so that they can undergo an inelastic collision when they meet at the top and rise vertically upwards to a height h measured from the top of the planes.

Knowing the height H of the inclined planes and their angles α and β, find the initial velocity imparted to the body that moves on the side that makes an angle α with the horizontal.

The gravitational acceleration g is known.

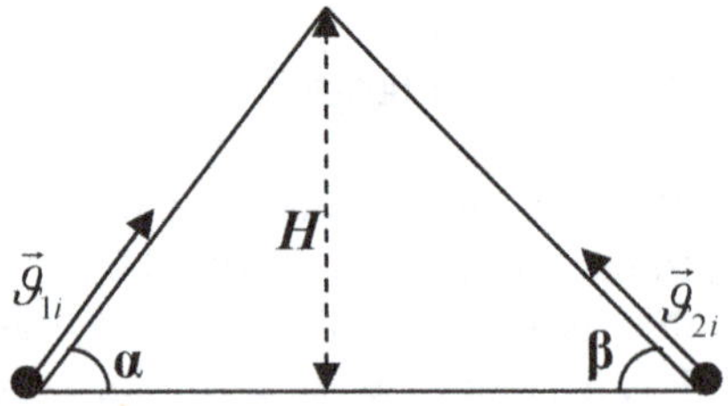

Figure 75

76. A cylindrical body having an elastic constant k is released from rest from a height h over a horizontal plane (see Figure 76). Knowing that on the impact with the ground it loses a fraction z of its energy, find the height h so that after the impact it can no longer rise. We know the weight of the body W. Neglect the deformation due to its own weight.

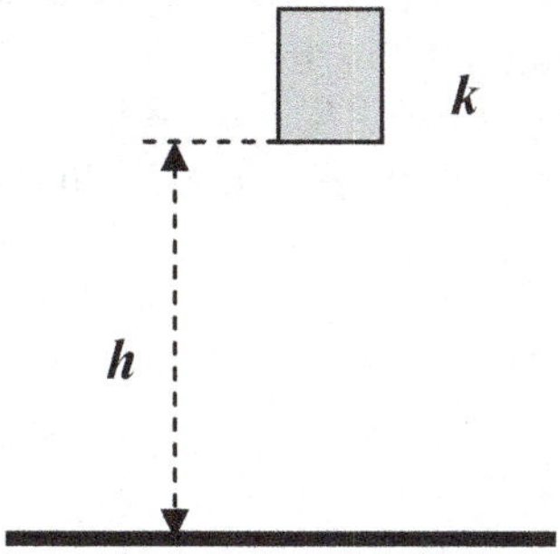

Figure 76

77. Consider the system of bodies in Figure 77 that have the ratio of the masses $k = \frac{m_1}{m_2}$. After imparting a small impulse to the body of mass m_1, it starts sliding on surface BD of the inclined plane. Finally it reaches point C on the ground. Point C which is on a horizontal plane is in the same vertical line with point D. The mass m_1 keeps a fraction f of its energy after it makes inelastic collision with the ground.

Calculate the acceleration of the system just before the collision.

We know the heights as $BF=H$ and $BE=h$. We assume that the string is long enough for the body of mass m_2 to stay on plane AB during the motion. All frictions are neglected.

The gravitational acceleration g is known.

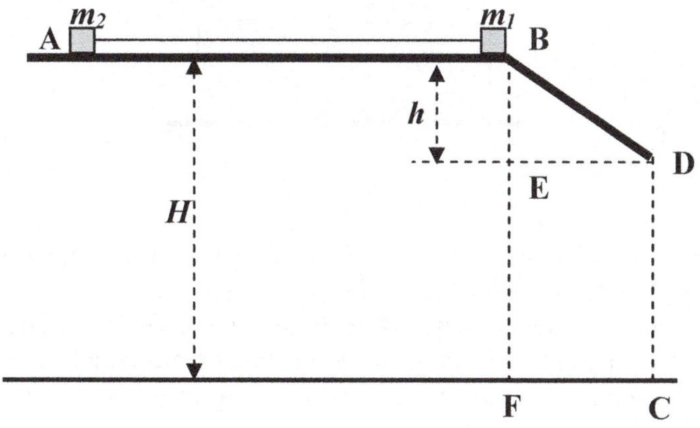

Figure 77

78. Two bodies of masses M and m move along a frictionless horizontal plane in the same direction with velocities ϑ_M (which is known) and ϑ_m where $\vartheta_M > \vartheta_m$ (see Figure 78).

Between what values can the velocity of the body of mass m be in order for it to remain stationary on the body of mass M (on its horizontal surface), supposing that portion BC is frictionless and the coefficient of friction between the bodies on portion AB is μ? What are the final velocities of the system in the two extreme points A and B? (The height h and length l are known).

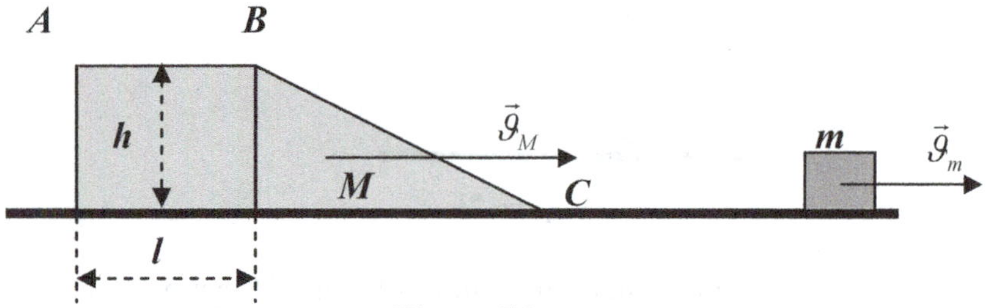

Figure 78

79. Three identical cubes of side l, having masses m_1, m_2 and m_3 are placed on a horizontal plane (see Figure 79). A velocity ϑ is given to the masses m_1 and m_2 .Then m_1 undergoes a head-on inelastic collision with the mass m_3 and then they stick and move together.

Consider that friction exists only between the bodies of masses m_2 and m_3.. Determine the coefficient of friction between them if, after the collision, the body of mass m_2 is perfectly superposed on the body of mass m_3.

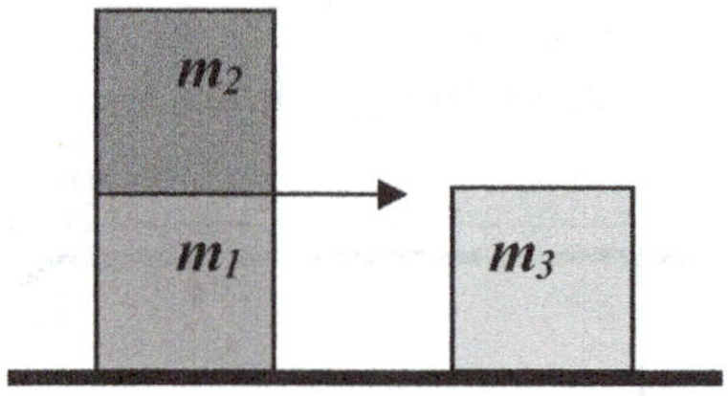

Figure 79

80. Consider the system in Figure 80 situated in a horizontal plane. Body 1 undergoes an inelastic collision with body 2 which is attached to the end of a rigid rod of length l and of negligible mass. The other end of the rod is attached to a joint. The masses of the bodies are equal. We know the velocity ϑ of body 1 before the collision and the angle α it makes with the rod.

Knowing that after the collision, body 2 covers a quarter of a complete circular path until it stops; determine the coefficient of friction between body 2 and the horizontal plane on which it moves.

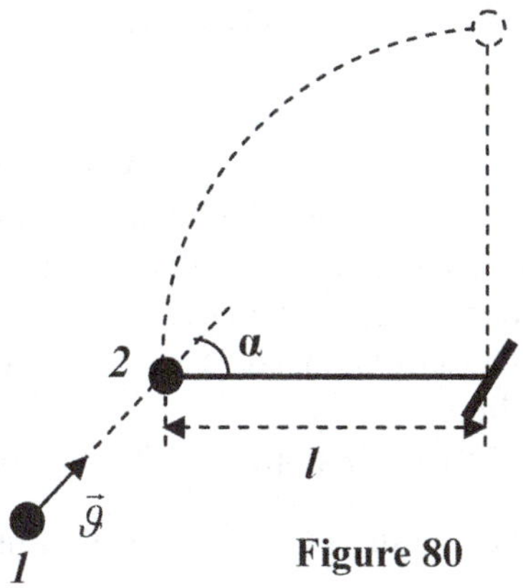

Figure 80

81. Many identical shells are fired one by one and each of them is divided into two equal parts by explosion in air. It was observed that the maximum time difference recorded between the flying time intervals of the parts of a shell is Δt until they reach the ground.

Calculate the energy produced after the shell explodes, knowing its mass m and the gravitational acceleration g.

82. Consider the bodies of masses m_1 and m_2 in Figure 82 where their velocities and dimensions are also specified. The horizontal plane is frictionless.

After the interaction, the body of mass m_1 remains on the top of the other.

Determine the quantity of heat released following this process.

The gravitational acceleration g is known.

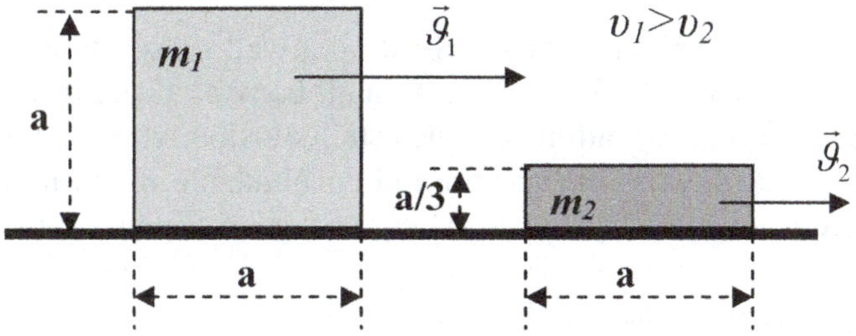

Figure 82

83. Suppose that the interaction of the bodies in the previous problem does not liberate heat. Determine the length of the side a knowing that the common velocity of the bodies after they come into contact with each other (superposed) is the arithmetic average of their initial velocities.

The gravitational acceleration g is known.

84. Consider the system in Figure 84. A ball with mass m is attached to one end of an inelastic string whose the other end is fixed at point O. After it is released it undergoes an inelastic collision with the body of mass M placed on a rough horizontal plane. The coefficient of friction between mass M and the plane is μ. The collision takes place when the string makes an angle α with the vertical line.

When the body of mass M stops, the distance between the left end of it and point O' is twice the length of the string. Determine the ratio $\frac{m}{M}$.

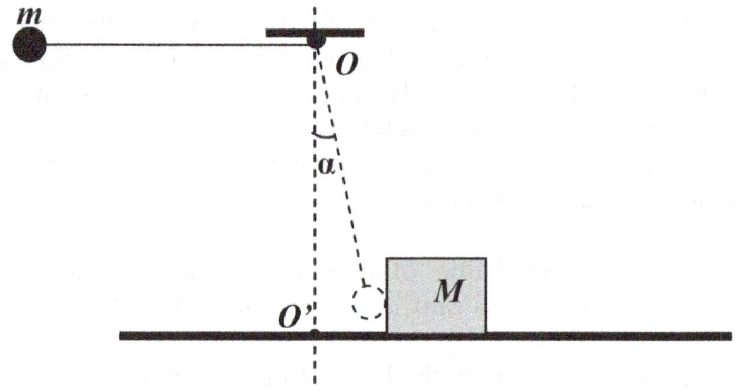

Figure 84

85. A frictionless board fixed on a wall makes an angle α above the horizontal as shown in Figure 85. A small body at a height H above the floor is released from rest and makes inelastic collision with the top of the board. Then it slides down on the board and encounters a rough horizontal surface with a coefficient of friction μ. After it covers a distance s on the horizontal plane, it stops.

Determine the length of the board.

The gravitational acceleration g is known.

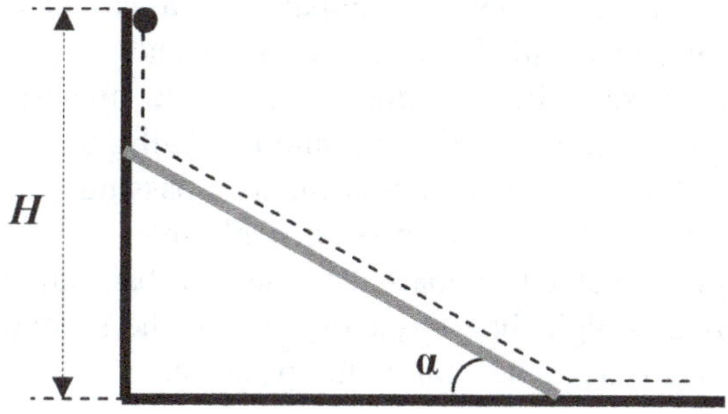

Figure 85

86. From a height h, two balls are released from rest and the time interval between the moments they are released is τ. If the first ball undergoes a perfectly elastic collision with the floor, determine the time interval τ so that the balls meet at the half of the height from where they were released.

The gravitational acceleration g is known.

Numerical application: h=10 m; g=10 m/s^2.

87. A dumbbell held horizontally is released from rest from a height H=4 m and collides with the floor. After collision, one of the ends remains on the floor while the other one making a perfectly elastic collision rises by following a circular arc.

When the dumbbell reaches vertical position, the contact between the first end and the floor disappears and the dumbbell becomes free.

Calculate the maximum length of the dumbbell so that it may rise when it reaches the vertical position.

88. A cart of mass M is placed on a horizontal plane, and a ball of mass m is fired towards it from a distance s (see Figure 88). The mechanical work necessary for the projectile is W.

Find the velocity imparted to the cart if the ball undergoes an elastic collision with its bottom.

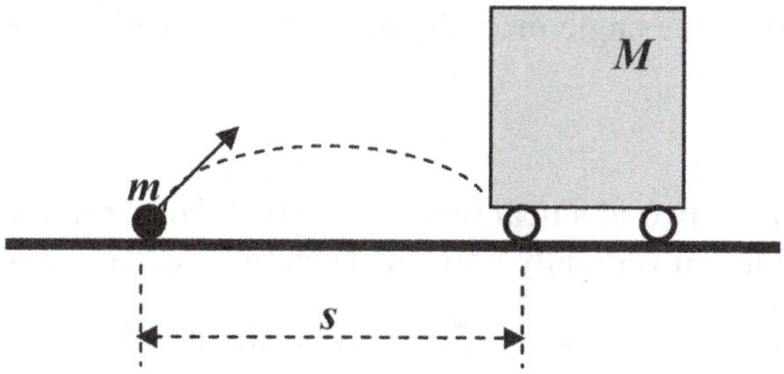

Figure 88

89. A horizontal velocity is imparted to a ball attached to one end of an inelastic string of length l, whose the other end is fixed (see Figure 89). Thus it follows a semicircular trajectory. At the highest point it makes a perfect head-on elastic collision with another ball attached to one end of a vertical rigid rod that can rotate about the axis passing through the other end of it. The rod's length is L and its mass is negligible.

Find the initial velocity imparted to the first ball, knowing that after the collision it has a straight line trajectory, while the second one stops at the moment when the rod reaches horizontal position.

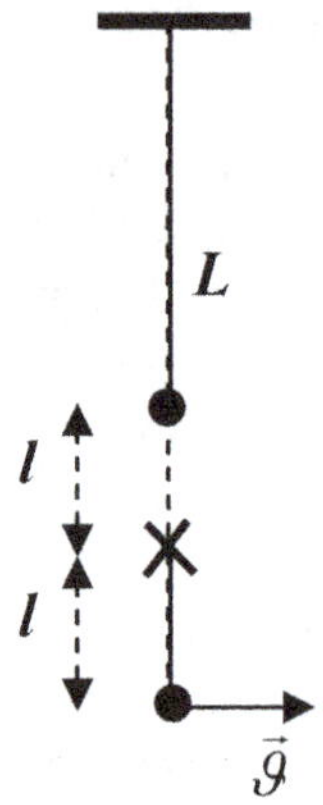

Figure 89

90. From the bottom of a frictionless inclined plane of an angle α, two bodies are thrown simultaneously (towards the incline) with the same initial velocities and with the same angles relative to the horizontal.

The first one undergoes a perfectly elastic collision, and turns back following the same path to the point from where it was thrown, while the other one makes inelastic collision with the plane and reaches its bottom at the same instant with the first body.

Determine the angle made by the initial velocities of the bodies with the horizontal.

91. One of two identical balls is released from rest at a height h. The second ball is thrown vertically upward. Then they undergo a perfectly elastic collision at the height $h_1 = \frac{h}{2}$ .If the balls are directed horizontally after collision, find the distance between the points where they fall on the ground.

92. Consider the system in Figure 92. We know the masses of the bodies: m, M where $M>m$. The distances AB and BC are covered in equal time intervals by the body of mass m, and at point B it undergoes an elastic collision with a stationary body of mass m_o (unknown). The wire passing over the first pulley has a very big elastic constant.

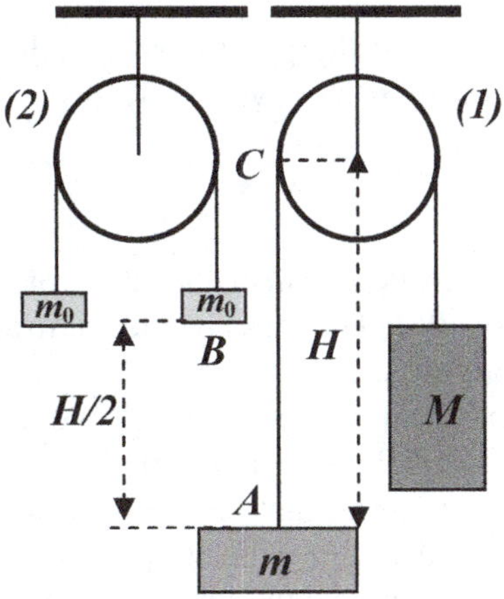

Figure 92

How long time after this collision does the string of the pulley (2) become tight again? Assume that $AB = BC = \frac{H}{2}$. Find out the value of the masses, m_o, of identical bodies hung by the pulley (2).

The gravitational acceleration g is known.

Numerical application: M=3 kg; m=1 kg; H=2 m; $g=10\frac{m}{s^2}$.

93. A ball is launched at an angle β above the horizontal from point A which is at the bottom of a double inclined plane, as shown in Figure 93. (The ball is able to make elastic collision with side BC).The inclined planes have angle α and height h. Determine the initial velocity of the ball at point A so that it can cover the distance between B and C by sliding.

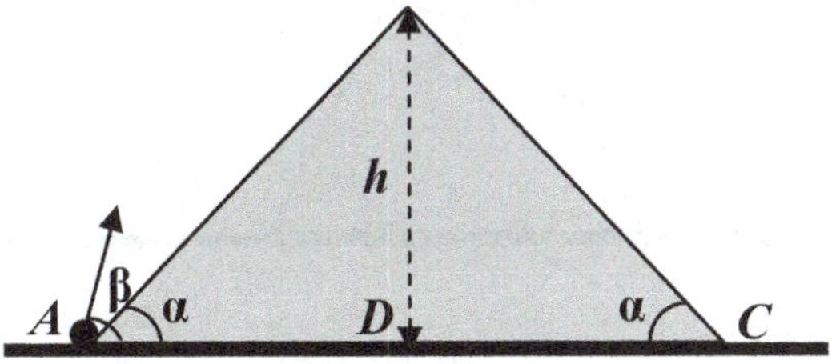

Figure 93

94. Two tennis players are training by passing the ball one to another by having the ball hit a wall that has the shape of a circular arc of radius R, with the center on the players' side. One of them sends the ball towards the wall from a certain point situated very close to the bisector of the angle subtended by the circular wall. The trajectory of the ball is parallel to the bisector.

The second player is at the point corresponding to the center of the circular arc. What distance does he have to cover along the bisector in order to easily catch the ball?

95. A squirrel is inside a wheel that can rotate about a frictionless axis at point O (see Figure 95). The mass of the squirrel is m and the mass of the wheel is M, and its radius is R.

The squirrel starts moving at point C and reaches point B where radius OB makes an angle α below the horizontal. Since it gets tired, it clings to the wheel at point B. Supposing that before this, the squirrel was standing still relative to the ground, determine the frequency of rotation of the wheel just before the squirrel clings, knowing that it stops when the squirrel is at the maximum height above the ground.

The gravitational acceleration g is known.

Numerical application: m=0.4kg; M=1.6 kg; α=30°; R=0.5m; $g=10\frac{m}{s^2}$.

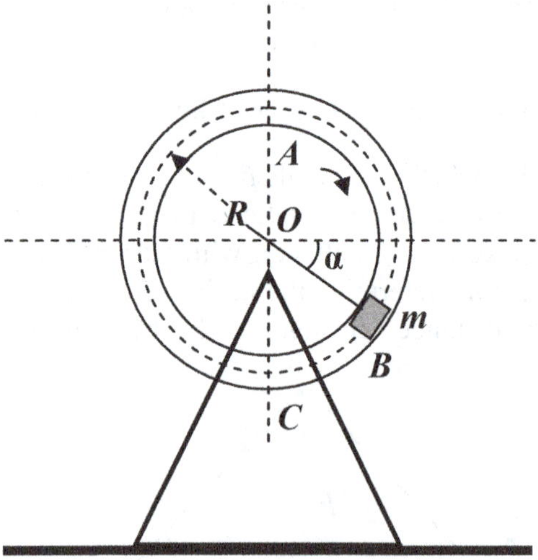

Figure 95

96. Each of two rigid rods in Figure 96, of length $2l$ has a body of mass M attached to its end, and a body of mass m at its middle. The bodies of mass M can undergo elastic collision between them, while those of mass m undergo inelastic collision. The rod on the left side is released from rest when it makes an angle of α with the vertical.

Calculate the angular velocities of the rods, just after the interactions between the pairs of bodies.

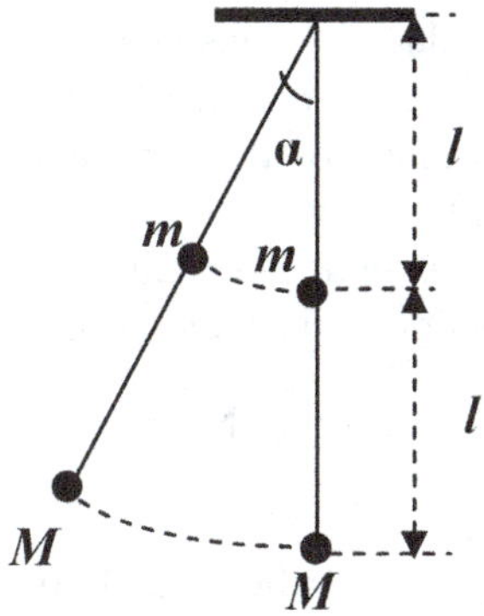

Figure 96

97. A rigid rod of negligible mass and is placed on a frictionless horizontal plane. Two bodies of masses m_1 and m_2 are attached to its ends. Just near the center of masses a vertical rigid axle is fixed to the horizontal plane. The second body is attached by a light inelastic string of length l to another one of mass m_3 (see Figure 97). Initially m_3 is at rest at a distance d from the m_2 on the same line joining m_1 and m_2.

In the direction perpendicular to the rod a velocity ϑ is imparted to the body of mass m_3 then it makes a one-dimensional motion with constant velocity on the horizontal plane until the string becomes perfectly tight. Find

a) the time necessary to perform this motion;
b) the velocities of the bodies of masses m_1 and m_2 just after the string becomes tight.

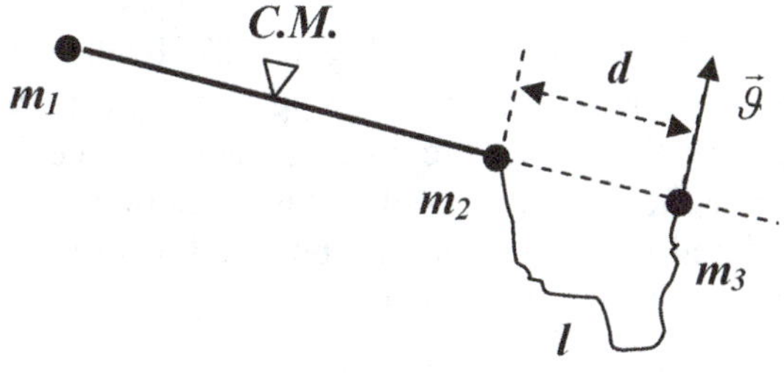

Figure 97

98. Find the maximum number of base sides of a regular prism placed on a plane inclined at an angle α, so that it does not roll down.

The coefficient of friction satisfies the formula $\mu > tg\alpha$, and the prism base plane is in the vertical.

99. On a cart of mass M placed on a horizontal plane there is a pendulum consisting of a rigid rod of negligible mass, that has a body of mass m at its free end.

The pendulum is placed in unstable equilibrium position and then it is unbalanced. At the moment it reaches the horizontal position, a force (F) (contained in the rotation plane of the pendulum) is exerted on the cart in a direction opposite the pendulum.

Determine the horizontal acceleration of the system. The frictions will be neglected; the gravitational acceleration g is known.

Numerical application: F=50 N; m=2 kg; M=3 kg; $g=10\frac{m}{s^2}$.

100. On a rectangular parallelepiped body of mass M which is at rest on a horizontal plane, a pendulum consisting of a rigid rod of negligible mass stands in unstable equilibrium, with a body of mass m at its end.

After the pendulum is unbalanced, one can observe that the body of mass M on the plane moves at the moment when the rod makes the angle α with the vertical line.

Determine the coefficient of friction between the plane and the body.

101. A pendulum consisting of a rod of negligible mass, with a body of mass m at its end, is placed on another one of mass M which is on a horizontal plane and the coefficient of friction between M and the plane is μ. The pendulum swings with the angular amplitude α.

Find out the force that should be exerted horizontally in the direction of motion of the pendulum that is descending over the cart, in order to change its stationary position when the rod makes the angle β with the vertical.

The gravitational acceleration g is known.

102. Consider the system in Figure 102. Each of the cords of equal lengths sustains the body attached by a ring to one of the vertical cylindrical rods. The diameters of the rings are much greater than the diameters of rods.

Determine the minimum coefficient of friction between the rings and the rods (considered to be the same on both rods), so that the body remains stationary. We know the angle made by the cords with the horizontal α.

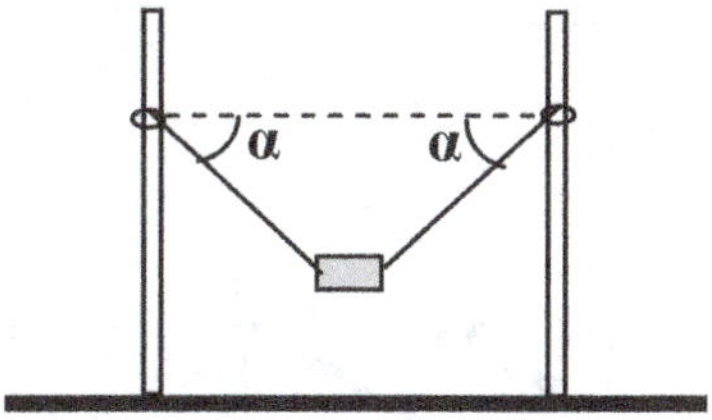

Figure 102

103. Consider the system in Figure 103. One of the ends of the rod of mass m is on the floor and the other end leans on a rectangular parallelepiped body of mass M.

Knowing the coefficient of friction μ between the floor and the body of mass M, find the minimum angle made by the rod with the horizontal, so that the system remains in equilibrium. Exclude the possibility of overturning of the body while the rod acts on it.

Numerical application: m= 1 kg; M= 4 kg; μ=0.5.

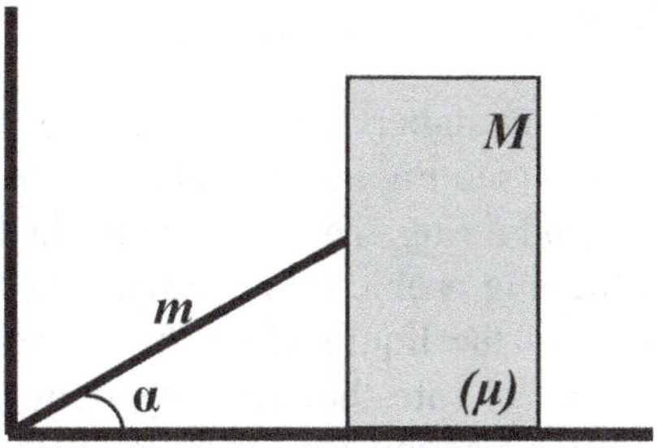

Figure 103

104. Two identical homogenous rods are leaning on separate vertical walls which are parallel. The distance between the walls is smaller than the sum of the lengths l_1 and l_2 of the two rods but greater than the length of each rod.

Find an expression relating the angles made by the rods on the walls to the lengths of the rods if they are in equilibrium.

Frictions are neglected.

105. A rod with a mass m and length l is leaning on an object with a mass m_1, making an angle α with the horizontal as shown in Figure 105. What is the maximum distance, s, which a person with a mass M at point A can cover on the rod? It is assumed that the rod is fixed at point A on the ground. The coefficient of friction between the object with mass m_1 and the ground is μ.

Numerical application: m_1=40 kg; l=2 m; m= 20 kg; M= 60 kg; μ=0.3; α=30°.

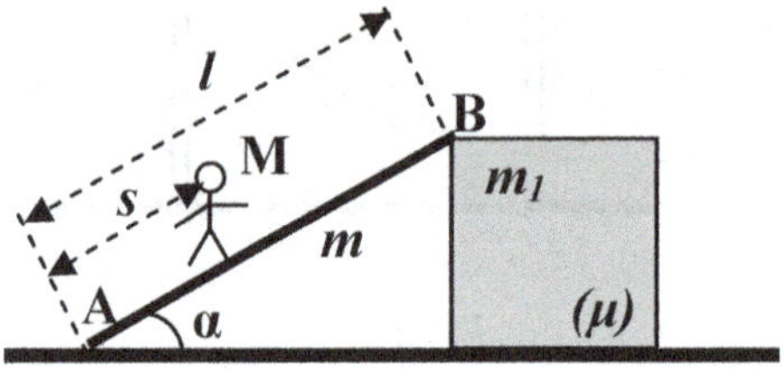

Figure 105

106. A body is immersed into the water in a container to a certain depth. When it is released, it rises towards the surface of the water.

Knowing that the time necessary for the body to reach the maximum height, measured from the moment it leaves the liquid, is k times longer than the time necessary to travel through the liquid, find the density of the body, if we know the water density ρ_o.

107. In a tubular chamber there is a homogenous liquid in which there is a ball of density ρ (see Figure 107) attached to a wire by means of a cord of negligible mass and a ring. The wire is attached to the interior part of the tube, along it, and the ring is able to move without friction.

Find the density of the liquid, if the ball covers the entire length of the wire as the chamber accelerates horizontally along the wire by covering a distance which is equal to a fraction f of the length of the chamber.

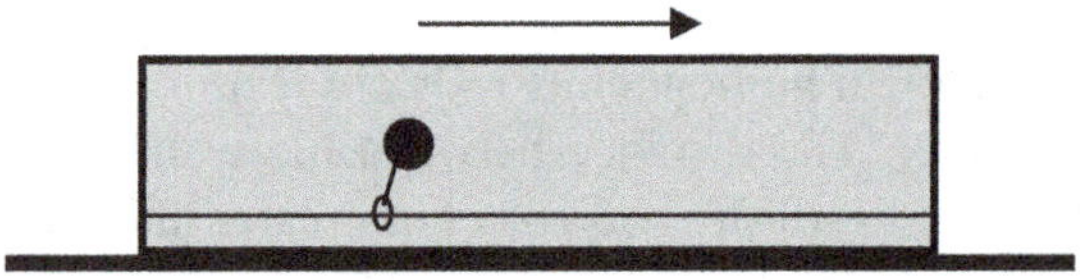

Figure 107

108. A ball having the density n times lower than the density of water is thrown horizontally near the edge of a pool from a height h above the water level.

Knowing the length L of the pool, find the initial velocity of the ball so that at the moment it leaves the water, it can reach the other edge of the pool.

Neglect the resistance to motion in liquid.
The gravitational acceleration g is known.

109. When the tap R in Figure 109 is opened, water flows with the volume debit Q through a U-shaped uniform pipe with a cross-sectional area S. Then it spurts out of the right arm of the pipe and strikes the cover suspended from the ceiling at a height h by means of a spring. The surface area of the cover is much larger than S.

Calculate the mass of the cover if the spring turns to its relaxed position during the interaction between the water and the cover. Consider that this interaction is inelastic.

Hint: Note that before and during the interaction the cover is in the horizontal. The gravitational acceleration g is known.

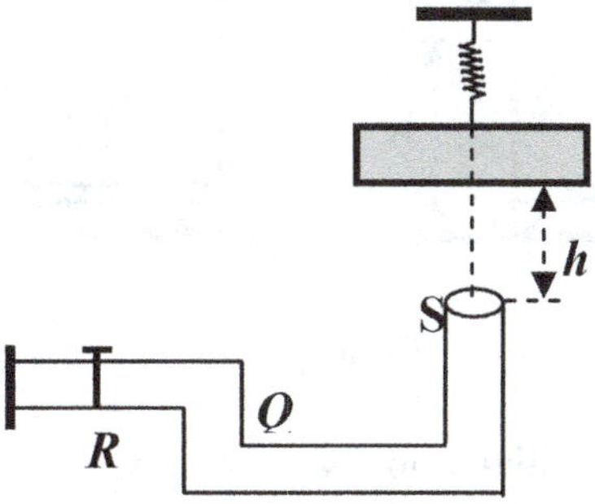

Figure 109

110. A rectangular parallelepiped container full of water of total mass M is placed on an inclined plane of angle α. The coefficient of friction between the container and the incline is μ. In order to keep the container stationary it has to be tied to a wall with an inextensible string as shown in Figure 110. The container has two orifices with the cross-sectional areas S_1 and S_2. The piston at the first orifice is pushed inside by a spring and the second one has a blocked cover.

Calculate the tension in the spring so that, when the second cover is opened, for just one moment the presence of the string is not necessary to keep the container still. The gravitational acceleration g is known.

Numerical application: α=30°; S_1=20 cm^2; S_2=40 cm^2; μ=0.3; M=4 kg, g=10 m/s^2.

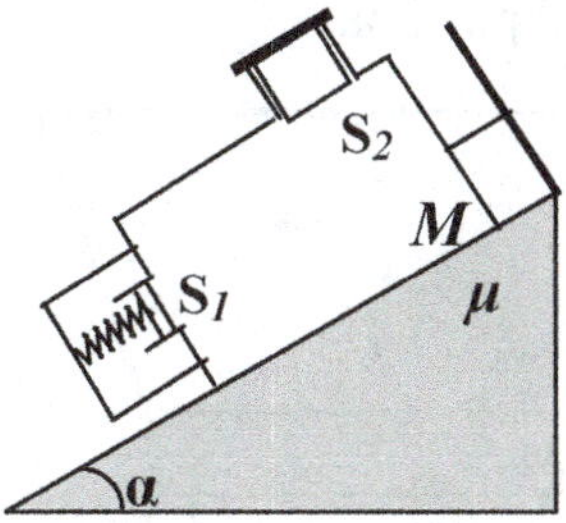

Figure 110

111. A container of length l, mounted on a cart (see Figure 111), is filled with water up to the height h. We make an orifice E on the right wall at the height H from the bottom.

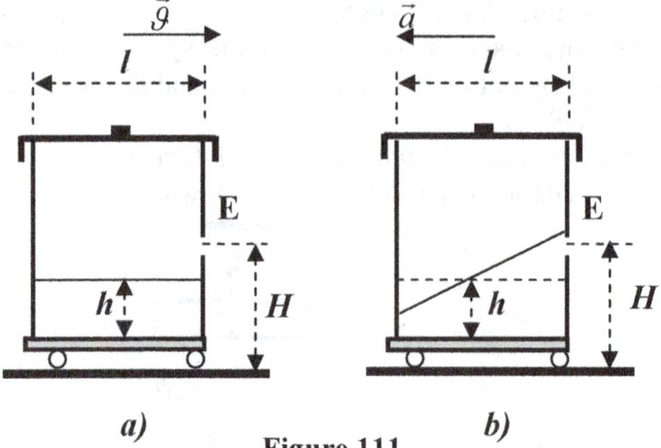

Figure 111

The cart whose initial velocity is ϑ slows down with an acceleration a and stops in a time interval.

Knowing the gravitational acceleration as g, find out the height h of the water level in the container before breaking, so that until it stops the cart wheels do not enter the portion of the floor, wetted by the water spurting out through the orifice.

112. A container having the shape of a prism with a trapezoidal section of bases L and l and with negligible mass is placed on a cart of mass m (see Figure 112). Then it is filled with water of quantity M. When the tap mounted at the bottom of the container is opened, water leaves the container horizontally and the cart begins to move without friction.

Find the ratio of its acceleration when the container is full to the acceleration when the height of the water is equal to a fraction $f > 0$, of the height of the container. Consider that during motion, the free surface of the water maintains in horizontal position.

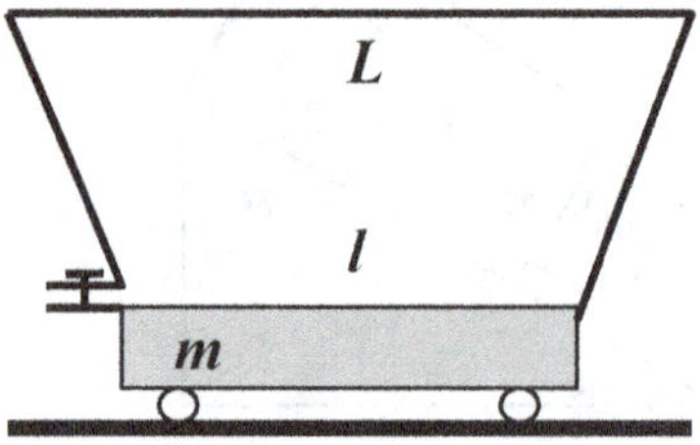

Figure 112

113. A container of negligible mass and a rectangular parallelepiped in shape, whose base is a square, is placed on horizontal plane as shown in Figure 113. On one of the vertical faces of the container there is a closed orifice whose horizontal side is equal to that of the face of the container, while the vertical side represents the nth part of the height of the container.

Find the height of the center of the orifice so that the container overturns just after the orifice is opened. We know that $AB=l$ and $AD=H$.

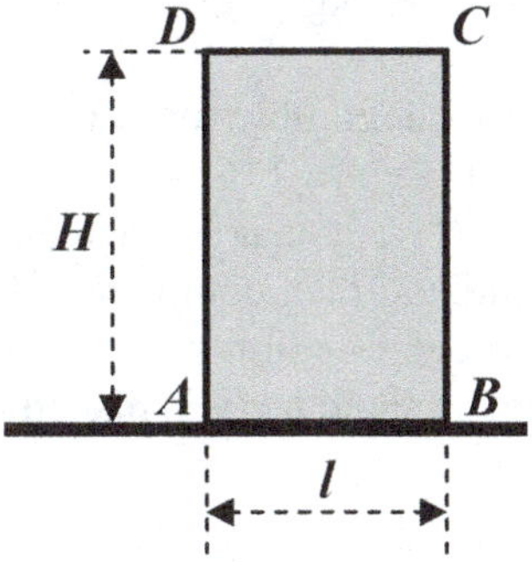

Figure 113

114. The two containers in Figure 114, each having the shape of a rectangular parallelepiped with identical square sections, are placed on a horizontal plane and the distance between them is l. We fill container 1 with water up to the height H and then make an orifice at a height h on its side near container 2, where $h < H$.

Find the height h_x of the side of container 2 which is near container 1, so that it may be completely filled by the water coming out from the first, without any loss of water. Suppose that the opposite side of container 2 is high enough not to let water pass over it.

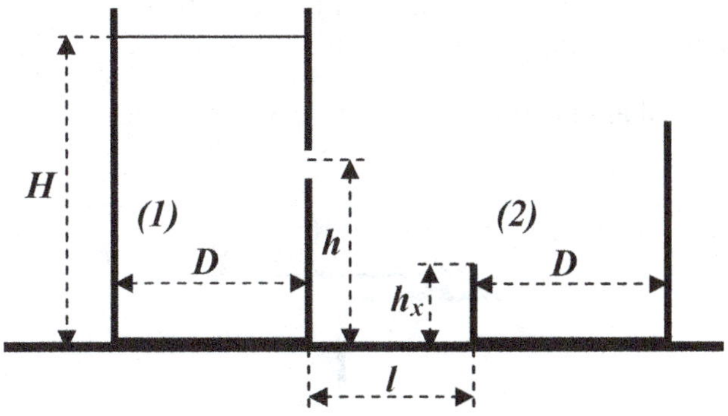

Figure 114

115. Two bodies of masses m_1 and m_2 are placed on a frictionless horizontal plane and attached one to another by means of a spring of negligible mass and spring constant k.

If we move the bodies away from each other, the spring stretches, and afterwards we let the system free.

Find the period of the oscillatory motion of the system.

Numerical application: m_1=2 kg; m_2=5 kg; k=10 N/m.

116. A rigid platform of negligible mass is attached to two identical springs of length l as shown in Figure 116. We know that when a body is released from rest at a height $H+l$, it makes an inelastic collision with the platform and the springs extend and then compress. The maximum extension is twice longer than maximum compression during the motion of the system. Also we know that in the case the same body is placed gently on the platform, each spring extends $l/2$.

Find H.

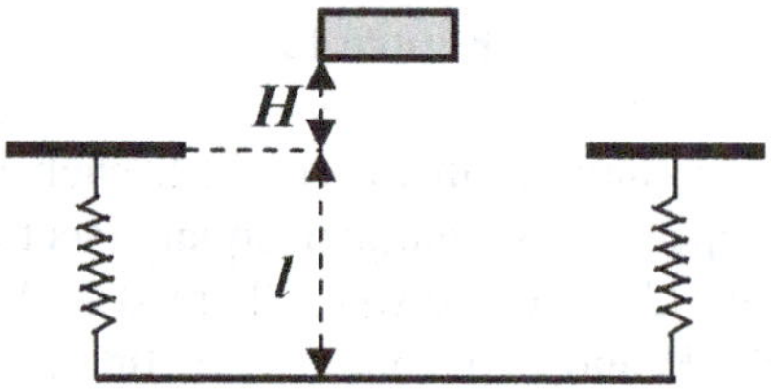

Figure 116

117. A body is attached to a inextensible string and placed on a table. Find the acceleration that must be horizontally given for a long time to the right end of the string as shown in Figure 117 so that after the body leaves the edge of the table, it descends a distance h in the vertical.

We know the length l of the string.

Numerical application: l=1 m; h=0.7 m; $g=10\frac{m}{s^2}$.

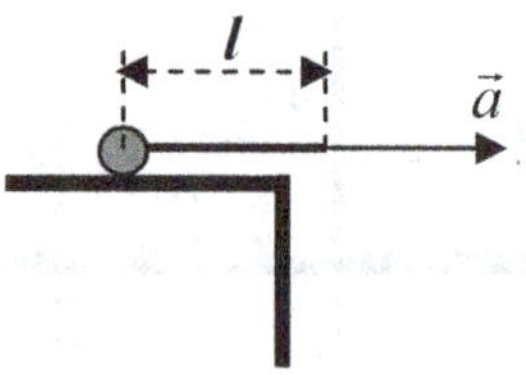

Figure 117

118. Consider the system in Figure 118. The ratio of the mass of body 1 to the mass of body 2 immersed in a liquid is n. Body 2 which is cylindrical in shape has the height h.

Knowing that the volume remaining out of the liquid is a fraction f of the total volume of body 2, find the period of the oscillatory motion of the system. The gravitational acceleration g is known.

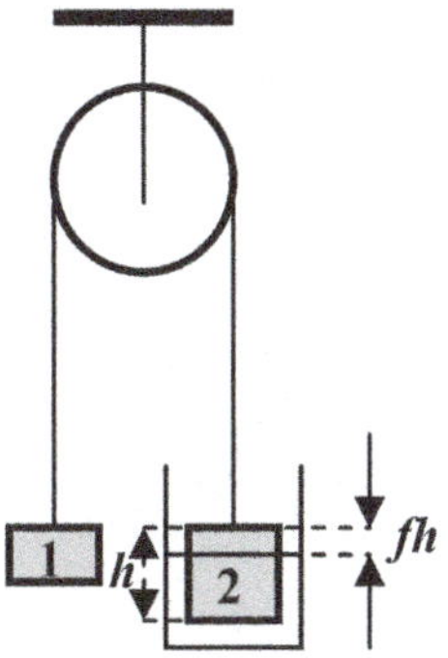

Figure 118

119. Two identical balls of mass m are connected by an elastic string having the length l_0 in unstretched state and the elastic constant k.

The system thus formed in the horizontal is released from rest when the string is tight but not stretched. After covering a distance h in the vertical, the string clings to a nail right in the middle.

If the collision between the balls is considered to be inelastic, find the amplitude of the oscillation of the balls. Suppose that the balls collide when the string is at its maximum extension. The gravitational acceleration g is known.

120. Consider the system in Figure 120. Inside the U-shaped tube there is a quantity M of liquid up to the height L. Above the tube; two pistons of negligible masses are suspended by a spring of spring constant k.

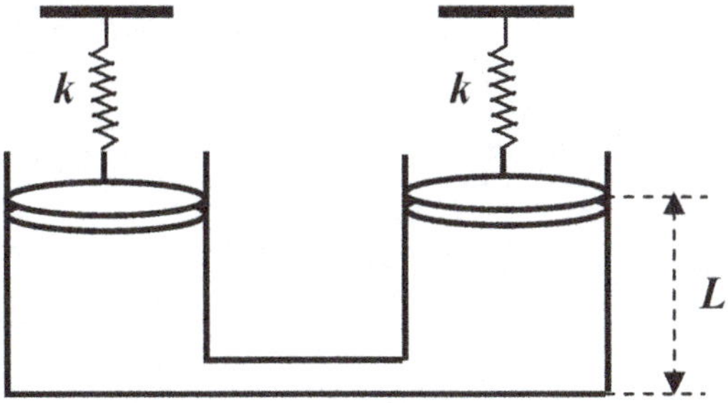

Figure 120

Find the period of oscillatory motion of the system described above.

Numerical application: M=2 kg; L=0.5 m; k=10 N/m; $g=10\frac{m}{s^2}$.

SOLUTIONS

1. Supposing that the locomotive is initially at point B (see Figure 1), in order to reach point D situated at the distance l from point C from where to be able to subsequently move on circular arc CE, it will cover a distance

$$s_1 = R\frac{\pi}{2} + l \qquad (1.1)$$

The subsequent motion up to point F requires a distance

$$s_2 = R\frac{\pi}{2} + l \qquad (1.2)$$

while the distance left up to the original position (FB) is given by the expression

$$s_3 = l + 2R \qquad (1.3)$$

Therefore, the total distance

$$s = 3 \cdot l + R \cdot (2 + \pi) \qquad (1.4)$$

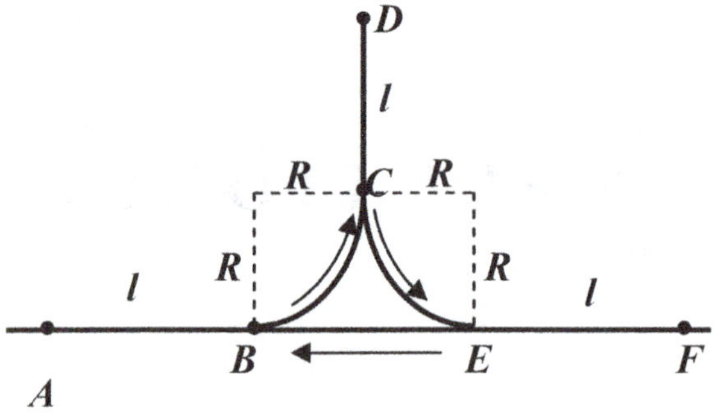

Figure 1

2. For the body of mass m (see Figure 2), by imposing the condition

$$a_m = 0, \qquad (2.1)$$

we obtain

$$T = m \cdot g = 700\ \text{N} \qquad (2.2)$$

As for the body of mass M, we can write

$$M \cdot a_M = T - M \cdot g \qquad (2.3)$$

from the expressions 2.2 and 2.3 we obtain a_M as

$$a_M = \frac{m \cdot g - M \cdot g}{M} = 7.5\ \text{m/s}^2 \qquad (2.4)$$

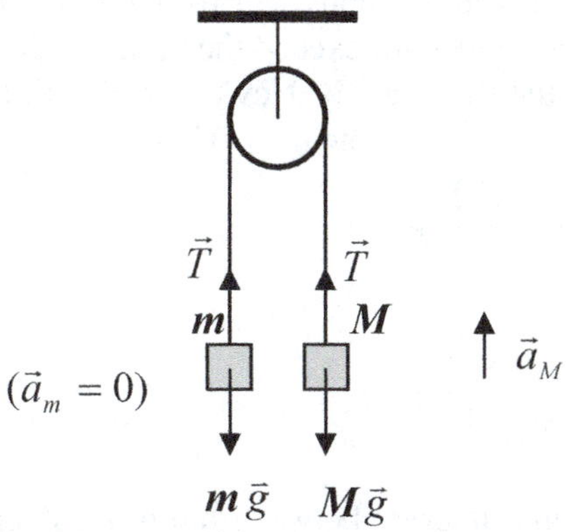

Figure 2

3. The direction of the velocity gained by the body coincides with the direction of the acceleration given to it by the force F and the weight acting simultaneously. Therefore, according to Figure 3, we can write

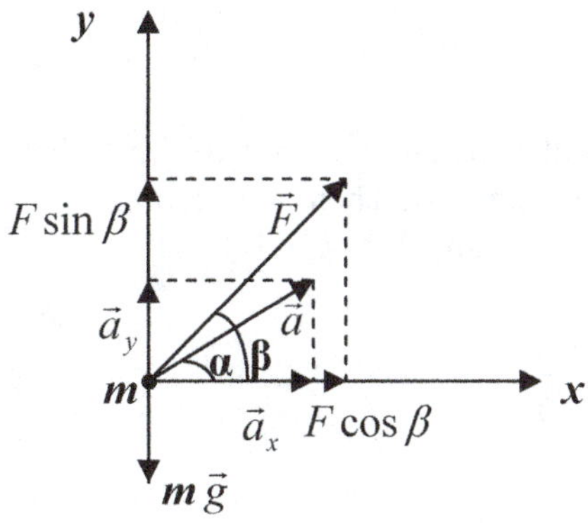

Figure 3

$$Oy: F\cdot\sin\beta - m\cdot g = m\cdot a_y \qquad (3.1)$$

$$Ox: F\cdot\cos\beta = m\cdot a_x \qquad (3.2)$$

$$\tan\alpha = \frac{a_y}{a_x} \qquad (3.3)$$

Therefore

$$\tan\alpha = \tan\beta - \frac{m\cdot g}{F}\cdot\frac{1}{\cos\beta} \qquad (3.4)$$

4. In order to prevent the conveyor from sliding relative to the ground, the maximum force on it must not exceed the value of the force of friction.

According to the third law of Newton, this will be equal to the force that produces the displacement of the man. Therefore

$$a_1 = \frac{\mu \cdot (2 \cdot m + M)}{M} \cdot g \qquad (4.1)$$

and

$$a_2 = \frac{\mu \cdot (2 \cdot m + M)}{2 \cdot m} \cdot g \qquad (4.2)$$

5. Since the time interval between the trains decreases as the second train moves ($\Delta t_2 < \Delta t_1$), we deduce that the second train has a greater velocity than the first one. Therefore

$$\vartheta_2 = \vartheta_r + \vartheta_1 \qquad (5.1)$$

where ϑ_r is the relative velocity of the second train relative to the first one; on the other hand, the velocity of the first train will be given by the expression

$$\vartheta_1 = \frac{L}{\tau} \qquad (5.2)$$

Consider T_1 and T_2 as the moments of time when the first train passes through the two subway stations. Then, the second one will reach the stations at the moments $T_1' = T_1 + \Delta t_1$ and $T_2' = T_2 + \Delta t_2$.

Therefore:

$$\vartheta_1 = \frac{l}{T_2 - T_1} \qquad (5.3)$$

then

$$T_2 - T_1 = \frac{l}{\vartheta_1} \qquad (5.4)$$

and

$$\vartheta_2 = \frac{l}{(T_2 + \Delta t_2) - (T_1 + \Delta t_1)} \qquad (5.5)$$

Therefore

$$\vartheta_2 = \frac{l \cdot \vartheta_1}{l + \vartheta_1 (\Delta t_2 - \Delta t_1)} \qquad (5.6)$$

If we take into account the expression (5.2), we obtain

$$\vartheta_2 = \frac{l \cdot L}{\tau \cdot l + L(\Delta t_2 - \Delta t_1)} \quad (5.7)$$

By substituting the expressions (5.2) and (5.7) into the expression (5.1), we obtain

$$\vartheta_r = L\left[\frac{l}{\tau \cdot l + L(\Delta t_2 - \Delta t_1)} - \frac{1}{\tau}\right] \quad (5.8)$$

The condition in order for the problem to be valid is $T_2 - T_1 > \Delta t_1 - \Delta t_2$.

6. According to Figure 6, the distances covered by each runner will be

$$O_1C = s_1 = s + (n-1) \cdot s = n \cdot s \quad (6.1)$$

$$AB = s_2 = 2(n-1) \cdot s \quad (6.2)$$

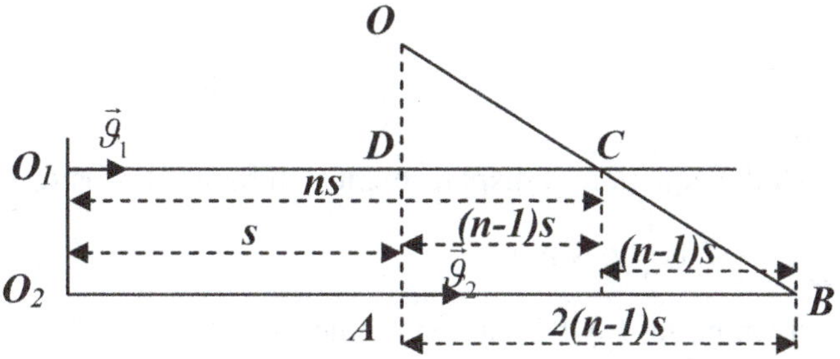

Figure 6

On the other hand

$$s_1 = \vartheta_1 \cdot t \quad (6.3)$$

and

$$s_2 = \vartheta_2 \cdot t \quad (6.4)$$

By eliminating the time from the last two equations and by taking into account the other expressions, we obtain

$$\vartheta_2 = \frac{2(n-1)}{n} \cdot \vartheta_1 \quad (6.5)$$

7. The equations of motion for the two bodies will be

$$x_1 = \vartheta_{01} t + a_1 \cdot \frac{t^2}{2} \quad (7.1)$$

$$x_2 = x_{02} + \vartheta_{02} \cdot t + a_2 \cdot \frac{t^2}{2} \tag{7.2}$$

$$\vartheta_1 = \vartheta_{01} + a_1 \cdot t \tag{7.3}$$

and

$$\vartheta_2 = \vartheta_{02} + a_2 \cdot t \tag{7.4}$$

By writing the condition for them to meet

$$x_1 = x_2 \tag{7.5}$$

and the condition that the two velocities will be equal at that time

$$\vartheta_1 = \vartheta_2 \tag{7.6}$$

by making the calculations, we obtain

$$x_{02} = \frac{(\vartheta_{01} - \vartheta_{02})^2}{2 \cdot (a_2 - a_1)} = 2m \tag{7.7}$$

8. On portion AC (see Figure 8), the expression for the falling time will be

$$t = \sqrt{\frac{2 \cdot h}{g}} \tag{8.1}$$

and on portion AB the equation of displacement will be written as follows

$$h\frac{1}{\sin\alpha} = \vartheta \cdot t + \frac{1}{2} g \cdot \sin\alpha \cdot t^2 \tag{8.2}$$

where the velocity at point A will be given by the expression

$$\vartheta = \sqrt{2 \cdot g(H - h)} \tag{8.3}$$

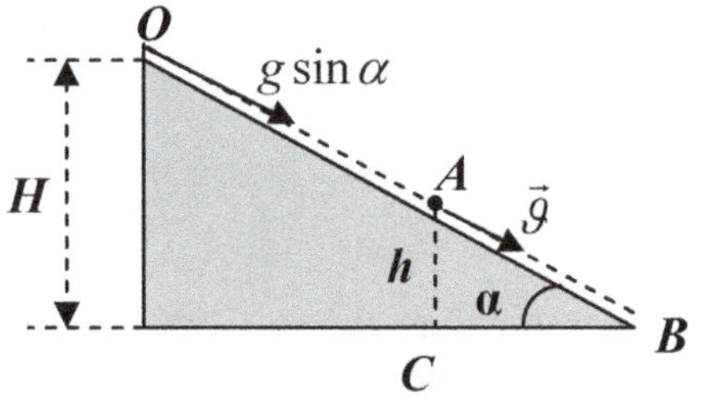

Figure 8

After making the calculations, we can obtain

$$h = \frac{4 \cdot \sin^2\alpha}{(1 - \sin\alpha)^2 + 4 \cdot \sin^2\alpha} \cdot H \tag{8.4}$$

9. The equation of motion on the inclined plane (see Figure 9) is

$$\frac{h}{\sin\alpha} = \vartheta \cdot t + \frac{1}{2} g \cdot t^2 \cdot \sin\alpha \qquad (9.1)$$

and in the case of the vertical motion

$$h = -\vartheta \cdot t + \frac{1}{2} g \cdot t^2 \qquad (9.2)$$

By eliminating time from the equations above, we obtain

$$\vartheta = \sqrt{g \cdot h} \cdot \frac{1 - \sin\alpha}{\sqrt{2 \cdot \sin\alpha}} \qquad (9.3)$$

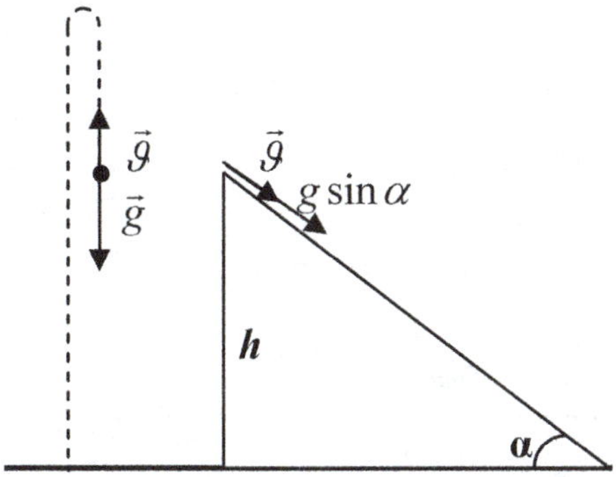

Figure 9

10. From the equation of motion of the body moving along the inclined plane

$$\frac{h}{\sin\alpha} = \vartheta \cdot t + \frac{1}{2} g \cdot t^2 \cdot \sin\alpha \qquad (10.1)$$

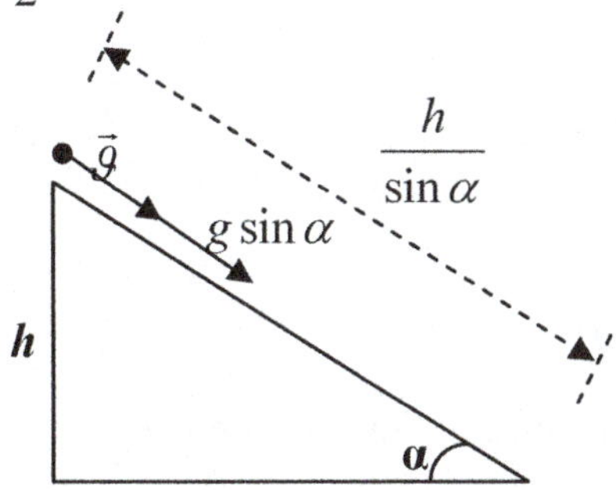

Figure 10

and the equation of displacement in the case of a free fall

$$h = \frac{1}{2} g \cdot t^2 \tag{10.2}$$

by eliminating time, we obtain

$$\vartheta = \frac{\cos^2 \alpha}{\sin \alpha} \cdot \sqrt{\frac{h \cdot g}{2}} = 4.74 \text{ m/s} \tag{10.3}$$

11. In order to break the ice, the ball should reach a maximum height greater or at least equal to *h*, (see Figure 11).

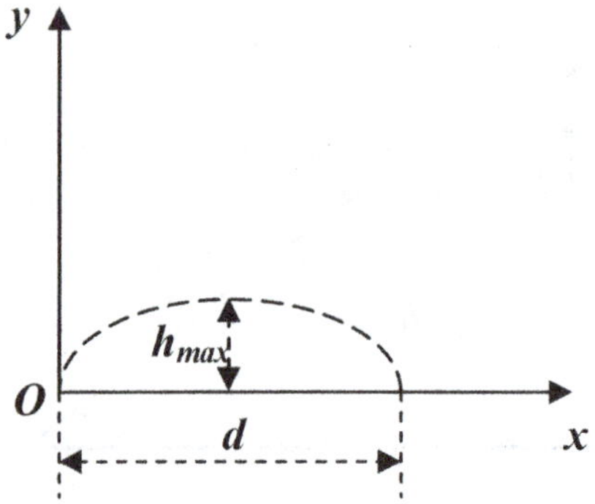

Figure 11

Therefore

$$h_{\max} = h \tag{11.1}$$

But

$$h_{\max} = \frac{\vartheta_0^2}{2 \cdot g} \cdot \sin^2 \alpha \tag{11.2}$$

and

$$d = 2\frac{\vartheta_0^2}{g} \sin\alpha \cdot \cos\alpha \tag{11.3}$$

By making the calculations, we obtain

$$d = \frac{2}{g}\sqrt{2gh\left(\vartheta_0^2 - 2gh\right)} = 3{,}8m \tag{11.4}$$

12. For the ball to be broken when colliding with the inclined plane, the condition is that the component of the velocity which is perpendicular to the plane at the moment of collision must be equal to the final velocity reached by the ball falling from rest from the height h (see Figure 12)

Therefore

$$\vartheta' = \sqrt{2 \cdot g \cdot h} \tag{12.1}$$

where

$$\vartheta' = \vartheta_y \cdot \cos\alpha - \vartheta \cdot \sin\alpha, \tag{12.2}$$

ϑ_y is the vertical component of the velocity of the ball just before the impact, and has the expression:

$$\vartheta_y = \sqrt{2 \cdot g \cdot H} \tag{12.3}$$

where H is the distance covered by the ball on the vertical until the moment of the impact.

On the other hand, we know that

$$s = H \cdot \cot\alpha \tag{12.4}$$

where s is the distance covered on the horizontal.

Therefore

$$s = \vartheta \cdot t \tag{12.5}$$

$$H = \frac{1}{2} \cdot g \cdot t^2 \tag{12.6}$$

By making the calculations, we obtain

$$\vartheta = \frac{1}{\sin\alpha} \cdot \sqrt{2 \cdot g \cdot h} = 10\,\frac{\text{m}}{\text{s}} \tag{12.7}$$

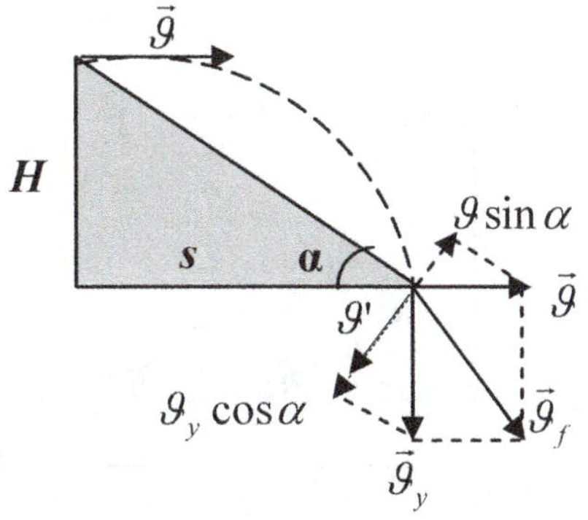

Figure 12

13. We know that

$$b = \frac{\vartheta_0^2}{g}\sin 2\alpha \tag{13.1}$$

and

$$h_\alpha = \frac{\vartheta_0^2}{2g}\sin^2\alpha \tag{13.2}$$

$$h_\beta = \frac{\vartheta_0^2}{2g}\sin^2\beta \tag{13.3}$$

$$\Delta h = \frac{\vartheta_0^2}{2g}\left(\sin^2\beta - \sin^2\alpha\right) \tag{13.4}$$

but

$$\alpha = \frac{\pi}{2} - \beta \tag{13.5}$$

Therefore

$$\Delta h = \frac{\vartheta_0^2}{2g}\left(\cos^2\alpha - \sin^2\alpha\right) \tag{13.6}$$

the answer demanded will be

$$\frac{b}{\Delta h} = \frac{\frac{\vartheta_0^2}{g}\sin 2\alpha}{\frac{\vartheta_0^2}{2g}\cos 2\alpha} \tag{13.7}$$

then

$$\frac{b}{\Delta h} = \frac{2}{\cot 2\alpha} \tag{13.8}$$

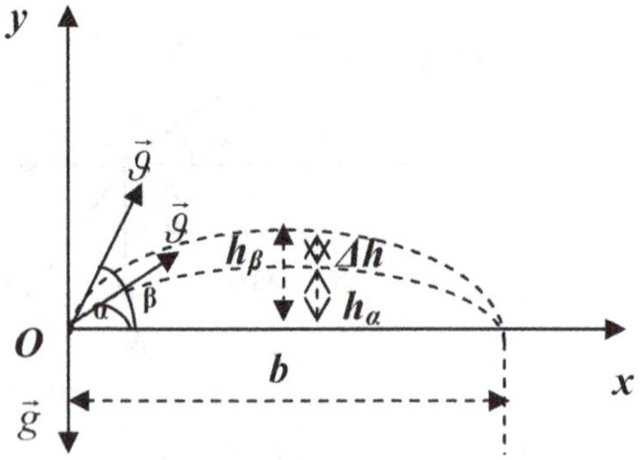

Figure 13

14. In the case of throwing the object from the ground (see Figure 14a), the expression of the distance covered in the horizontal in the flying time will be

$$b = 2\frac{\vartheta_0^2}{g} \cdot \sin\alpha \cdot \cos\alpha \qquad (14.1)$$

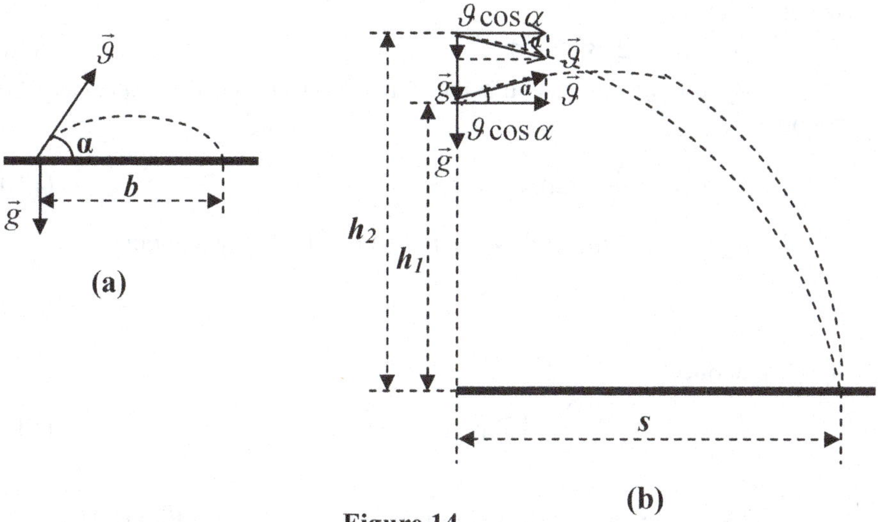

Figure 14

Since the distance covered on the horizontal is the same (s) in the case of throwing from heights h_1 and h_2 (see Figure 14b) also the projections of the initial velocities in the two cases are equal, we deduce that the flying time intervals will also be equal

$$t_1 = t_2 = \frac{s}{\vartheta_0 \cdot \cos\alpha} \qquad (14.2)$$

By applying the equation of displacement on the vertical in the two cases, we obtain

$$h_1 = \frac{1}{2} \cdot g \cdot t_1^2 - \vartheta_0 \cdot \sin\alpha \cdot t_1 \qquad (14.3)$$

$$h_2 = \frac{1}{2} \cdot g \cdot t_2^2 + \vartheta_0 \cdot \sin\alpha \cdot t_2 \qquad (14.4)$$

By first adding and then subtracting the expressions above, we obtain

$$h_1 + h_2 = \frac{1}{2} \cdot g \cdot \left(t_1^2 + t_2^2\right) \qquad (14.5)$$

and

$$h_2 - h_1 = \vartheta_0 \cdot \sin\alpha \cdot \left(t_1 + t_2\right) \qquad (14.6)$$

If we take into account (14.2)

$$h_2 + h_1 = \frac{1}{2} \cdot g \cdot 2 \frac{s^2}{\vartheta_0^2 \cdot \cos^2 \alpha} \tag{14.7}$$

$$h_2 - h_1 = 2\vartheta_0 \cdot \sin \alpha \frac{s}{\vartheta_0 \cdot \cos \alpha} \tag{14.8}$$

which means

$$h_2 - h_1 = 2 \cdot s \cdot \tan \alpha \tag{14.9}$$

By taking into account the expression (14.1), the expression (14.7) becomes

$$h_2 + h_1 = \frac{s^2}{b} \cdot \tan \alpha \tag{14.10}$$

By dividing the expression (14.9) by (14.10), we obtain

$$\frac{h_2 - h_1}{h_2 + h_1} = 2 \frac{b}{s} \tag{14.11}$$

then we deduce

$$h_2 = h_1 \cdot \frac{s + 2b}{s - 2b} = 15 \text{ m} \tag{14.12}$$

15. In the case of throwing from the ground (see Figure 15a), we can write

$$b = 2 \frac{\vartheta^2}{g} \cdot \sin \alpha \cdot \cos \alpha \tag{15.1}$$

In the case of throwing from the height *h*, the following equations of motion can be written

$$h = \frac{1}{2} \cdot g \cdot t^2 - \vartheta \cdot \sin \alpha \cdot t \tag{15.2}$$

and

$$s = \vartheta \cdot \cos \alpha \cdot t \tag{15.3}$$

By eliminating time and taking into account that $h=b$, we obtain

$$b = \frac{1}{2} \cdot g \cdot \frac{s^2}{\vartheta^2 \cdot \cos^2 \alpha} - s \cdot \tan \alpha \tag{15.4}$$

In the case of throwing on the horizontal from the height H (see Figure 15b), the equations of motion will be

$$H = \frac{1}{2} \cdot g \cdot t'^2 \tag{15.5}$$

$$S = \vartheta \cdot t' \tag{15.6}$$

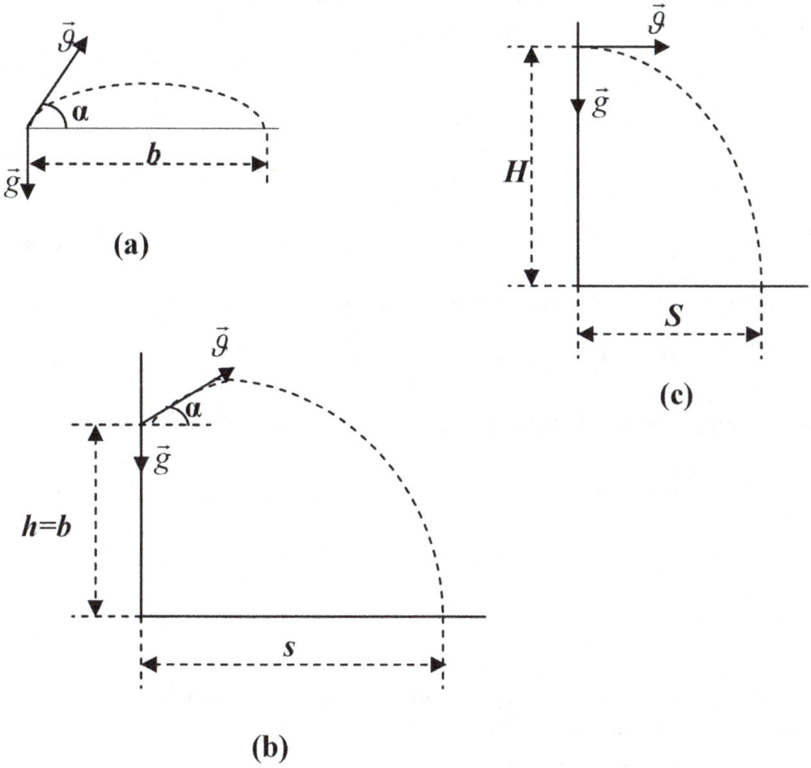

Figure 15

By eliminating the falling time t', we obtain

$$S = \vartheta \cdot \sqrt{\frac{2 \cdot H}{g}} \tag{15.7}$$

If we solve the equations (15.1) and (15.4), the initial velocity will be given by the following expression

$$\vartheta = \sqrt{\frac{s^2 (s-b)^2 + b^4}{2 \cdot s \cdot b \cdot (s-b)} \cdot g} \tag{15.8}$$

If we substitute it in the expression (15.7), it follows that

$$S = \sqrt{\frac{s^2 (s-b)^2 + b^4}{s \cdot b \cdot (s-b)} \cdot H} = 6.32 \text{ m} \tag{15.9}$$

16. Consider h to be the height from where the two bodies are thrown (see Figure 16); for the first body, we can write

$$h = \frac{1}{2} \cdot g \cdot t^2 \quad (16.1)$$

$$d = \vartheta \cdot t \quad (16.2)$$

By eliminating time, we obtain

$$h = \frac{1}{2} \cdot g \cdot \frac{d^2}{\vartheta^2} \quad (16.3)$$

The displacement covered by the balloon is

$$\Delta x = \sqrt{h^2 + d^2} \quad (16.4)$$

the velocity with which it must move will be

$$\vartheta' = \frac{\sqrt{h^2 + d^2}}{t} \quad (16.5)$$

where

$$t = \frac{d}{\vartheta} \quad (16.6)$$

By substituting the expressions (16.3) and (16.6) in (16.5) and by making the calculations, we obtain

$$\vartheta' = \frac{1}{2 \cdot \vartheta} \sqrt{g^2 d^2 + 4 \cdot \vartheta^4} = 7.76 \text{ m/s} \quad (16.7)$$

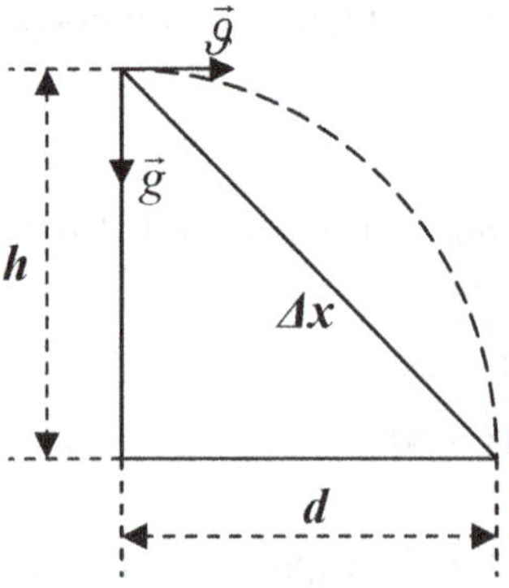

Figure 16

17. If we analyze Figure 17, we can notice that

$$s_1 = \vartheta\sqrt{\frac{2}{g}} \cdot \sqrt{h} \tag{17.1}$$

$$s_1 + s_2 = \vartheta \cdot \sqrt{\frac{2}{g}} \cdot \sqrt{2 \cdot h} \tag{17.2}$$

that is

$$s_2 = \vartheta\sqrt{\frac{2}{g}} \cdot \sqrt{h} \cdot (\sqrt{2} - 1) \tag{17.3}$$

and by generalization

$$s_k = \vartheta \cdot \sqrt{\frac{2h}{g}}\left(\sqrt{k} - \sqrt{k-1}\right) \tag{17.4}$$

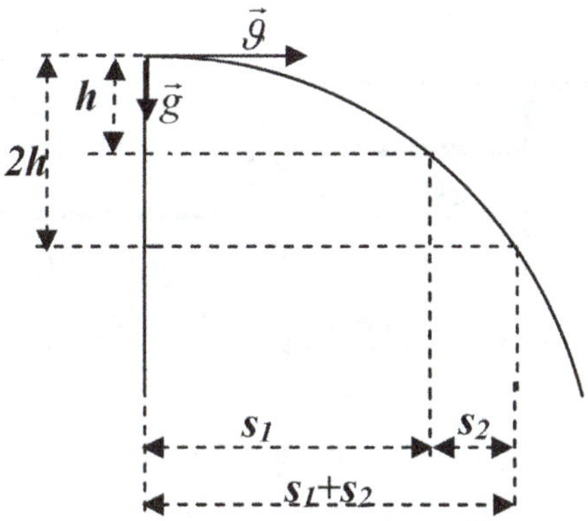

Figure 17

18. By analyzing Figure 18, we can see that:

$$l_1 = s_1 = \vartheta \cdot \sqrt{\frac{2 \cdot h}{g}} \tag{18.1}$$

$$l_2 = 2 \cdot s_1 + s_2 = 2 \cdot \vartheta \cdot \sqrt{\frac{2 \cdot h}{g}} + \vartheta \cdot \sqrt{\frac{2 \cdot h}{g}} \cdot \left(\sqrt{2} - 1\right) \tag{18.2}$$

(see Problem 17).

$$l_3 = 2 \cdot (s_1 + s_2) + s_3 = 2 \cdot \vartheta \cdot \sqrt{\frac{2 \cdot h}{g}} \cdot \sqrt{2} + \vartheta \cdot \sqrt{\frac{2 \cdot h}{g}} \cdot \left(\sqrt{3} - \sqrt{2}\right) \quad (18.3)$$

That is

$$l_3 = \vartheta \sqrt{\frac{2 \cdot h}{g}} \cdot (\sqrt{3} + \sqrt{2}) \quad (18.4)$$

Therefore

$$l_n = \vartheta \cdot \sqrt{\frac{2 \cdot h}{g}} \cdot \left(\sqrt{n} + \sqrt{n-1}\right) \quad (18.5)$$

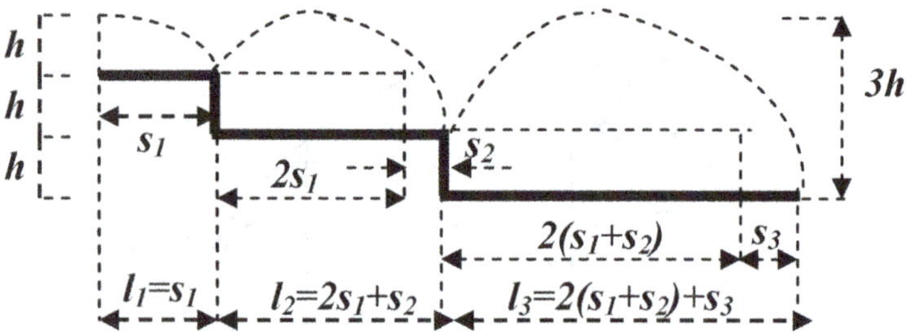

Figure 18

19. Consider Δt as the time interval necessary for the ball to cover the distance H between the wheels, which is a time interval that is equal to a quarter of the rotation period of the wheels, therefore

$$\Delta t = \frac{1}{4 \cdot \nu} \quad (19.1)$$

and on the other hand

$$H = \vartheta \cdot \Delta t + \frac{1}{2} \cdot g \cdot \Delta t^2 \quad (19.2)$$

where

$$\vartheta = \sqrt{2 \cdot g \cdot h} \quad (19.3)$$

By solving equations above, we obtain

$$h = \frac{\left(32 \cdot \nu^2 \cdot H - g\right)^2}{128 \cdot g \cdot \nu^2} = 0{,}378m \quad (19.4)$$

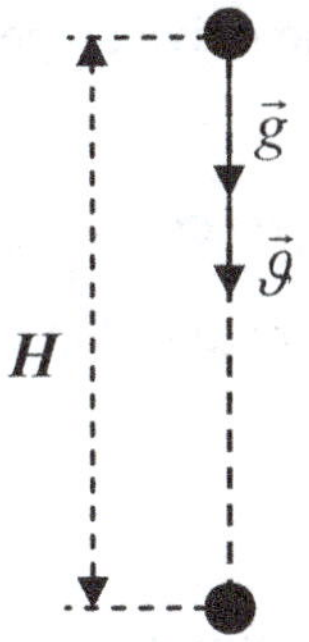

Figure 19

20. The decrease in the tension in the spring by which the pipe is attached is due to the presence of the resultant force of its weight and the centrifugal force exerted on the ball during the circular motion performed inside the pipe. The projection of the centrifugal force in the vertical will be maximum at the highest point of the pipe.

Initially, the tension in the spring is

$$T = M \cdot g \tag{20.1}$$

then

$$T' = M \cdot g - \left(m \cdot \frac{\vartheta^2}{R} - m \cdot g \right) \tag{20.2}$$

If we take into account that

$$T' = \frac{T}{n} \tag{20.3}$$

and make the calculations, we obtain

$$M = \left(\frac{n}{n-1} \right) \cdot \left(\frac{m}{R \cdot g} \right) \cdot \left(\vartheta^2 - R \cdot g \right) \tag{20.4}$$

21. Consider ϑ_0 as the velocity of the rod before entering on the last horizontal segment of the toboggan. Then

$$\vartheta_0 = \sqrt{2 \cdot g \cdot (H - h)} \tag{21.1}$$

where h is the height of the horizontal surface relative to the ground.

On the segment having a positive slope the following expression is valid (see Figure 21.)

$$\vartheta_1^2 = \vartheta_0^2 - 2 \cdot g \cdot d \cdot \tan \alpha \tag{21.2}$$

where

$\alpha = \alpha_1 = |\alpha_2|$.

The final velocity on the negative slope segment will be given by the expression

$$\vartheta_2^2 = \vartheta_0^2 - 2 \cdot g \cdot \frac{d}{\cos\alpha} \cdot \left(\mu \cdot \cos\alpha - \sin\alpha\right) \tag{21.3}$$

By imposing the condition required in the problem,

$$\vartheta_1 = \vartheta_2 \tag{21.4}$$

we obtain

$$\mu = 2 \cdot \tan\alpha \tag{21.5}$$

The time necessary to perform a complete rotation can be given by the expression

$$T = \frac{2 \cdot \pi \cdot \frac{l}{2}}{\vartheta_y} \tag{21.6}$$

where υ_y is the projection of the final velocity of each body on the vertical direction

$$\vartheta_y = \vartheta_1 \cdot \sin\alpha \tag{21.7}$$

The time necessary for the center of mass to descend the distance h will be

$$t = \sqrt{\frac{2 \cdot h}{g}} \tag{21.8}$$

By imposing the condition required in the problem, from the expressions (21.6), (21.7) and (21.8) it follows that

$$\frac{\pi \cdot l}{\sin\alpha \cdot \sqrt{\vartheta_0^2 - 2 \cdot g \cdot d \cdot \tan\alpha}} = \sqrt{\frac{2 \cdot h}{g}} \tag{21.9}$$

If we take into account the expression (21.1), we can write

$$\frac{\pi \cdot l}{\sin\alpha \cdot \sqrt{2 \cdot g \cdot (H - h) - 2 \cdot g \cdot \tan\alpha}} = \sqrt{\frac{2 \cdot h}{g}} \tag{21.10}$$

By solving the equation (21.10) for $h_{1,2}$, we obtain

$$h_{1,2} = \frac{H - d \cdot \tan\alpha \pm \sqrt{\left(H - d \cdot \tan\alpha\right)^2 - \frac{\pi^2 \cdot l^2}{\sin^2\alpha}}}{2} \tag{21.11}$$

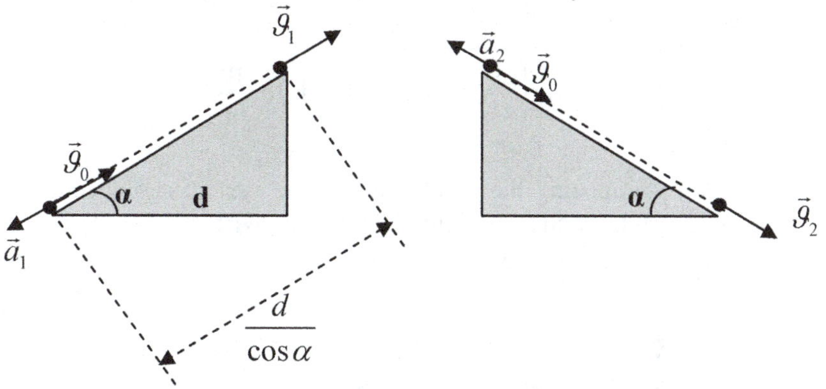

Figure 21

22. In order to assist the body of mass M to detach from the wall, the tension in the string must cancel the component of its weight along the incline

$$T = M \cdot g \cdot \sin\alpha \quad (22.1)$$

At the moment when the body of mass m is imparted a velocity ϑ (on the horizontal), a centrifugal force will act on it vertically downwards, because the body will perform a circular motion of radius $h = s \cdot \sin\alpha$.

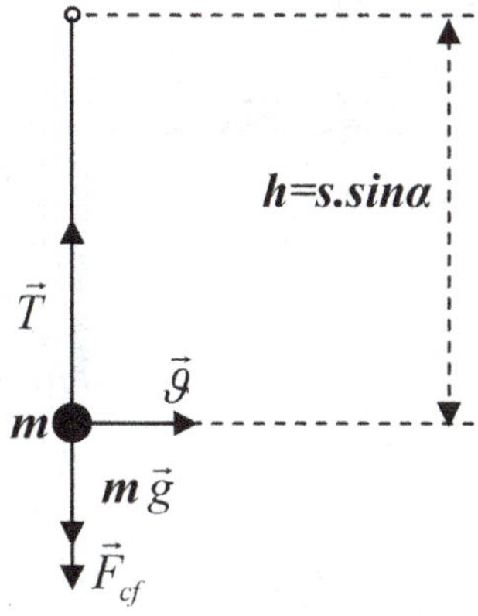

Figure 22

$$T = m \cdot g + F_{cf} \quad (22.2)$$

where

$$F_{cf} = m\frac{\vartheta^2}{s \cdot \sin\alpha} \quad (22.3)$$

By making the calculations, we obtain

$$\vartheta = \sqrt{s \cdot g \cdot \sin\alpha\left(\frac{M}{m} \cdot \sin\alpha - 1\right)} = 4.36\ \frac{\mathrm{m}}{\mathrm{s}} \qquad (22.4)$$

23. By imposing the condition that the system should not move, so that m_2 does not descend (see Figure 23), we can write

$$m_2 \cdot g = \mu \cdot m_1 + m_{31} \cdot g \qquad (23.1)$$

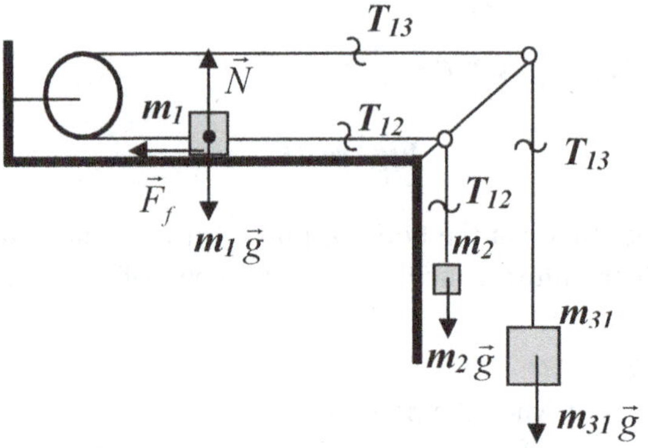

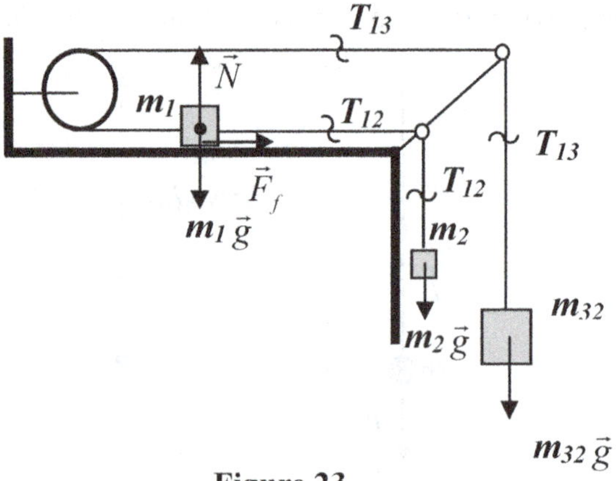

Figure 23

And if we impose that the third body does not descend, we obtain

$$m_{32} \cdot g = \mu \cdot m_1 \cdot g + m_2 \cdot g \qquad (23.2)$$

where m_{31} and m_{32} are the extreme values of the mass of the third body. After making the calculations, we obtain

$$m_3 \in (m_2 - \mu m_1; m_2 + \mu m_1) \qquad (23.3)$$

24. Consider α to be the angle required in the problem; by taking into account that the expression of the maximum force of traction is equal to the force of friction, we obtain the expression of the maximum climbing acceleration

$$a = g(\mu \cos\alpha - \sin\alpha) \tag{24.1}$$

From Figure 24b we can deduce the ratio of the distance covered up to the exit of the workshop to the depth where it is built

$$s = \frac{h}{\sin\alpha} \tag{24.2}$$

Since the motion takes place without an initial velocity, the following equation of motion can be written

$$s = \frac{1}{2} a \cdot t^2 \tag{24.3}$$

By replacing the expressions (24.1) and (24.2) into the expression above, we obtain

$$t = \sqrt{\frac{2h}{g \cdot \sin\alpha(\mu \cdot \cos\alpha - \sin\alpha)}} \tag{24.4}$$

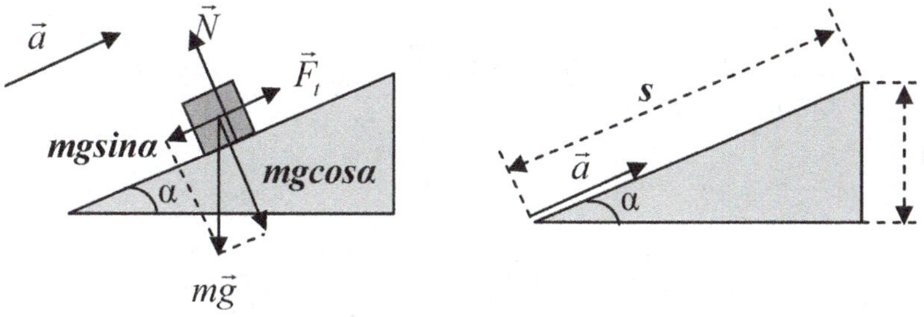

(a) (b)

Figure 24

In order for the climbing time to be minimum, we will impose the condition that the expression $E(\alpha)=\sin\alpha(\mu\cdot\cos\alpha - \sin\alpha)$ must be maximum.

Since $\mu = \frac{\sin\varphi}{\cos\varphi}$, $E(\alpha)$ can also be written as

$$E(\alpha) = \frac{\sin\alpha(\sin\varphi \cdot \cos\alpha - \sin\alpha \cdot \cos\varphi)}{\cos\varphi} \tag{24.5}$$

and then

$$E(\alpha) = \frac{\cos(2\alpha - \varphi) - \cos\varphi}{2\cos\varphi} \tag{24.6}$$

where $E(\alpha)$ that becomes maximum when

$$\cos(2\alpha - \varphi) = 1, \tag{24.7}$$

then we can obtain α as

$$\alpha = \frac{\arctan \mu}{2} \tag{24.8}$$

where $\arctan \mu = \varphi$ so,

$$\alpha = \frac{\varphi}{2} \tag{24.9}$$

25. From the conditions of equilibrium imposed on the body of the person in the vertical and horizontal axes (see Figure 25) we obtain

$$N = m \cdot a \cdot \sin\alpha + m \cdot g \tag{25.1}$$

$$F_t = m \cdot a \cdot \cos\alpha \tag{25.2}$$

and

$$F_t = F_f = \mu \cdot N \tag{25.3}$$

then

$$a = \frac{\mu}{\cos\alpha - \mu \cdot \sin\alpha} \cdot g = 14.13\,\frac{\text{m}}{\text{s}^2} \tag{25.4}$$

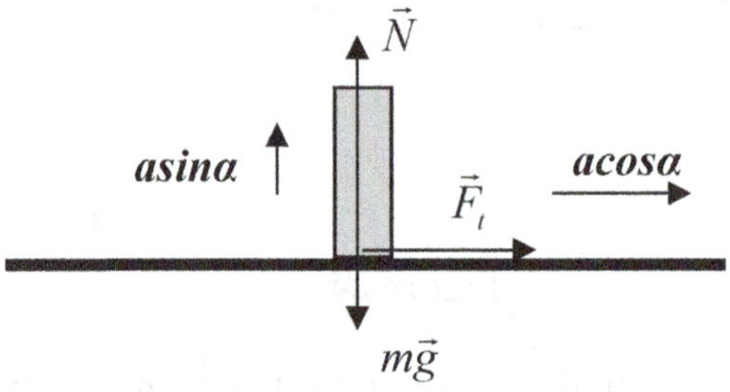

Figure 25

26. Initially by covering the distance s_1 (see Figure 26) at the bottom of the plane, the cyclist will reach the velocity:

$$\vartheta = \sqrt{2 \cdot \mu \cdot g \cdot s_1} \tag{26.1}$$

By imposing the condition of stopping on the inclined plane at point C, we can write

$$\vartheta = \sqrt{2 \cdot f \cdot s \cdot g \cdot (\sin\alpha - \mu \cdot \cos\alpha)} \tag{26.2}$$

where s is the total length of the hill. Therefore

$$\mu \cdot s_1 = f \cdot s \cdot (\sin\alpha - \mu\cos\alpha) \tag{26.3}$$

By remaking the calculations in the case when the distance s_2 is initially covered, we obtain

$$\mu \cdot s_2 = s \cdot (\sin\alpha - \mu\cos\alpha) \tag{26.4}$$

therefore

$$s_2 = s_1 \cdot \frac{1}{f} \tag{26.5}$$

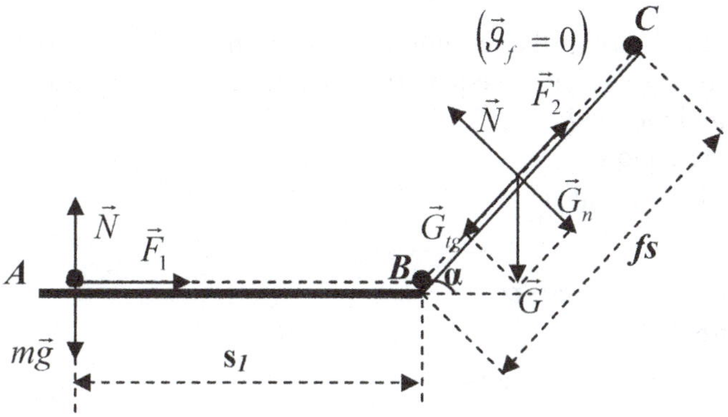

Figure 26

27. Starting from the condition of equilibrium along the perpendicular axis to the direction of motion Figure 27, we can write

$$\vec{F}_{cf} + \vec{F}_f = 0 \tag{27.1}$$

and we obtain

$$m \cdot \omega^2 \cdot R = \mu \cdot m \cdot g \tag{27.2}$$

where $\omega = \dfrac{2\pi}{t}$ and then

$$\frac{4 \cdot \pi^2}{t^2} \cdot R = \mu \cdot g \tag{27.3}$$

Therefore

$$R = \frac{\mu \cdot g}{4 \cdot \pi^2} \cdot t^2 \tag{27.4}$$

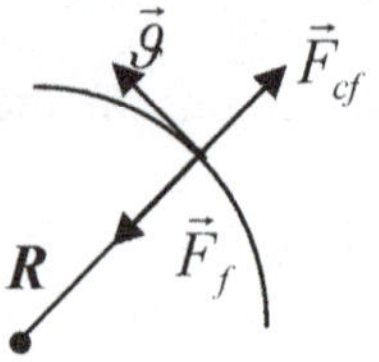

Figure 27

28. During the climbing or descending, the maximum force of traction of the car will be equal to the maximum force of friction between the wheels and the road.

Therefore

$$F_t = \mu \cdot N \tag{28.1}$$

and

$$N = m \cdot g \cdot \cos\alpha \tag{28.2}$$

Therefore

$$F_t = \mu \cdot m \cdot g \cdot \cos\alpha \tag{28.3}$$

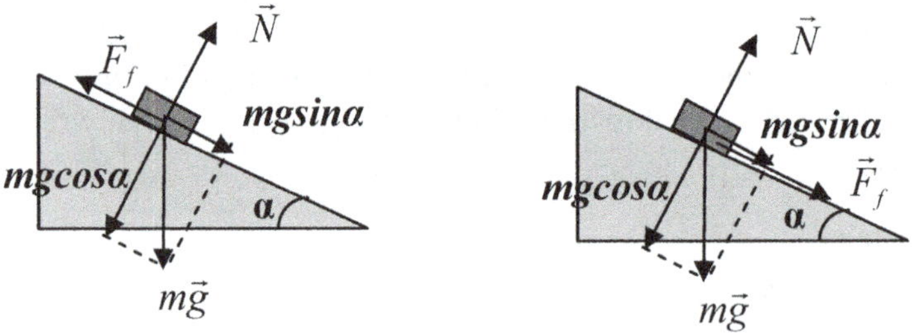

Figure 28

In the case of climbing, we will obtain

$$m \cdot a_c = F_t - m \cdot g \cdot \sin\alpha \tag{28.4}$$

and for descending we can write

$$m \cdot a_d = F_t + m \cdot g \cdot \sin\alpha \tag{28.5}$$

then

$$a_c = \mu \cdot g \cdot \cos\alpha - g \cdot \sin\alpha \tag{28.6}$$

$$a_d = \mu \cdot g \cdot \cos\alpha + g \cdot \sin\alpha \tag{28.7}$$

By solving the system above, we obtain

$$a_d = g \cdot \left(2 \cdot \sin\alpha + \frac{a_c}{g} \right) \tag{28.8}$$

29. Consider that ϑ is the launching velocity of the jump from one platform to another. Since our interest is the shortest time possible, the jumping velocity must be gained so that the distance covered horizontally, in the air, must be equal to the distance between the two platforms (see Figure 29). Therefore

$$l = \frac{\vartheta^2 \cdot \sin 2\alpha}{g} \tag{29.1}$$

then

$$\vartheta^2 = l \cdot g \cdot \frac{1}{\sin 2\alpha} \tag{29.2}$$

and the flight time will be given by the expression

$$t_f = \frac{2 \cdot \vartheta}{g} \cdot \sin\alpha \qquad \text{where } t_f \text{ is the flight time} \tag{29.3}$$

The maximum acceleration with which the car can climb is given by the expression

$$ma = F_{t\max} - m \cdot g \cdot \sin\alpha \tag{29.4}$$

where F_{tmax} is the maximum force of traction.

Therefore

$$F_{t\max} = \mu \cdot m \cdot g \cdot \cos\alpha \tag{29.5}$$

from where

$$a = g \cdot (\mu \cdot \cos\alpha - \sin\alpha) \tag{29.6}$$

The time necessary to reach the jumping velocity will be given by the expression

$$t_c = \frac{\vartheta}{a} \tag{29.7}$$

where t_c is climbing time, that is,

$$t_c = \frac{\sqrt{\dfrac{l \cdot g}{\sin 2\alpha}}}{g \cdot (\mu \cdot \cos\alpha - \sin\alpha)} \tag{29.8}$$

If we take into account the expressions (29.3) and (29.7), we obtain

$$t_f = 2 \cdot a \cdot t_c \cdot \frac{\sin\alpha}{g} \tag{29.9}$$

The expression of the braking acceleration will be the same as the expression calculated before. Therefore the time necessary to stop the car just after the jump (thus having the same initial velocity ϑ) will also be the same as the time necessary to reach the velocity ϑ.

Therefore

$$t_b = t_c \tag{29.10}$$

Since two consecutive jumps are to be performed, by neglecting the time necessary for the car to turn around, we obtain the following expression for the total time

$$t_t = 2 \cdot (t_c + t_f + t_b) \tag{29.11}$$

If we take into account the expressions above, we can write

$$t_t = \frac{4 \cdot \sqrt{\dfrac{l}{g \cdot \sin 2\alpha}}}{\mu \cdot \cos\alpha - \sin\alpha} \cdot [1 + (\mu \cdot \cos\alpha - \sin\alpha) \cdot \sin\alpha] \tag{29.12}$$

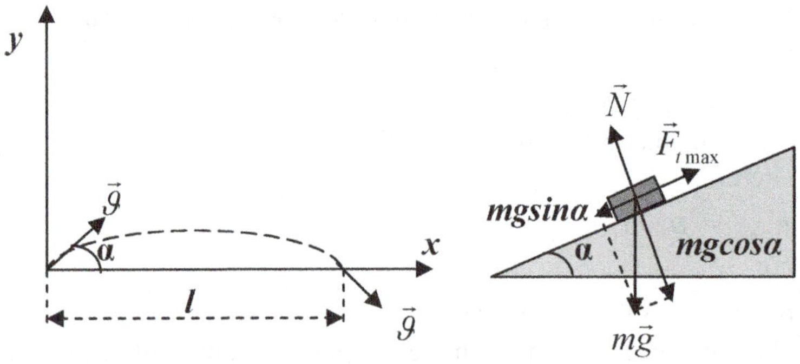

Figure 29

30. The force acting on the body cannot have the vertical component greater than the body's weight (otherwise the body would take off). (see Figure 30)

Therefore

$$F \cdot \sin\alpha = m \cdot g \tag{30.1}$$

On the other hand

$$F \cdot \cos\alpha = m \cdot a \tag{30.2}$$

The force of friction, regardless of the value of the coefficient, is not taken into consideration because, in this extreme situation, the normal force is cancelled.

Therefore, after the calculations we obtain

$$a = g \cdot \cot \alpha \tag{30.3}$$

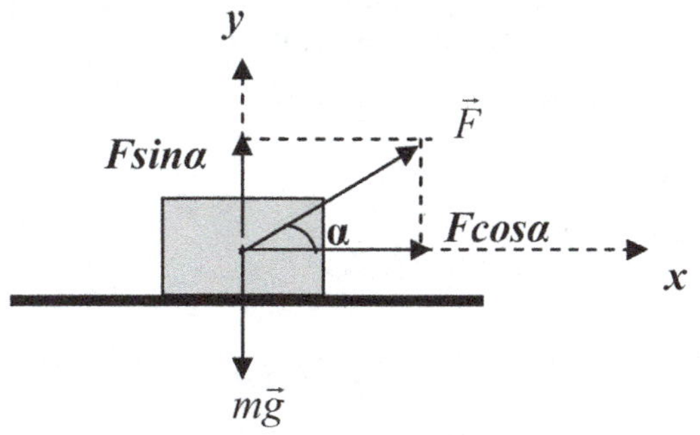

Figure 30

31. If α is the angle made by the string with the horizontal (see Figure 31), for the first body we can write

$$N = m_1 \cdot g - T \cdot \sin \alpha \tag{31.1}$$

$$F_{\mathrm{f}} = \mu \cdot N \tag{31.2}$$

$$m_1 \cdot a = T \cdot \cos \alpha - F_f \tag{31.3}$$

and as far as the second body is concerned

$$T = m_2 \cdot g \cdot \cos \beta - m_2 \cdot a \cdot \cos \alpha \tag{31.4}$$

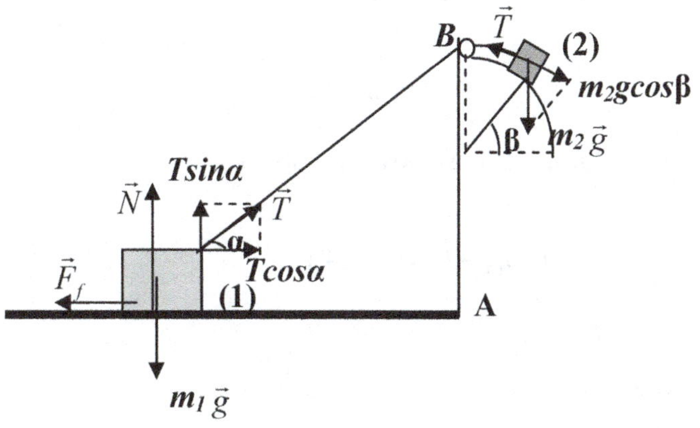

Figure 31

From the equations above we obtain

$$a = g\frac{m_2 \cos\beta(\cos\alpha + \mu\sin\alpha) - \mu m_1}{m_1 + m_2(\cos\alpha + \mu\sin\alpha)\cos\alpha} \tag{31.5}$$

32. As

$$T = k_1 \cdot \Delta l_1 \tag{32.1}$$

$$T = k_2 \cdot \Delta l_2 \tag{32.2}$$

it follows that

$$k_1 \Delta l_1 = k_2 \cdot \Delta l_2 \tag{32.3}$$

On the other hand

$$l = l_{01} + \Delta l_1 + l_{02} + \Delta l_2 \tag{32.4}$$

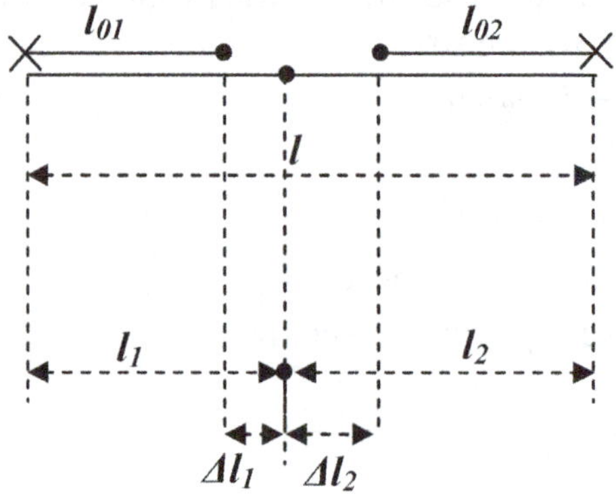

Figure 32

By solving the equations above, we obtain

$$\Delta l_1 = \frac{k_2}{k_1 + k_2} \cdot (l - l_{01} - l_{02}) = 1.84 \text{ m} \tag{32.5}$$

$$\Delta l_2 = \frac{k_1}{k_1 + k_2} \cdot (l - l_{01} - l_{02}) = 1.15 \text{ m} \tag{32.6}$$

$$T = \frac{k_1 \cdot k_2}{k_1 + k_2} \cdot (l - l_{01} - l_{02}) = 9.23 \text{ N} \tag{32.7}$$

33. Consider E as the elastic modulus characterizing the material which the body is made of.

Then, for the cable in the initial case, we will write

$$k_0 = \frac{E \cdot A}{L} \tag{33.1}$$

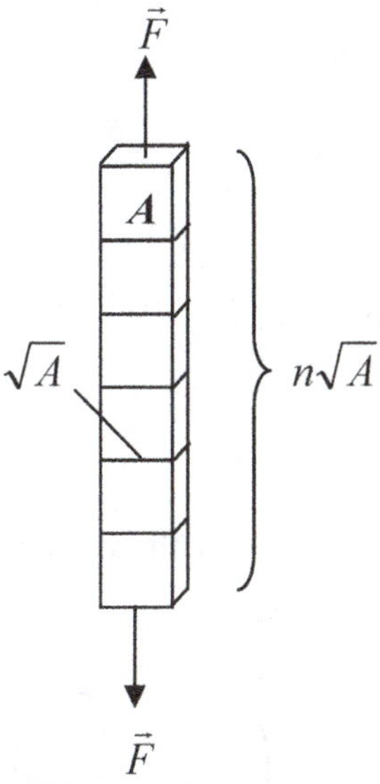

Figure 33

The new body (see Figure 33) will be characterized by a cross-sectional area A' perpendicular to the direction of tension and a length L' along this direction, given by the expressions

$$A' = \frac{L}{n} \cdot \sqrt{A} \tag{33.2}$$

and

$$L' = n \cdot \sqrt{A} \tag{33.3}$$

The spring constant has the following expression:

$$k' = \frac{E \cdot A'}{L'} \tag{33.4}$$

we obtain

$$\frac{k'}{k_0} = \frac{E \cdot A'}{L'} \cdot \frac{L}{E \cdot A} \tag{33.5}$$

If we take into account the expressions (33.2) and (33.3), we obtain

$$\frac{k'}{k_0} = \frac{L^2}{n^2 \cdot A} \tag{33.6}$$

34. Consider k'' as the spring constant of the new body (see Figure 34). Then

$$k'' = \frac{E \cdot A''}{L''} \tag{34.1}$$

where

$$L'' = \sqrt{A} \tag{34.2}$$

and

$$A'' = \frac{1}{n} \cdot L \cdot \sqrt{A} \cdot n \tag{34.3}$$

then we obtain the ratio

$$\frac{k''}{k_0} = \frac{L^2}{A} \tag{34.4}$$

Therefore, we notice that the required ratio does not depend on the number n.

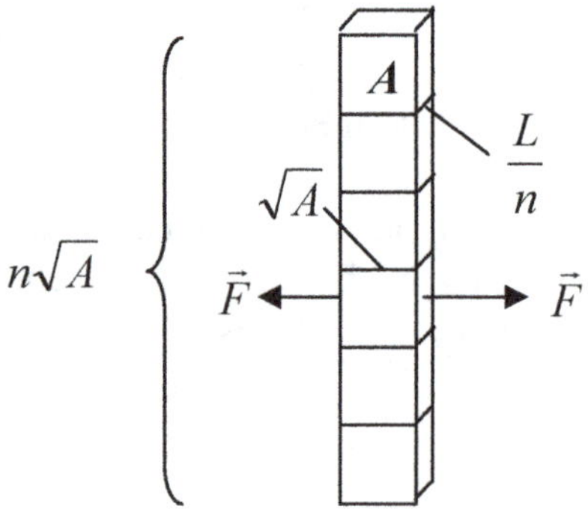

Figure 34

35. Consider T as the tension necessary to break the cable and A as its cross-sectional area. Hence we obtain

$$\varphi = \frac{T}{A} \tag{35.1}$$

Due to the fact that the string is thinner on a certain segment, here the breaking tension decreases proportionally with the section, so that

$$\frac{T'}{T} = \frac{A'}{A} \tag{35.2}$$

where T' is the new breaking tension and A' the cross-sectional area in the thinner segment.

Therefore

$$T' = \frac{A'}{A} \cdot T \qquad (35.3)$$

On the other hand

$$A' = \frac{A}{n} \qquad (35.4)$$

from where

$$T' = \frac{T}{n} \qquad (35.5)$$

The absolute extension of the cable when it undergoes the tension T' will consist of the sum of the extension of the segment whose cross-sectional area remained unchanged and the extension of the thinner section, hence

$$\Delta l = \Delta l_1 + \Delta l_2 \qquad (35.6)$$

Consider k as the elastic constant of the string in the initial situation (i.e. before one segment of it got thinner) and l_o as its length, and k_1 and k_2 as the spring constants characterizing the two segments of the cable, having the same cross-sectional areas A and A', respectively.

Hence, we can write

$$k = \frac{E \cdot A}{l_0} \qquad (35.7)$$

$$k_1 = \frac{E \cdot A}{(1 - f) \cdot l_0} \qquad (35.8)$$

$$k_2 = \frac{E \cdot A'}{f \cdot l_0} \qquad (35.9)$$

then

$$k_1 = \frac{k}{1 - f} \qquad (35.10)$$

$$k_2 = \frac{k}{f \cdot n} \qquad (35.11)$$

On the other hand, we can write

$$T' = k_1 \cdot \Delta l_1 \qquad (35.12)$$

and

$$T' = k_2 \cdot \Delta l_2 \qquad (35.13)$$

Taking into account the expressions (35.6), (35.10), (35.12) and (35.13), we obtain

$$\Delta l = \frac{T'}{k} \cdot (1 - f + f \cdot n) \qquad (35.14)$$

By replacing the expressions (35.1), (35.5) and (35.7) in the expression above and by dividing it by l_o, we obtain

$$\frac{\Delta l}{l_0} = \varphi \cdot \frac{1 - f + f \cdot n}{n \cdot E} \tag{35.15}$$

36. The liquid begins to leave the tube during its circular motion at the moment its tension relative to section a is equal or greater than the tensile stress.

$$T' = \sigma \cdot a \tag{36.1}$$

According to Figure 36, we notice that

$$F_{cf} = 2 \cdot T' \cdot \sin\alpha \tag{36.2}$$

with

$$F_{cf} = \Delta m \cdot 4 \cdot \pi^2 \cdot \nu^2 \cdot \frac{l}{2 \cdot \pi} \tag{36.3}$$

and

$$\Delta m = \frac{2 \cdot \alpha}{2 \cdot \pi} \cdot m \tag{36.4}$$

(with $\alpha \ll 1$), where

$$m = \rho \cdot (A - a) \cdot l \tag{36.5}$$

By solving the equations above, we obtain

$$\nu = \frac{1}{l} \cdot \sqrt{\frac{\sigma \cdot a}{(A - a) \cdot \rho}} \tag{36.6}$$

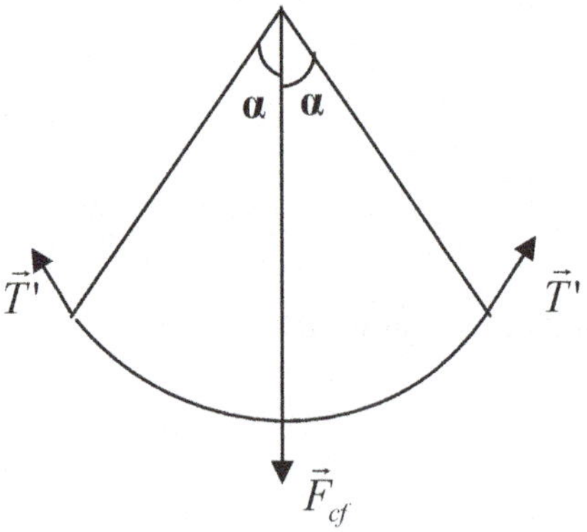

Figure 36

37. If we take into account the enunciation of the problem, we can write

$$g_1 = \sqrt{g_2 \cdot g_3} \quad (37.1)$$

so

$$\frac{G \cdot M_1}{R_1^2} = \frac{\sqrt{G \cdot M_2 \cdot G \cdot M_3}}{R_2 \cdot R_3} \quad (37.2)$$

where

$$M_1 = \rho_1 \cdot V_1 \quad (37.3)$$

$$M_2 = \rho_2 \cdot V_2 \quad (37.4)$$

$$M_3 = \rho_3 \cdot V_3 \quad (37.5)$$

Therefore, by making the calculations, we obtain

$$\rho_1 \cdot R_1 = \sqrt{\rho_2 \cdot \rho_3} \cdot \sqrt{R_2 \cdot R_3} \quad (37.6)$$

By taking into account

$$\rho_1 = \sqrt{\rho_2 \cdot \rho_3} \quad (37.7)$$

we obtain

$$R_1 = \sqrt{R_2 \cdot R_3} \quad (37.8)$$

(and the radius of the first planet represents the geometrical mean of the radii of the other two)

38. By imposing the condition of cancellation of the gravitational field at point A (see Figure 38):

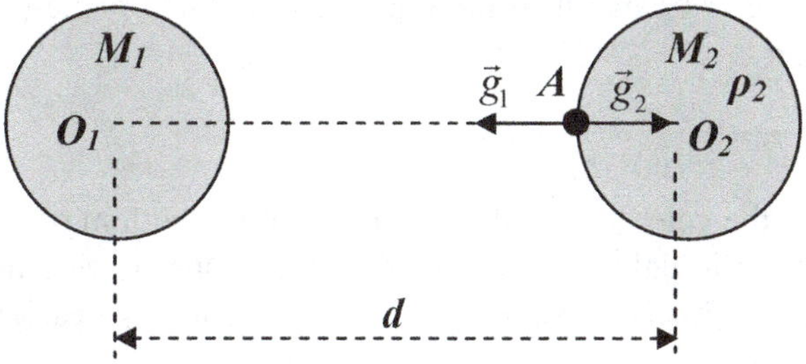

Figure 38

$$g = 0 \quad (38.1)$$

it follows that

$$g_1 = g_2 \quad (38.2)$$

where

$$g_1 = \frac{G \cdot M_1}{(d - R_2)^2} \tag{38.3}$$

and

$$g_2 = \frac{G \cdot M_2}{R_2^2} \tag{38.4}$$

On the other hand

$$R_2 = \left(\frac{3}{4 \cdot \pi}\right)^{\frac{1}{3}} \cdot \left(\frac{M_2}{\rho_2}\right)^{\frac{1}{3}} \tag{38.5}$$

By solving the equations above, we obtain

$$d = \left(\frac{3}{4 \cdot \pi}\right)^{\frac{1}{3}} \cdot \left(\frac{M_2}{\rho_2}\right)^{\frac{1}{3}} \cdot \frac{M_2^{\frac{1}{2}} + M_1^{\frac{1}{2}}}{M_2^{\frac{1}{2}}} \tag{38.6}$$

39. Starting from the expression of the efficiency

$$\eta = \frac{\Delta PE}{W_m} \tag{39.1}$$

where ΔPE is the change in potential energy of the body and W_m is the mechanical work to carry it to the top of the inclined plane (see Figure 39), then we obtain

$$\eta = \frac{1}{(1 + \mu \cdot \cot\alpha)} \tag{39.2}$$

Since the velocities of the containers at the bottom of the platform are the same as their initial velocities, their accelerations are zero as they descend on the platform. This is possible only if the following expression is valid:

$$\mu = \tan\alpha \tag{39.3}$$

Returning to expression (39.2), we obtain

$$\eta = \frac{1}{2} \tag{39.4}$$

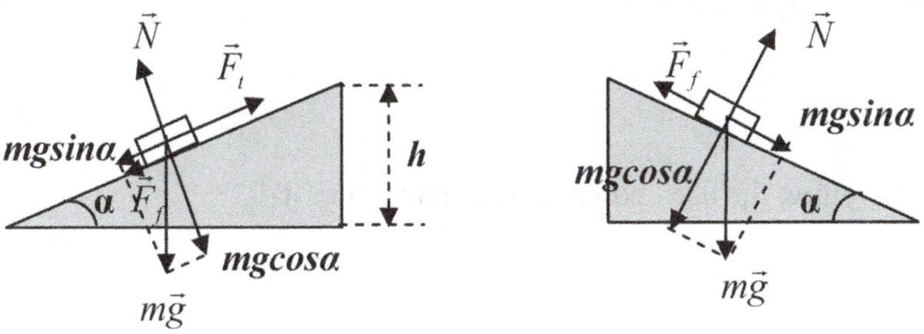

Figure 39

40. Starting from

$$\eta = \frac{P_e}{P_c} \tag{40.1}$$

we obtain

$$P_c = \frac{W_e}{\eta \cdot t} \tag{40.2}$$

Therefore, consider W_e as the effective mechanical work necessary for certain materials to move on a level difference h. Since this quantity is constant, depending on the mass of the materials, height difference and gravitational acceleration and, since the condition imposed is that the consumed power is maximum, from the expression (40.2) we deduce that

$$\eta \cdot t = \text{minimum}, \tag{40.3}$$

where t is the time necessary to transport materials along the entire platform (see Figure 40.R), therefore along a distance s:

$$s = \frac{h}{\sin\alpha} \tag{40.4}$$

Then, if ϑ is the transport speed, we can write

$$t = \frac{h}{\vartheta \cdot \sin\alpha} \tag{40.5}$$

Therefore

$$\eta \cdot t = \frac{h}{\vartheta} \cdot \frac{1}{\sin\alpha + \mu\cos\alpha} \tag{40.6}$$

If we take into account that $\mu = \tan\varphi$, the expression becomes

$$\eta \cdot t = \frac{h}{\vartheta} \cdot \frac{\cos\varphi}{\sin(\alpha + \varphi)} \tag{40.7}$$

Therefore, the product $\eta \cdot t$ becomes minimum if

$$\sin(\alpha + \varphi) = \text{maximum} \tag{40.8}$$

or

$$\alpha = \frac{\pi}{2} - \varphi \tag{40.9}$$

Therefore, the used power will be maximum if

$$\cot\alpha = \mu \tag{40.10}$$

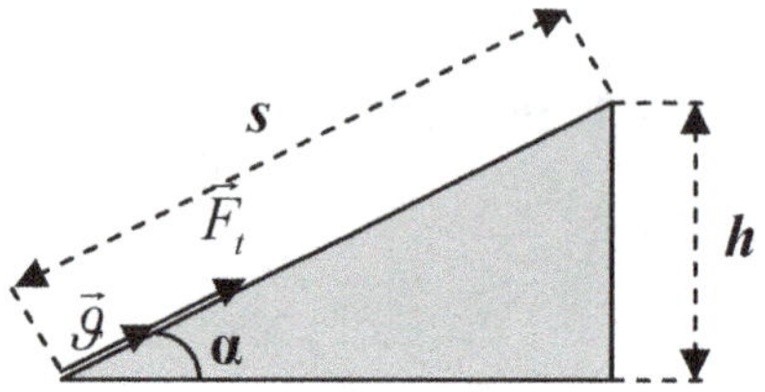

Figure 40

41. The mechanical work of the forces of friction between the body and the inclined plane, and also horizontal plane will be equal to change in mechanical energy of the body.

The initial and final potential energies of the body will be (see Figure 41):

$$PE_i = m \cdot g \cdot y_i \tag{41.1}$$

$$PE_f = m' \cdot g \cdot y_f \tag{41.2}$$

where

$$y_i = h - \frac{l \cdot \sin\alpha}{2} \tag{41.3}$$

$$y_f = \frac{l \cdot (1 - f)}{2} \cdot \sin\alpha \tag{41.4}$$

and

$$m' = (1 - f) \cdot m \tag{41.5}$$

On the other hand

$$\Delta E = W \tag{41.6}$$

where

$$\Delta E = PE_f - PE_i \tag{41.7}$$

and

$$W = W_1 + W_2 + W_2' \tag{41.8}$$

$$W_1 = -\mu_1 \cdot m \cdot g \cdot \cos\alpha \cdot s_1 \tag{41.9}$$

$$s_1 = \frac{h}{\sin\alpha} - l \tag{41.10}$$

and

$$W_2 = -\mu_2 \cdot \frac{m \cdot f}{2} \cdot g \cdot f \cdot l \tag{41.11}$$

and

$$W_2' = -\mu_1 \cdot (1-f) \cdot m \cdot g \cdot f \cdot l \cdot \cos\alpha \tag{41.12}$$

By solving the equations above, we obtain

$$h = \frac{l}{2(1-\mu_1 \cot\alpha)} \left\{ 2\mu_1 (1-f) f \cos\alpha + \mu_2 f^2 + \frac{1}{2} \sin\alpha \left[1 + (1-f)^2 \right] - \mu_1 \cos\alpha \right\} \tag{41.13}$$

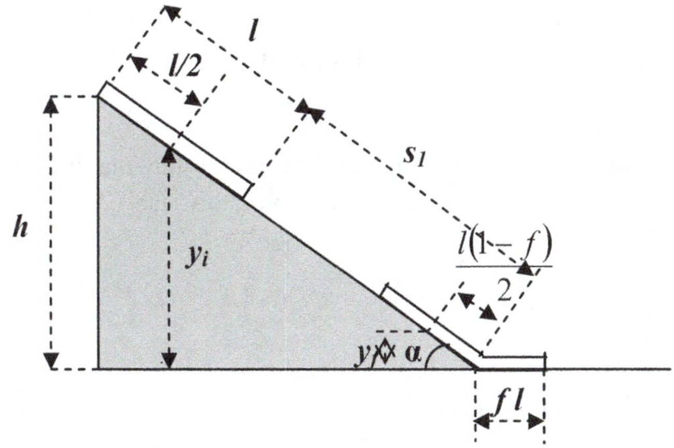

Figure 41

42. We must check if the distance at which the dog can go relative to the stake is longer or shorter than the length S.

If we apply the law of conservation of energy, we notice that the work done by the dog during its displacement on the distance L is stored as potential energy in the string (in the initial and final positions, the dog is at rest).

Hence

$$W = \frac{k \cdot (L - l_0)^2}{2} \tag{42.1}$$

where

$$W = F_m \cdot L \tag{42.2}$$

and F_m is the maximum force of friction (of adherence) between the dog and the ground.

$$F_m = F_f \tag{42.3}$$

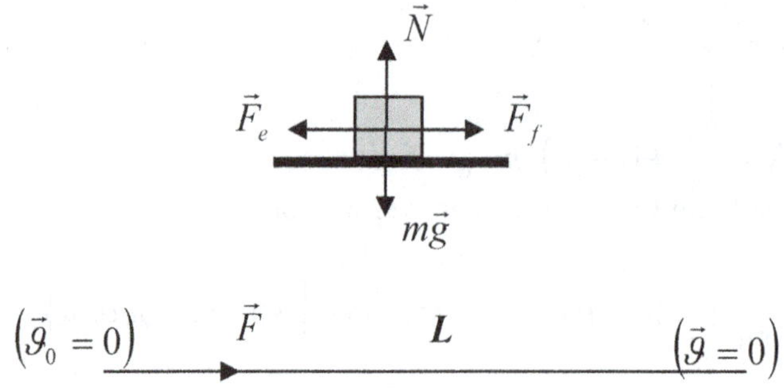

Figure 42

From the condition of equilibrium at the maximum extension of string where the dog can stay stationary we can write

$$\vec{F}_f + \vec{F}_e = 0 \tag{42.4}$$

$$F_f = F_e$$

also

$$F_e = k \cdot (l - l_0) \tag{42.5}$$

so

$$F_m = k \cdot (l - l_0) \tag{42.6}$$

If we return to expression (42.1), we obtain

$$k \cdot (l - l_0) \cdot L = \frac{k \cdot (L - l_0)^2}{2} \tag{42.7}$$

By solving the equation above, it follows that

$$L = l + \sqrt{l^2 - l_0^2} \tag{42.8}$$

that is

$$L = 8\ \mathrm{m} \qquad (L < S)$$

Therefore, one can enter the yard!

43. If we take into account the solution of the previous problem, we know that the force of friction between the dog and the ground can be written as

$$F_f = k \cdot (l - l_0) \tag{43.1}$$

and also

$$F_f = \mu \cdot m \cdot g \tag{43.2}$$

where μ is the coefficient of friction and m dog's mass.

For the cage not to be moved, we must impose the condition of equality of the maximum tension in the string and the frictional force between the cage and the ground.

In other words, we need to find the expression of the maximum extension of the string. The extension can appear if the dog performs a maximum displacement with a maximum force of traction. In the circumstances imposed by the problem, this can happen when the dog begin to run just near the cage from rest.

When the displacement is over, the extension is maximum and the energy stored in the string will be equal to the work done by the dog during motion. If L is the final length, then we obtain

$$\frac{k \cdot (L - l_0)^2}{2} = F_t \cdot L \tag{43.3}$$

where

$$F_t = k \cdot (l - l_0) \tag{43.4}$$

Thus, by solving the equations above, it follows that

$$L = l + \sqrt{l^2 - l_0^2} \tag{43.5}$$

Therefore the expression for the elastic force in the string when the displacement is over is

$$F_e' = k \cdot \left(l - l_0 + \sqrt{l^2 - l_0^2}\right) \tag{43.6}$$

Now by imposing the condition of equilibrium for the cage (see Figure 43), we can write

$$\vec{N} + M \cdot \vec{g} = 0 \Rightarrow N = M \cdot g \tag{43.7}$$

$$\vec{F}_e' + \vec{F}_{fM} = 0 \Rightarrow F_e' = F_{fM} \tag{43.8}$$

where

$$F_{fM} = \mu \cdot N \tag{43.9}$$

therefore

$$\mu \cdot M \cdot g = k \cdot \left(l - l_0 + \sqrt{l^2 - l_0^2}\right) \tag{43.10}$$

If we take into account the expressions (43.1) and (43.2), we obtain

$$\frac{M}{m} = \frac{l - l_0 + \sqrt{l^2 - l_0^2}}{l - l_0} \tag{43.11}$$

by simplifying it, we get

$$\frac{M}{m} = 1 + \sqrt{\frac{l + l_0}{l - l_0}} = 4 \tag{43.12}$$

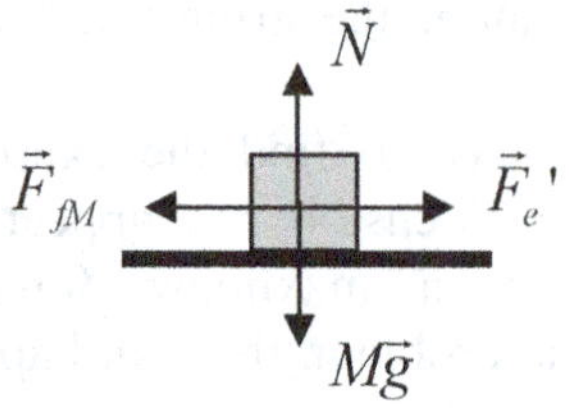

Figure 43

44. By imposing the condition of stopping in the velocity equation and by taking into account the expression of the maximum acceleration, we obtain

$$\Delta t = \frac{\vartheta}{\mu \cdot g} \tag{44.1}$$

According to Figure 44, the pressing force exerted by the outer rail horizontally corresponds to the centrifugal force, and the frictional force will be

$$F = \mu \cdot N \tag{44.2}$$

By imposing the condition that motion takes place uniformly, it follows that

$$F = F_f \tag{44.3}$$

where F is the force exerted by the engine.

If we write afterwards that

$$N = F_{cf} \tag{44.4}$$

where

$$F_{cf} = \frac{m \cdot \vartheta^2}{R} \tag{44.5}$$

and

$$P = F \cdot \vartheta \tag{44.6}$$

If we solve the equations above for P we obtain

$$P = \frac{\vartheta^4 \cdot m}{g \cdot \Delta t \cdot R} \quad (44.7)$$

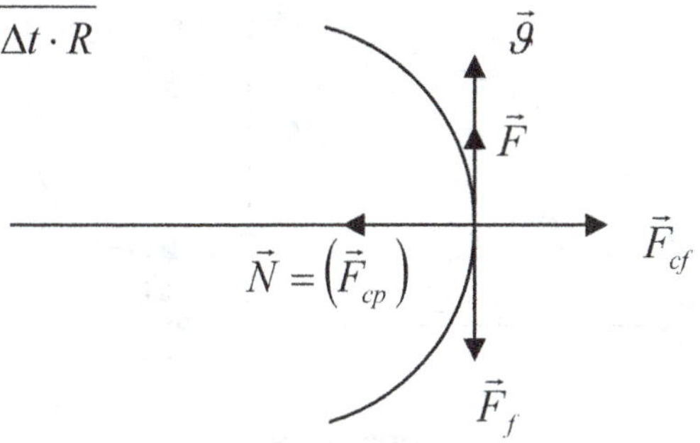

Figure 44

45. Motion is frictionless on portion CB (see Figure 45), at point B the body will have the energy

$$E_B = \frac{m \cdot \vartheta^2}{2} \quad (45.1)$$

and at point A

$$E_A = \frac{m \cdot \vartheta'^2}{2} + m \cdot g \cdot 2 \cdot R \quad (45.2)$$

Since

$$E_A = E_B \quad (45.3)$$

we obtain

$$\frac{m \cdot \vartheta'^2}{2} + m \cdot g \cdot 2 \cdot R = \frac{m \cdot \vartheta^2}{2} \quad (45.4)$$

On the other hand, as for the motion between points A and C we can write

$$2 \cdot R = \frac{1}{2} \cdot g \cdot t^2 \quad (45.5)$$

and

$$L = \vartheta' t \quad (45.6)$$

By solving the equations (45.4), (45.5) and (45.6) for ϑ we obtain

$$\vartheta = \frac{1}{2}\sqrt{\frac{\left(L^2 + 16R^2\right) \cdot g}{R}} = 10.54 \text{ m/s} \quad (45.7)$$

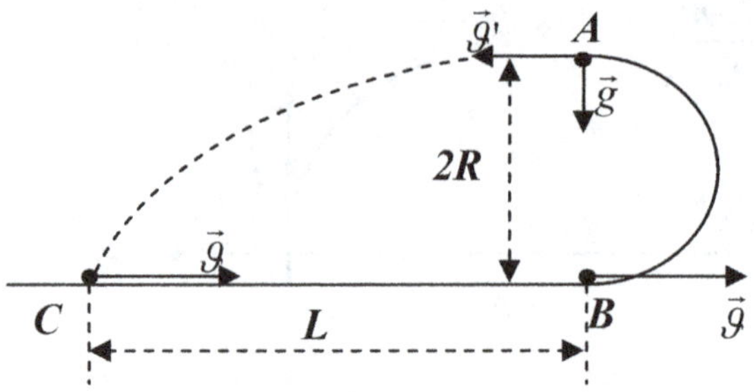

Figure 45.R

46. Since only up to the height h a constant-speed motion is possible, we deduce that at this point the tangential component of the weight is equal to the maximum force of traction that can be imparted by the engine to the wheel; therefore we can write

$$N = m \cdot g \cdot \cos\alpha + m \cdot \frac{\vartheta^2}{R} \tag{46.1}$$

$$F_t = \mu \cdot N \tag{46.2}$$

also

$$F_t = mg\sin\alpha \tag{46.3}$$

$$\sin\alpha = \frac{\sqrt{h(2R-h)}}{R} \tag{46.4}$$

and

$$\cos\alpha = \frac{R-h}{R} \tag{46.5}$$

then from the equations above, we can obtain

$$\vartheta^2 = g \cdot \left[\frac{\sqrt{h \cdot (2 \cdot R - h)}}{\mu} - R + h\right] \tag{46.6}$$

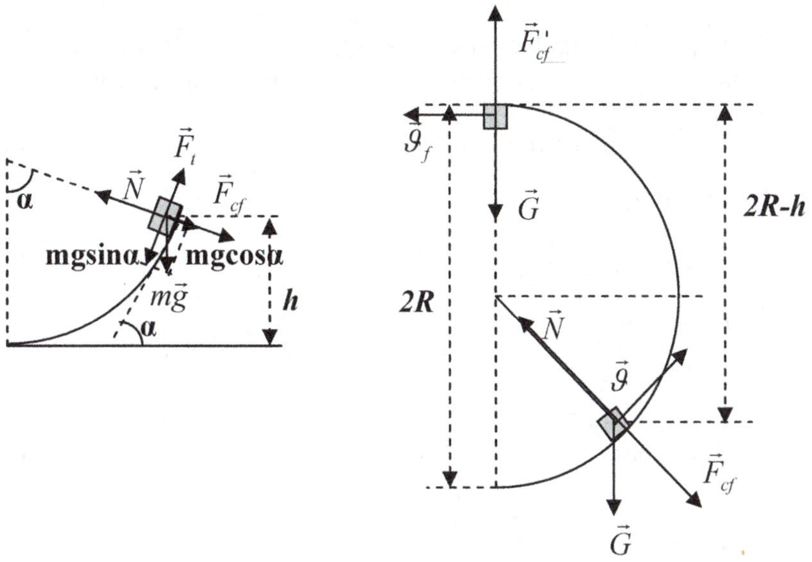

Figure 46

Since motion continues to take place under the single action of the weight, by applying the law of conservation of energy for motion up to the highest point (see Figure 46), we obtain

$$\vartheta_f^2 = \vartheta^2 - 2\cdot(2\cdot R - h)\cdot g \tag{46.7}$$

by imposing the condition

$$\frac{m\cdot\vartheta_f^2}{R} = m\cdot g \tag{46.8}$$

we will obtain, if we take into account (46.6)

$$\mu = \frac{1}{3}\cdot\sqrt{\frac{h}{2R-h}} \tag{46.9}$$

47. We consider that: AD=s_1, DC=s_2, BD=x, BC=l (see Figure 47)

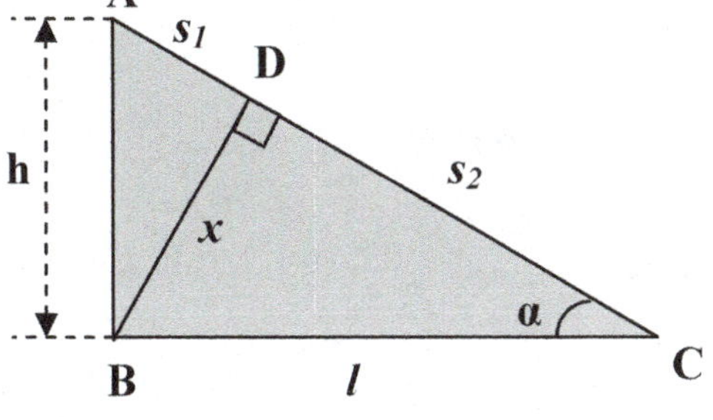

Figure 47

If we apply the law of conservation of energy for the motion of the body attached by the elastic string between points A and C, we may write

$$\frac{k \cdot s_1^2}{2} + m \cdot g \cdot h = \frac{k \cdot s_2^2}{2} \quad (47.1)$$

Therefore

$$k = \frac{2 \cdot m \cdot g \cdot h}{s_2^2 - s_1^2} \quad (47.2)$$

On the other hand, it follows that

$$s_1 \cdot s_2 = x^2 \quad (47.3)$$

$$x \cdot (s_1 + s_2) = h \cdot l \quad (47.4)$$

$$l = h \cdot \cot \alpha \quad (47.5)$$

and

$$\cot \alpha = \frac{s_2}{x} \quad (47.6)$$

By making the calculations, we obtain

$$k = \frac{2 \cdot m \cdot g}{h} \cdot \frac{1}{\cot^2 \alpha - 1} = 10 \frac{N}{m} \quad (47.7)$$

48. During the motion, the rod to which the body is attached always remains in the vertical. Until the angle between the two rods becomes α, the body has descended a distance in the vertical h relative to the initial position (see Figure 48), so that we can write

$$h = l(1 - \cos \alpha) \quad (48.1)$$

By applying the law of conservation of energy, we obtain

$$\frac{m \vartheta^2}{2} = mgh \quad (48.2)$$

or

$$\vartheta = \sqrt{2 \cdot g \cdot h} \quad (48.3)$$

By solving the equations above, for ϑ we can get it as

$$\vartheta = \sqrt{gl \cdot 2(1 - \cos \alpha)} \quad (48.4)$$

$$\vartheta = \sqrt{10} \text{ m/s} \quad (48.5)$$

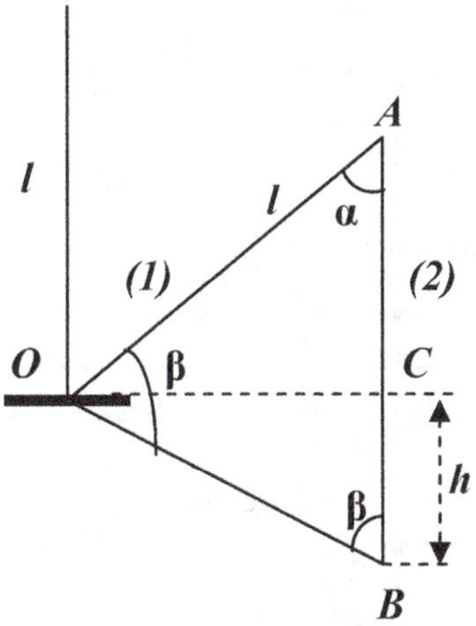

Figure 48

49. Consider y as the maximum compression undergone by the spring after the body of unknown mass m has fallen on the balance pan. In order to lift the body of mass M from the horizontal plane where it was placed, the following condition should be observed:

$$M \cdot g = k \cdot y \tag{49.1}$$

If we apply the law of conservation of energy to the motion of the body of mass m, we can write

$$m \cdot g \cdot (h + y) = \frac{k \cdot y^2}{2} \tag{49.2}$$

If we take into account the previous expression, we obtain

$$m = \frac{M^2 \cdot g}{2 \cdot (h \cdot k + M \cdot g)} \tag{49.3}$$

50. If we apply the law of conservation of energy for the motion of the body of mass m from the bottom of the body of mass M until the moment it stops (that is up to the maximum compression of the spring), we can write

$$\frac{m \cdot \vartheta_0^2}{2} = m \cdot g \cdot (s + x) \cdot \sin\alpha + \frac{k \cdot x^2}{2} \tag{50.1}$$

(see Figure 50a).

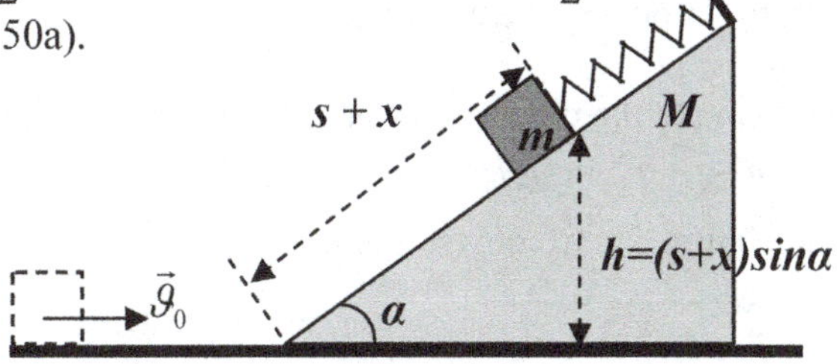

Figure 50 (a)

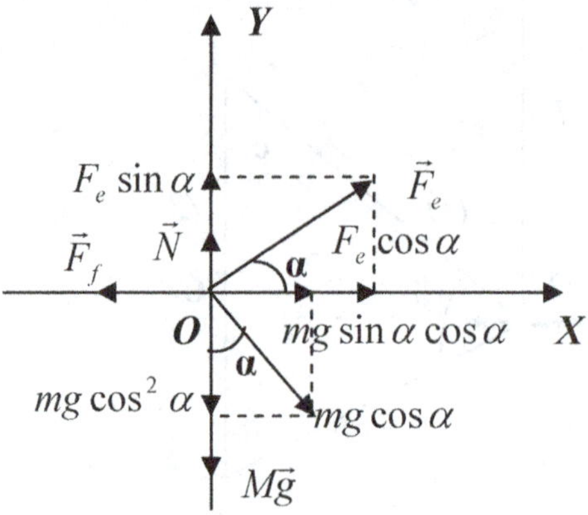

Figure 50 (b)

By imposing the conditions of equilibrium for the body of mass M in the vertical and, horizontal, the moment when the compression of the spring is maximum (x) (see Figure 50b), we obtain

$$N = M \cdot g + m \cdot g \cdot \cos^2 \alpha - F_e \cdot \sin \alpha \tag{50.2}$$

$$F_f = m \cdot g \cdot \cos \alpha \cdot \sin \alpha + F_e \cdot \cos \alpha \tag{50.3}$$

and

$$F_f = \mu \cdot N \tag{50.4}$$

By taking into account that

$$F_e = k \cdot x \tag{50.5}$$

and by solving the equations above for ϑ_0, we obtain

$$\vartheta_0 = \sqrt{2 \cdot g \left[s + \frac{g}{k} \cdot \left(\frac{\mu \cdot M + m \cdot \cos\alpha (\mu \cdot \cos\alpha - \sin\alpha)}{\cos\alpha + \mu \cdot \sin\alpha} \right) \right] + \frac{g^2 \cdot [\mu \cdot M + m \cdot \cos\alpha \cdot (\mu \cos\alpha - \sin\alpha)]^2}{mk(\cos\alpha + \mu \sin\alpha)^2}}$$

(50.6)

51. Starting by imposing the condition

$$N = 0 \tag{51.1}$$

which is necessary to make the detachment possible, we will be able to write

$$T \cdot \cos\alpha = m \cdot g + F_{cf} \cdot \cos\alpha \tag{51.2}$$

where, according to Figure 51, we observe that

$$F_{cf} = \frac{m \cdot \vartheta^2 \cdot \cos^2 \alpha}{r + \Delta l} \tag{51.3}$$

where

$$\cos\alpha = \frac{r}{r+\Delta l} \tag{51.4}$$

and ϑ is the velocity of the body at the time of detachment.

If we take into account that

$$T = k \cdot \Delta l \tag{51.5}$$

and, on the other hand, if we apply the conservation of energy:

$$m \cdot g \cdot r = \frac{m \cdot \vartheta^2}{2} + \frac{k}{2} \cdot \Delta l^2 \tag{51.6}$$

after solving the expressions above for m, we obtain

$$m = \frac{k \cdot \Delta l \cdot r \cdot \left[(r+\Delta l)^3 + r^2 \cdot \Delta l\right]}{g \cdot \left[(r+\Delta l)^4 + 2 \cdot r^4\right]} \tag{51.7}$$

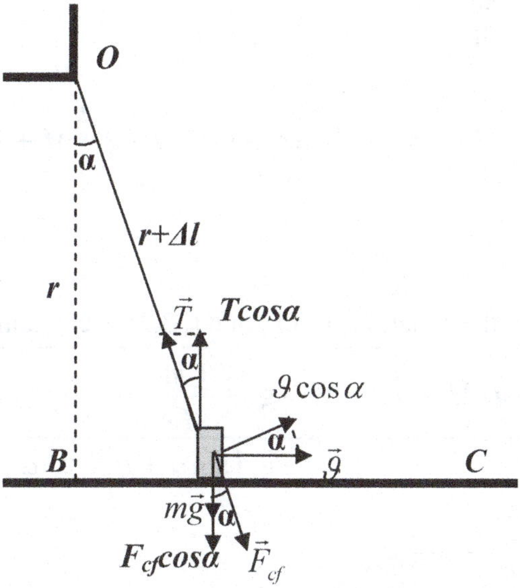

Figure 51

52. Just before hitting the balance pan, body 1 will reach the velocity

$$\vartheta = \sqrt{2 \cdot g \cdot h} \tag{52.1}$$

and after this moment, both bodies 1 and 2 will reach the same speed

$$\vartheta' = \frac{m}{M+m} \cdot \sqrt{2 \cdot g \cdot h} \tag{52.2}$$

As the body 2 will thus cover a circular arc of a radius equal to half of the length of the string, a centrifugal force will act on it, determining the accelerated motion of both bodies 2 and 3, in the vertical.

Hence

$$F_{cf} = \frac{2 \cdot M}{l} \cdot \vartheta'^2 \tag{52.3}$$

and

$$F_{cf} = 2 \cdot M \cdot a \tag{52.4}$$

Finally, we obtain

$$a = 2 \cdot g \cdot \frac{m^2}{(M+m)^2} \cdot \frac{h}{l} = 4 \frac{m}{s^2} \tag{52.5}$$

53. We consider the system consisting of two bodies and the cable. In the case of the cable, after applying the conservation of momentum, we will apply the theorem of conservation of energy.

We obtain

$$\Delta E = W \tag{53.1}$$

and

$$-\frac{1}{2} \cdot \frac{m^2}{M+m} \cdot \vartheta^2 + m' \cdot \frac{l}{2} \cdot (\sin\alpha) \cdot g = -\mu \cdot g \cdot \left(M + \frac{m'}{2} \cdot \cos^2\alpha \right) \cdot l \tag{53.2}$$

where

$$m' = \gamma \cdot l \tag{53.3}$$

From the equations (53.2) and (53.3), we obtain l as

$$l = \frac{-\mu \cdot g \cdot M + \sqrt{\mu^2 \cdot M^2 \cdot g^2 + \frac{m^2}{M+m} \cdot \vartheta^2 \cdot \gamma \cdot g \cdot \left(\sin\alpha + \mu \cdot \cos^2\alpha\right)}}{\gamma \cdot g \cdot \left(\sin\alpha + \mu \cdot \cos^2\alpha\right)} \tag{53.4}$$

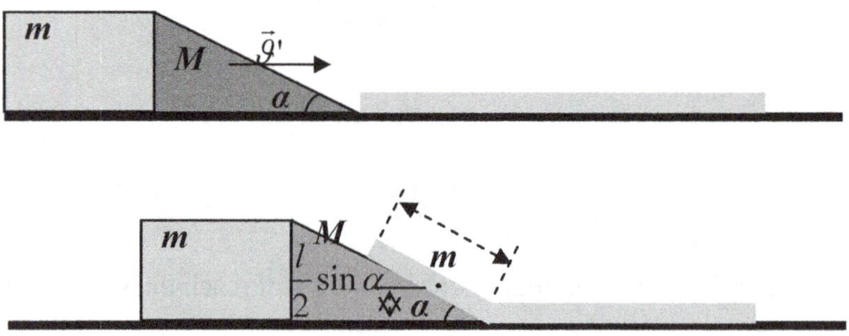

Figure 53

54. Consider $h=l\sin\alpha$ as the distance covered in the vertical by the body of mass M until the interaction with the body of mass m ceases, and $s=l\cos\alpha$ as the distance covered by m.

By applying the law of conservation of energy, we can write

$$M\cdot g\cdot l\cdot\sin\alpha=\frac{m}{2}\vartheta_1^2+\frac{M}{2}\vartheta_2^2 \tag{54.1}$$

As the motion is performed, we observe that

$$h=\frac{\vartheta_2}{2}\cdot\tau \tag{54.2}$$

where

$$h=l\cdot\sin\alpha \tag{54.3}$$

and

$$s=\frac{\vartheta_1}{2}\cdot\tau \tag{54.4}$$

where

$$s=l\cos\alpha \tag{54.5}$$

where ϑ_1 and ϑ_2 are the final velocities, and τ is the time interval of the motion.

Hence, we deduce that

$$\vartheta_2=\vartheta_1\cdot\tan\alpha \tag{54.6}$$

If we make the calculations, we obtain

$$\vartheta_1=\sqrt{\frac{2\cdot M\cdot g\cdot l\cdot\sin\alpha}{m+M\cdot\tan^2\alpha}}\cong 1{,}38\frac{m}{s} \tag{54.7}$$

$$\vartheta_2=\sqrt{\frac{2\cdot M\cdot g\cdot l\cdot\sin\alpha}{m+M\cdot\tan^2\alpha}}\cdot\tan\alpha\cong 2{,}38\frac{m}{s} \tag{54.8}$$

55. By decomposing the velocity of body 1 into its components in the horizontal and the vertical (see Figure 55), we obtain

$$\vartheta^2=\vartheta_x^2+\vartheta_y^2 \tag{55.1}$$

where ϑ_x represents its velocity in the horizontal, which is thus the same as the velocity of the other end.

On the other hand

$$\vartheta_y=\vartheta_x\cdot\cot\alpha \tag{55.1'}$$

If we apply the law of conservation of energy, we can write

$$m\cdot g\cdot R\cdot\sin\alpha=\frac{m}{2}\cdot\vartheta^2+\frac{m}{2}\cdot\vartheta_x^2 \tag{55.2}$$

By taking into account the expressions above, we obtain

$$\vartheta^2 = 2 \cdot g \cdot R \cdot \frac{\sin\alpha \cdot \left(1+\cot^2\alpha\right)}{2+\cot^2\alpha} \qquad (55.3)$$

In order to obtain the acceleration of the dumbbell at the required time, the force which is necessary is the one that has the magnitude at least equal to the magnitude of the projection of the centrifugal force in the horizontal.

Hence

$$F = F_{cf} \cdot \cos\alpha \qquad (55.4)$$

where

$$F_{cf} = 2 \cdot m \cdot g \cdot \sin\alpha \cdot \frac{1+\cot^2\alpha}{2+\cot^2\alpha} \qquad (55.5)$$

from where

$$F = m \cdot g \cdot \sin 2\alpha \cdot \frac{1+\cot^2\alpha}{2+\cot^2\alpha} = 13.84\,\mathrm{N} \qquad (55.6)$$

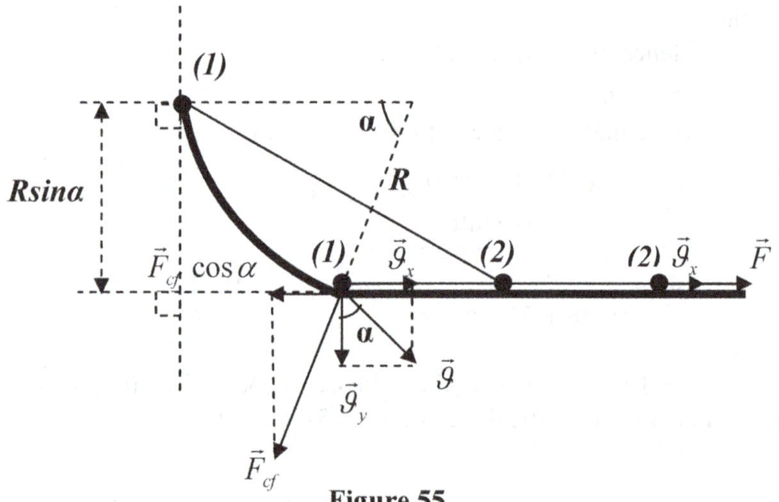

Figure 55

56. The acceleration a_0 (see Figure 56a) characterizing the bodies M_0 and M, in the horizontal in the direction opposite the motion, is due to the horizontal component of the force exerted on the string by means of the pulley.

$$a_0 = \frac{T}{M+M_0} \qquad (56.1)$$

On the other hand

$$T = m \cdot a_m \tag{56.2}$$

As for the motion of the body of mass M in the vertical, we can write

$$M \cdot g - T = M \cdot a_M \tag{56.3}$$

If we take into account (56.2), we obtain

$$M \cdot g - m \cdot a_m = M \cdot a_M \tag{56.4}$$

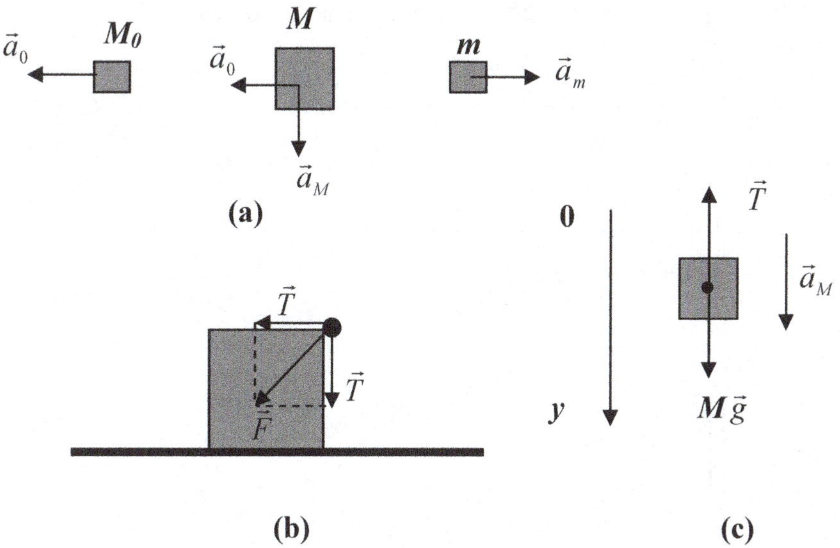

Figure 56

The motion of the body of mass M in the vertical consists of the sum of the motions of the other two bodies relative to an inertial mobile reference system moving with the velocity υ.

Therefore:

$$a_M = a_0 + a_m \tag{56.5}$$

If we apply the law of conservation of energy, we may write

$$\frac{(M + M_0 + m) \cdot \vartheta^2}{2} + M \cdot g \cdot l = \frac{(M + m) \cdot \vartheta'^2}{2} \tag{56.6}$$

where ϑ' is the velocity of the body of mass M just before striking the ground.

By applying the equation of velocity as a function of displacement referring to the vertical motion of the body of mass M, we can write

$$\vartheta'^2 = 2 \cdot a_M \cdot l \tag{56.7}$$

By solving the equations above, it can be written that

$$l = \frac{(M + M_0 + m) \cdot \vartheta^2 \cdot [M \cdot (2 \cdot m + M) + M_0 \cdot (M + m)]}{2 \cdot g \cdot M \cdot m^2} \tag{56.8}$$

57. The body will reach the maximum velocity relative to the ground at the moment it reaches the bottom of the assembly. The distance it covers relative to the assembly (the hypotenuse of the right triangle) will also represent the distance it covers relative to the ground (see Figure 57)

If we apply the law of conservation of energy, we can write

$$M \cdot g \cdot h = \frac{M \cdot \vartheta^2}{2} + \frac{3 \cdot m \cdot \vartheta^2 \cdot \cos^2 \frac{\alpha}{2}}{2} \tag{57.1}$$

Therefore

$$\vartheta = \sqrt{\frac{2 \cdot M \cdot g \cdot h}{M + 3 \cdot m \cdot \cos^2 \frac{\alpha}{2}}} \tag{57.2}$$

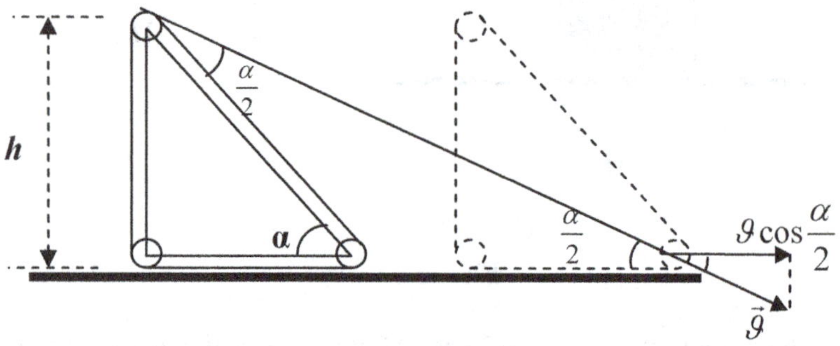

Figure 57

58. We notice three different situations:

I. The situation measured from the moment the motion starts until the end of the string reaches the floor;

II. The situation when the string has three different parts:

1) The part situated at the height h above the floor and is going to be made to move,
2) The straight line, vertical segment that is moving,
3) The segment that has already reached the floor.

III. The situation observed starting from the moment the last part of the string begins to move until the moment it reaches the floor.

The expression of time for each of them can be written as follows

$$t_I = \sqrt{\frac{2 \cdot h}{\frac{g}{2}}} = 2 \cdot \sqrt{\frac{h}{g}} \tag{58.1}$$

$$t_{II} = \frac{l - h}{\vartheta} \tag{58.2}$$

the uniform descending velocity ϑ of the string is a part of the expression:

$$m \cdot g \cdot \frac{h}{2} = m \cdot \frac{\vartheta^2}{2} \tag{58.3}$$

Therefore

$$t_{II} = \frac{l - h}{\sqrt{g \cdot h}} \tag{58.4}$$

The equation of the vertical motion of the last part of the string is

$$h = \vartheta \cdot t_{III} + \frac{1}{2} \cdot g \cdot t_{III}^2 \tag{58.5}$$

which means that

$$t_{III} = \sqrt{\frac{h}{g}} \cdot (\sqrt{3} - 1) \tag{58.6}$$

making the calculations, we obtain

$$t = \frac{1}{\sqrt{g}} \cdot \left[\sqrt{3h} + \frac{l}{\sqrt{h}} \right] \tag{58.7}$$

59. From the condition of losing the contact with the hemisphere (see Figure 59)

$$N = 0 \tag{59.1}$$

we obtain

$$m \cdot g \cdot \sin\alpha = \frac{m \cdot \vartheta^2}{R} \tag{59.2}$$

and

$$\sin\alpha = \frac{1}{2} \tag{59.3}$$

Therefore

$$\vartheta^2 = R \cdot \frac{g}{2} \tag{59.4}$$

If we apply the law of conservation of energy, it follows that

$$\frac{m \cdot \vartheta^2}{2} = \frac{m \cdot g \cdot R}{2} - |W| \qquad (59.5)$$

Therefore

$$|W| = \frac{m \cdot g \cdot R}{4} \qquad (59.6)$$

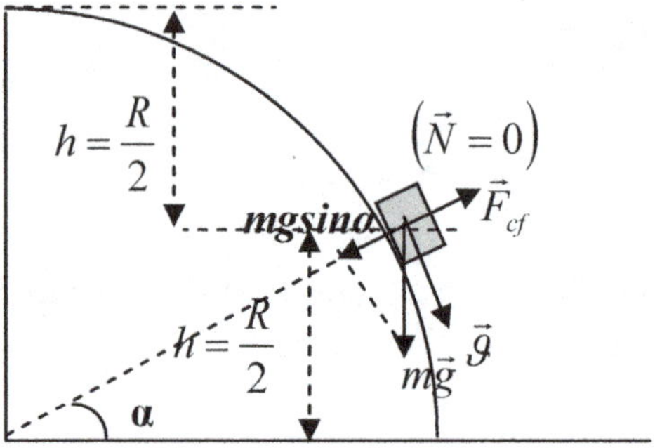

Figure 59

60. We can write the following expressions for each body:

$$m_1 \cdot a_1 = m_1 \cdot g - 2 \cdot T \qquad (60.1)$$

$$m_2 \cdot a_2 = m_2 \cdot g - 2 \cdot T \qquad (60.2)$$

As for the pulley to which none of the bodies is attached, we can write

$$2 \cdot T - T = 0 \qquad (60.3)$$

(The pulley is considered not to have any mass).

From here, we obtain

$$a_1 = a_2 = g \qquad (60.4)$$

Therefore

$$a_{cm} = g \qquad (60.5)$$

61. On portion AB (see Figure 61):

$$l = a_1 \cdot \frac{t_1^2}{2} \qquad (61.1)$$

where

$$a_1 = \frac{F}{m} \qquad (61.2)$$

and

$$\vartheta_1 = a_1 \cdot t_1 \qquad (61.3)$$

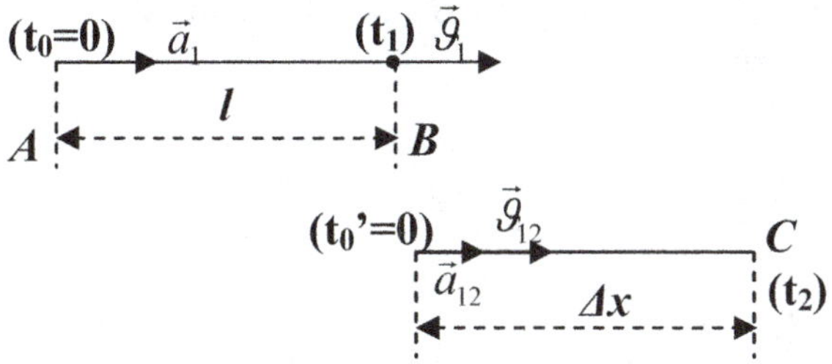

Figure 61

After the string is extended, the common velocity of the two bodies will be

$$\vartheta_{12} = \frac{1}{2} \cdot \vartheta_1 \qquad (61.4)$$

and the equation of motion starting with the moment of time t_1 can be written

$$\Delta x = \vartheta_{12} \cdot t_2 + \frac{1}{2} a_2 t_2^2 \qquad (61.5)$$

where

$$a_2 = \frac{F}{2 \cdot m} \qquad (61.6)$$

If we make the calculations, we obtain

$$\Delta x = \frac{l \cdot t_2 \cdot (t_2 + 2t_1)}{2 \cdot t_1^2} = 4m \qquad (61.7)$$

62. After giving an impulse I, the body of mass m_1 will have the velocity

$$\vartheta_1 = \frac{I}{m_1} \qquad (62.1)$$

After the string stretches at maximum amount, both bodies will move with the same velocity. So we can consider the phenomenon as an inelastic collision. Therefore

$$Q = \frac{1}{2} \cdot \frac{m_1 \cdot m_2}{m_1 + m_2} \cdot \vartheta_1^2 \qquad (62.2)$$

in conclusion

$$Q = \frac{1}{2} \cdot \frac{m_2 \cdot I^2}{(m_1 + m_2) \cdot m_1} = 5{,}33J \qquad (62.3)$$

63. Just before taking off, the dumbbell will spin around point *A* (see Figure 63) on the edge of the table. We want to find the velocity of the end *B* of the dumbbell. Since segments *AB* and *AC* spin with the same angular velocity, we can write

$$\frac{\vartheta'}{1-f} = \frac{\vartheta}{f} \tag{63.1}$$

which means that

$$\vartheta' = \vartheta \cdot (1-f) \cdot \frac{1}{f} \tag{63.2}$$

If we take into account the expression of the center of mass, we can find the velocity with which the dumbbell rises from the surface of the table:

$$\vartheta_{cm} = \frac{m \cdot \vartheta' + m \cdot (-\vartheta)}{m+m} \tag{63.3}$$

By taking into account the expression (63.2), we obtain

$$\vartheta_{cm} = \frac{1-2\cdot f}{2\cdot f} \cdot \vartheta \tag{63.4}$$

Then we can find of the maximum height:

$$h = \frac{(1-2\cdot f)^2}{4\cdot f^2} \cdot \left(\frac{\vartheta^2}{2\cdot g}\right) = 12.8 \text{ m} \tag{63.5}$$

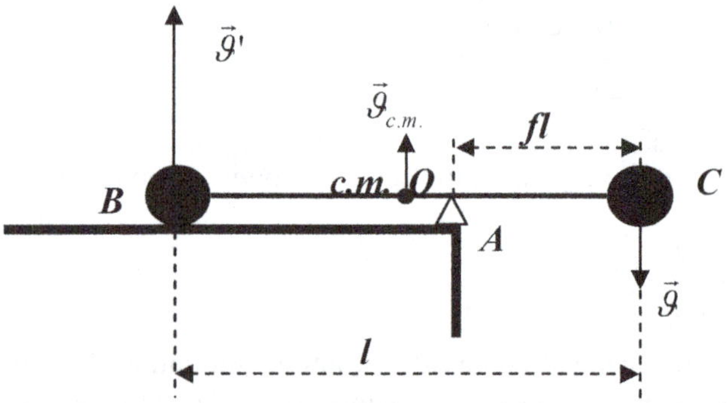

Figure 63

64. As the dumbbell returns to the table level where it is expected to be in the vertical position, its margin must be just under the lower end of the dumbbell. If the dumbbell had been hitting the table in another position at the time of the falling, although its center of mass would have been on the same vertical, the end that would have been towards the table could have touched it, even if it had been moved more. The center of mass keeps its position constant along the horizontal because, initially, the velocity was strictly imparted vertically in a very short time interval. If we analyze Figure 64, we notice that

$$\frac{\Delta l}{l} = \frac{1}{2} - f \tag{64.1}$$

where Δl is the magnitude of the displacement vector and l is the length of the dumbbell. Just after the velocity is imparted, the body on the table will reach the velocity upward as

$$\vartheta' = \frac{\vartheta \cdot (1 - f)}{f} \tag{64.2}$$

Therefore, the velocity of the center of mass will be (Figure 64a):

$$\vartheta_{cm} = \frac{1 - 2 \cdot f}{2 \cdot f} \cdot \vartheta \tag{64.3}$$

For the dumbbell to return the table in vertical position (see Figure 64b), we must impose the condition that time during which the center of mass reaches a height equal to half of its length is equal to the time necessary for the dumbbell to spin around the center with an angle $\alpha = \frac{\pi}{2}$.

Therefore,

$$t = \frac{T}{4} \tag{64.4}$$

where T is the period of dumbbell's rotation.

On the other hand, by taking into account the expression (64.3), it follows that

$$t = \frac{\vartheta}{g} \cdot \frac{1 - 2 \cdot f}{2 \cdot f} \tag{64.5}$$

and the expression of the period will be

$$T = \frac{2 \cdot \pi \cdot \frac{l}{2}}{\vartheta + \vartheta_{CM}} \tag{64.6}$$

which means that

$$T = 2 \cdot \pi \cdot l \cdot f \cdot \frac{1}{\vartheta} \tag{64.7}$$

Coming back to the expression (64.4), we obtain

$$\frac{\vartheta}{g} \cdot \frac{1 - 2 \cdot f}{2 \cdot f} = \frac{\pi \cdot f \cdot l}{2 \cdot \vartheta} \tag{64.8}$$

If we apply the equation of velocity as a function of displacement, referring to the translation motion of the center of mass, it follows that

$$\vartheta_{cm}^2 = 2 \cdot g \cdot l \cdot \frac{1}{2} \quad (64.9)$$

then

$$\frac{(1-2\cdot f)^2}{4\cdot f^2} \cdot \vartheta^2 = g \cdot l \quad (64.10)$$

If we take into account the expression above, in the expression (64.8) we can write

$$\frac{4}{1-2\cdot f} = \pi \quad (64.11)$$

therefore

$$f = \frac{1}{2} - \frac{2}{\pi} < 0 \quad (64.12)$$

So, the phenomenon is impossible.

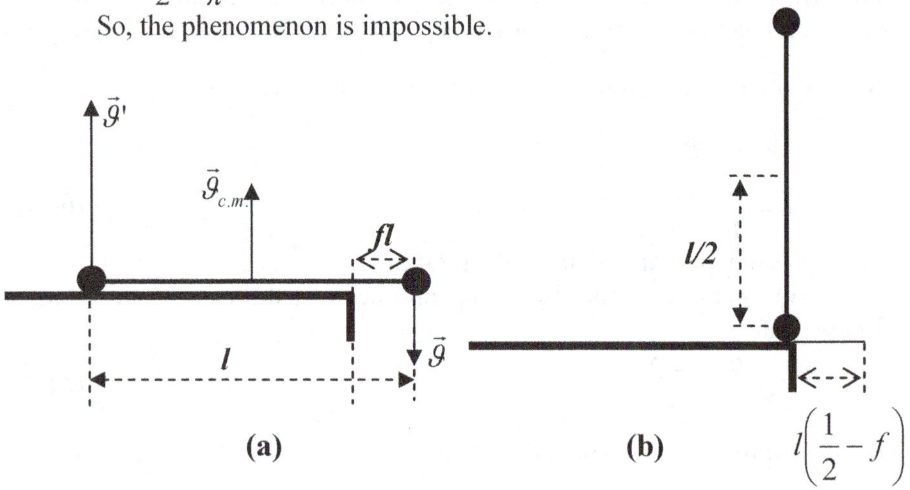

Figure 64

65. As motion takes place under the action of the gravitational forces, the center of mass of the system (initially at rest) will not move in the horizontal; it will keep its position, therefore at the end the velocities of the bodies that have moved only on the plane will cancel each other.

Then, the velocity of one of the bodies initially at the top relative to one of the other bodies at the bottom will be identical to the velocity relative to the ground.

By applying the law of conservation of energy, it follows that

$$\vartheta = \sqrt{2 \cdot g \cdot l} \tag{65.1}$$

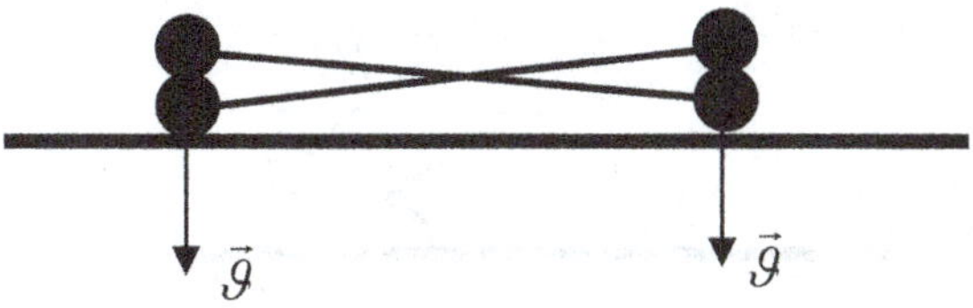

Figure 65

66. The frictional force that will act on one of the bodies that are in contact with the ground shall be

$$F_f = \mu \cdot N \tag{66.1}$$

By applying the condition of rotational equilibrium about point O (see Figure 66) for one of the dumbbells, we obtain

$$F_f \cdot \frac{l}{2} \cdot \sin\alpha + m \cdot g \cdot \frac{l}{2} \cdot \cos\alpha = m \cdot g \cdot \frac{l}{2} \cdot \cos\alpha + N \cdot \frac{l}{2} \cdot \cos\alpha \tag{66.2}$$

If we solve the expressions (66.1) and (66.2), we obtain

$$\cot\alpha = \mu \tag{66.3}$$

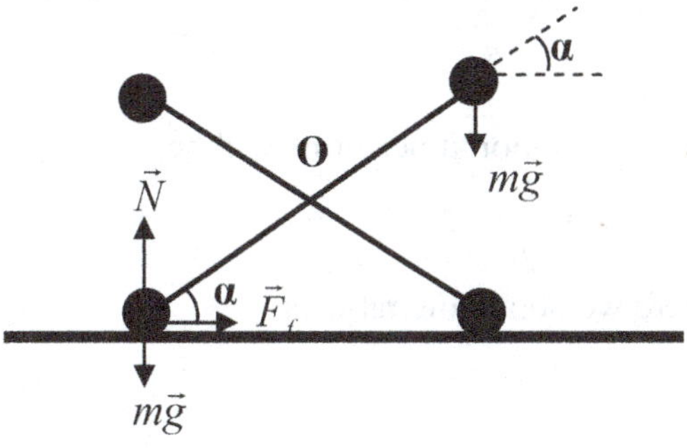

Figure 66

67. The motion of the rod is performed under the influence of both weight and the reaction force exerted on it vertically at the point of contact by the ground. The change in momentum in the horizontal is zero. Initially the rod was stationary and its center of mass maintains the horizontal coordinate constant during the motion. Consider l as the length of the rod; then, according to Figure 67a, compared to the projection of the center of mass on the ground, the end that has contact with the ground will be at the distance

$$l_1 = \frac{1}{2} \cdot l \cdot \cos\alpha \tag{67.1}$$

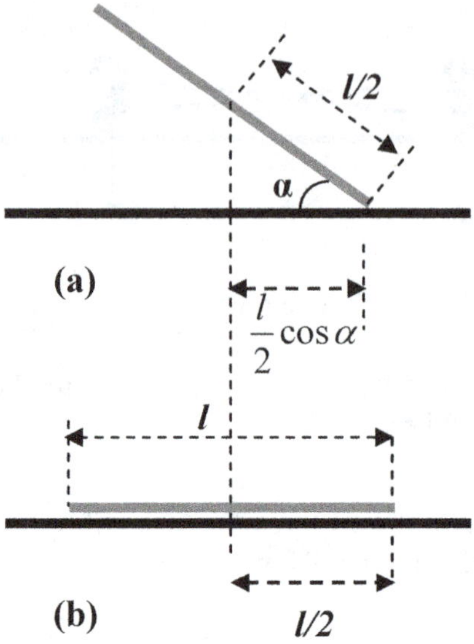

Figure 67

At the moment when the rod is on the ground in horizontal position, that end will be, relative to the same point, at the distance

$$l_2 = \frac{l}{2} \tag{67.2}$$

Therefore, the motion it performs will be

$$d = (1 - \cos\alpha) \cdot \frac{l}{2} \tag{67.3}$$

from where we obtain the ratio as

$$k = \frac{l}{d} \tag{67.4}$$

then

$$k = \frac{2}{(1 - \cos\alpha)} \tag{67.5}$$

68. Before leaving the table (where ball 1 moves horizontally), the speed of the two bodies will be given by the expression

$$2 \cdot \frac{m \cdot \vartheta^2}{2} = m \cdot g \cdot l \tag{68.1}$$

and after leaving the table, by applying conservation of momentum in the vertical , we obtain the common velocity of the two balls

$$m \cdot \vartheta = 2 \cdot m \cdot \vartheta' \qquad (68.2)$$

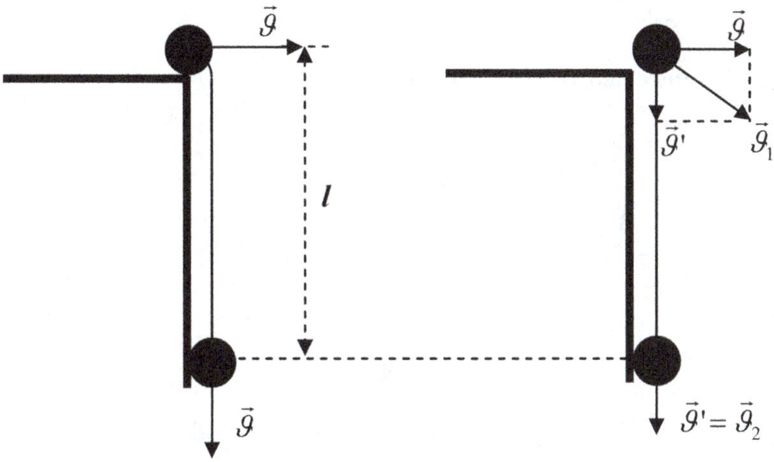

Figure 68

Since at this moment the change in momentum in the horizontal does not take place (because the string is in the vertical), the velocity of ball 1 in the horizontal will remain constant. Therefore, we can write

$$\vartheta_1 = \sqrt{\vartheta^2 + \vartheta'^2} \qquad (68.3)$$

and

$$\vartheta_2 = \vartheta' \qquad (68.4)$$

If we take into account the expressions (68.1) and (68.2), we obtain

$$\vartheta_1 = \frac{\sqrt{5 \cdot g \cdot l}}{2} = 2{,}95 \, \frac{\mathrm{m}}{\mathrm{s}} \qquad (68.5)$$

and

$$\vartheta_2' = \frac{1}{2} \cdot \sqrt{g \cdot l} = 1{,}32 \, \frac{\mathrm{m}}{\mathrm{s}} \qquad (68.6)$$

69. Consider ϑ_1 and ϑ_2 as the velocities of the bodies just before the second one reaches the ground (see Figure 69). If we apply the law of conservation of energy for the motion of the entire system, we can write

$$m \cdot g \cdot (l_1 + l_2) \cdot \sin\frac{\pi}{4} = m \cdot g \cdot l_1 + \frac{m}{2} \cdot \left(\vartheta_1^2 + \vartheta_2^2\right) \qquad (69.1)$$

with

$$\frac{\vartheta_1}{l_1} = \frac{\vartheta_2}{l_2} \tag{69.2}$$

since the momentum is conserved in the horizontal, we can find that

$$\vartheta = \frac{\vartheta_1}{2} \tag{69.3}$$

By making the calculations, we obtain

$$\vartheta = \frac{l_1}{2} \cdot \sqrt{\frac{g \cdot \sqrt{2} \cdot \left[l_2 - l_1 \cdot \left(\sqrt{2} - 1\right)\right]}{l_1^2 + l_2^2}} \tag{69.4}$$

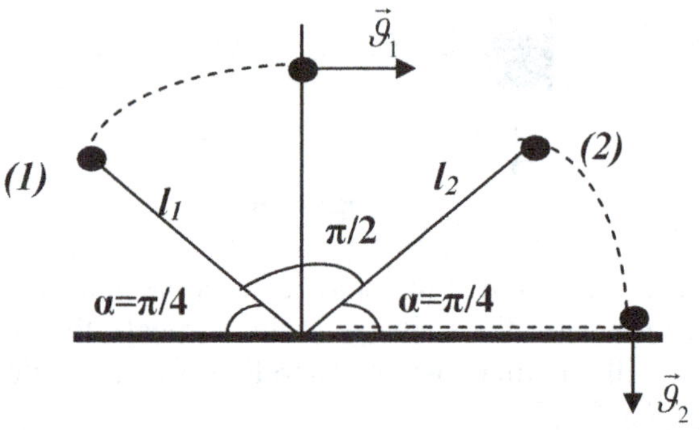

Figure 69

70. We can write about the projectile motion of the monkey that:

$$b = 2 \cdot \vartheta_{2x} \cdot \frac{\vartheta_{2y}}{g} \tag{70.1}$$

with

$$\vartheta_{2y} = \sqrt{2 \cdot g \cdot h} \tag{70.2}$$

If we apply conservation of momentum in horizontal for the moment when the monkey leaves from the swing (see Figure 70), we can write

$$\vartheta_1 = \frac{m_2}{m_1} \cdot \vartheta_{2x} \tag{70.3}$$

and about the motion of the swing afterwards

$$\frac{m_1}{2}\cdot\vartheta_1^2 = m_1\cdot g\cdot l\cdot(1-\cos\alpha) \tag{70.4}$$

By solving the equations above, we obtain

$$\sin\frac{\alpha}{2} = \frac{1}{4}\cdot\frac{m_2}{m_1}\cdot\frac{b}{\sqrt{l\cdot h}} \tag{70.5}$$

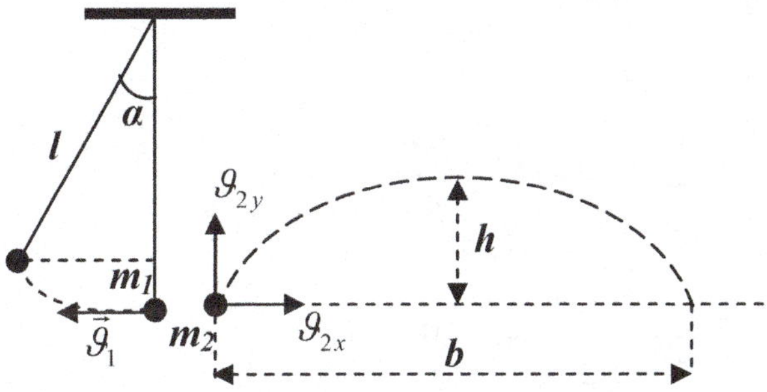

Figure 70

71. The horizontal component of the velocity of the first body just after the impact will be the same as its initial velocity (see Figure 71a). If μ is the coefficient of friction, the distance covered until it stops will be given by the expression

$$s = \frac{\vartheta^2}{2\cdot\mu\cdot g} \tag{71.1}$$

If ϑ_y is the vertical component of the velocity of the second body just before the impact (see Figure 71b), then it will rise from the ground, having the vertical component of the velocity as

$$\vartheta_y' = (1-f)\vartheta_y \tag{71.2}$$

But,

$$\vartheta_y = \sqrt{2\cdot g\cdot h} \tag{71.3}$$

therefore

$$\vartheta_y' = (1-f)\sqrt{2\cdot g\cdot h} \tag{71.4}$$

Then the displacement covered along the horizontal until the body returns to the ground will be given by the expression:

$$b = \vartheta \cdot t \tag{71.5}$$

where t is the time interval during which the motion takes place, and is given by the expression:

$$t = 2 \cdot \frac{(1-f)\sqrt{2 \cdot g \cdot h}}{g} \tag{71.6}$$

therefore

$$b = 2 \cdot \vartheta \cdot (1-f)\sqrt{\frac{2 \cdot h}{g}} \tag{71.7}$$

From the condition

$$s = b \tag{71.8}$$

we obtain

$$\frac{\vartheta^2}{2 \cdot \mu \cdot g} = 2 \cdot \vartheta \cdot (1-f)\sqrt{\frac{2 \cdot h}{g}} \tag{71.9}$$

than we can get μ as

$$\mu = \frac{\vartheta}{4(1-f)} \cdot \frac{1}{\sqrt{2 \cdot g \cdot h}} = 0.316 \tag{71.10}$$

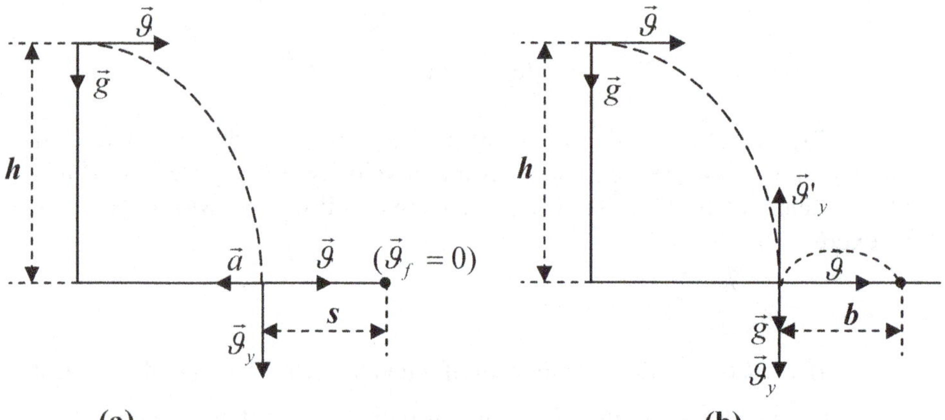

Figure 71

72. In the horizontal, the velocity will remain constant after the body makes inelastic collision with the ground. That is, the kinetic energy gained by the body during falling is lost in the collision.

In order for the body not to overturn at the moment of impact with C, we must impose the condition that the kinetic energy of the body on the plane is smaller than, or at the most equal to the mechanical work necessary to bring the body to the position where the diagonal of its cross-sectional area is in the vertical (the position before overturning).

Therefore

$$\frac{m \cdot \vartheta^2}{2} \leq m \cdot g \cdot \left(\frac{\sqrt{l^2 + a^2}}{2} - \frac{l}{2} \right) \quad (72.1)$$

Then, if we take into account the condition imposed in the text

$$\vartheta = \sqrt{g \cdot l} \quad (72.2)$$

we obtain

$$l \leq a \cdot \frac{\sqrt{3}}{3} \quad (72.3)$$

73. By applying the laws of conservation of momentum (in the horizontal) and energy, we may write

$$m \cdot \vartheta' = M \cdot \vartheta \quad (73.1)$$

and

$$\frac{m \cdot \vartheta'^2}{2} + \frac{M \cdot \vartheta^2}{2} = m \cdot g \cdot \frac{l \cdot \sin\alpha}{2} \quad (73.2)$$

Hence, we obtain

$$\vartheta = m \cdot \sqrt{\frac{g \cdot l \cdot \sin\alpha}{M \cdot (M + m)}} \quad (73.3)$$

74. Initially, the center of mass of the rod (see Figure 74) is at the height

$$h = \frac{l \cdot \sin\alpha}{2}$$

therefore, its potential energy is

$$PE = \frac{m \cdot g \cdot l \cdot \sin\alpha}{2} \quad (74.1)$$

Just before undergoing the inelastic collision, the right end of the rod undergoes a translational motion in the horizontal, while the left end continues to move on the inclined plane.

By decomposing the velocity at point A (see Figure 74), we obtain its components in the horizontal and vertical respectively; because the first of them is the same as the velocity of point B, we can consider it to be equal to the horizontal component of the velocity of the center of mass.

As for the motion in the vertical, we observe that it takes place around the right end (that remains in stationary position on this direction), therefore, it is a circular motion.

The kinetic energy of the dumbbell before collision will be

$$KE_i = \frac{m \cdot \vartheta_A^2}{2} + \frac{m \cdot \vartheta^2}{2} \tag{74.2}$$

where

$$\vartheta_A^2 = \vartheta^2 + \vartheta_y^2 \tag{74.3}$$

and

$$\vartheta_y = \vartheta \cdot \tan\alpha \tag{74.4}$$

If we take into account that:

$$PE_i = KE_f \tag{74.5}$$

we obtain

$$\vartheta = \sqrt{\frac{l \cdot g \cdot \sin\alpha}{2 + \tan^2\alpha}} = 1.46 \text{ m/s} \tag{74.6}$$

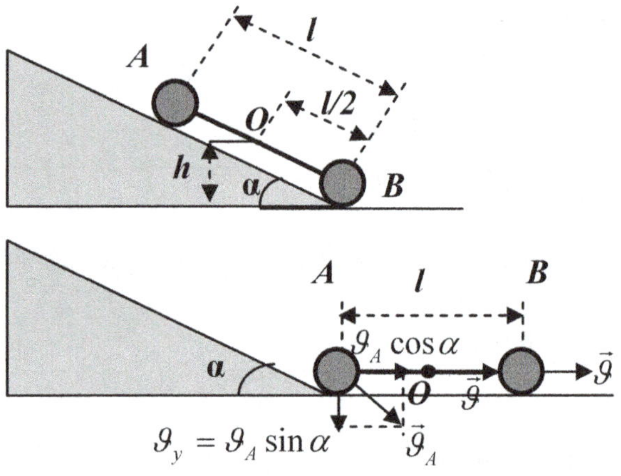

Figure 74

75. The fact that the displacement after collision takes place rectilinearly in the vertical means that the total momentum in the horizontal is zero (see Figure 75a), therefore

$$\vartheta_2 \cdot \cos\beta = \vartheta_1 \cdot \cos\alpha \tag{75.1}$$

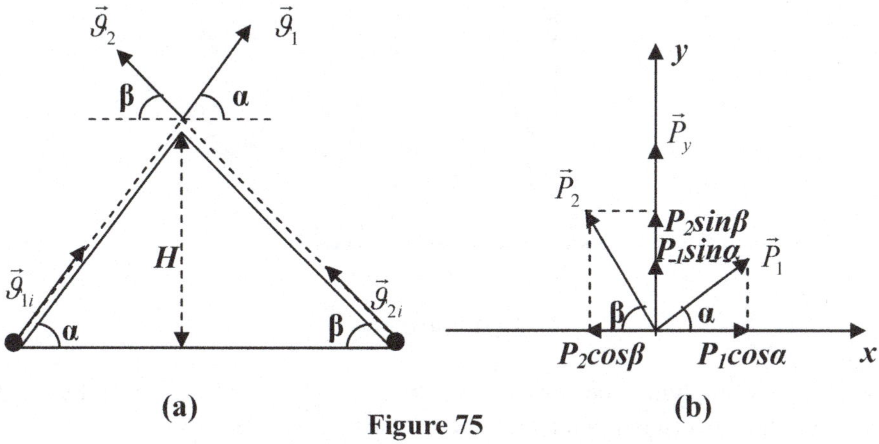

Figure 75

If we apply the conservation of momentum in the vertical, it follows that (see Figure 75b)

$$p_1 \cdot \sin\alpha + p_2 \cdot \sin\beta = p_y \quad (75.2)$$

then

$$m \cdot \vartheta_1 \cdot \sin\alpha + m \cdot \vartheta_2 \cdot \sin\beta = 2 \cdot m \cdot \vartheta \quad (75.3)$$

On the other hand

$$h = \frac{\vartheta^2}{2 \cdot g} \quad (75.4)$$

Additionally, regarding the motion of the first body on the side inclined with the angle α above horizontal, we can write

$$\vartheta_{1i}^2 = \vartheta_1^2 + 2 \cdot g \cdot H \quad (75.5)$$

By solving the equations above, we obtain

$$\vartheta_{1i} = \sqrt{2 \cdot g \cdot \left[H + \frac{4 \cdot h}{(\cos\alpha \cdot \tan\beta + \sin\alpha)^2} \right]} \quad (75.6)$$

76. Consider Δl as the deformation undergone by the cylinder at the time of impact (see Figure 76). Therefore, the center of weight will be lowered by

$$y = \frac{\Delta l}{2} \quad (76.1)$$

relative to the situation when it would be placed on the plane, (that is, when it is non-deformed).

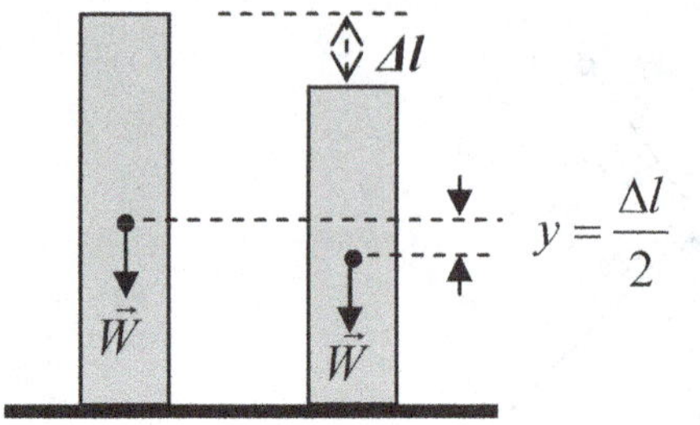

Figure 76

By applying the law of conservation of energy and by taking into account the specification made in the problem, we can write

$$(1-z)\cdot W\cdot\left(h+\frac{\Delta l}{2}\right)=\frac{k\cdot\Delta l^2}{2} \qquad (76.2)$$

By imposing the condition that the cylinder does not rise from the ground, we obtain

$$\frac{k\cdot\Delta l^2}{2}=W\cdot\frac{\Delta l}{2} \qquad (76.3)$$

or:

$$\Delta l=\frac{W}{k} \qquad (76.4)$$

Coming back to the expression (76.2), we obtain:

$$h=\frac{W}{2\cdot k}\cdot\frac{z}{1-z} \qquad (76.5)$$

77. Consider ϑ_2 and ϑ_1 as the velocities of the two bodies before the collision undergone by the body of mass m_1, at point C (see Figure 77).

By applying the law of conservation of energy, we obtain:

$$m_1\cdot g\cdot H=\frac{1}{2}\cdot m_2\cdot\vartheta_2^2+\frac{1}{2}\cdot m_1\cdot\vartheta_1^2 \qquad (77.1)$$

On the other hand:

$$\frac{m_1\cdot\vartheta_{1x}^2}{2}=\frac{f\cdot m_1\cdot\vartheta_1^2}{2} \qquad (77.2)$$

and

$$\vartheta_1^2=\vartheta_2^2+\vartheta_{1x}^2 \qquad (77.3)$$

(The vertical component of the velocity of the body of mass m_1 is the same as the velocity of the body of mass m_2).

$$\vartheta_1^2 = \vartheta_2^2 + f \cdot \vartheta_1^2 \tag{77.4}$$

that is

$$\vartheta_1^2 \cdot (1 - f) = \vartheta_2^2$$

Returning to (77.1), we obtain

$$\vartheta_1^2 = \frac{2 \cdot m_1 \cdot g \cdot H}{m_2 \cdot (1 - f) + m_1} \tag{77.5}$$

and also

$$\vartheta_{1x}^2 = \frac{2 \cdot g \cdot m_1 \cdot H \cdot f}{m_2 \cdot (1 - f) + m_1} \tag{77.6}$$

Thus we can find the expression of the centrifugal force acting on the first body, along the string (therefore, in the vertical). As motion takes place around point *D*, the radius characterizing it will be

$$R = H - h \tag{77.7}$$

Therefore

$$F_{cf} = \frac{m_1 \cdot \vartheta_{1x}^2}{R} \tag{77.8}$$

and taking into account the expressions (77.6) and (77.7), we obtain

$$F_{cf} = \frac{2 \cdot m_1^2 \cdot g \cdot H}{(H - h) \cdot [m_2 \cdot (1 - f) + m_1]} \tag{77.9}$$

If we analyze the motion of the two bodies along the string, we obtain

-for the body of mass m_1

$$m_1 \cdot a = F_{cf} + m_1 \cdot g - T \tag{77.10}$$

- as for the body of mass m_2:

$$m_2 \cdot a = T \tag{77.11}$$

by adding the expressions (77.10) and (77.11), we obtain:

$$a \cdot (m_1 + m_2) = F_{cf} + m_1 \cdot g \tag{77.12}$$

By making the calculations, we find

$$a = \frac{m_1 g \{2 m_1 H f + (H - h)[m_2 (1 - f) + m_1]\}}{(m_1 + m_2)(H - h)[m_2 (1 - f) + m_1]} \tag{77.13}$$

then

$$a = \frac{k g \{2 k H f + (H - h)[(1 - f) + k]\}}{(k + 1)[(1 - f) + k](H - h)} \tag{77.14}$$

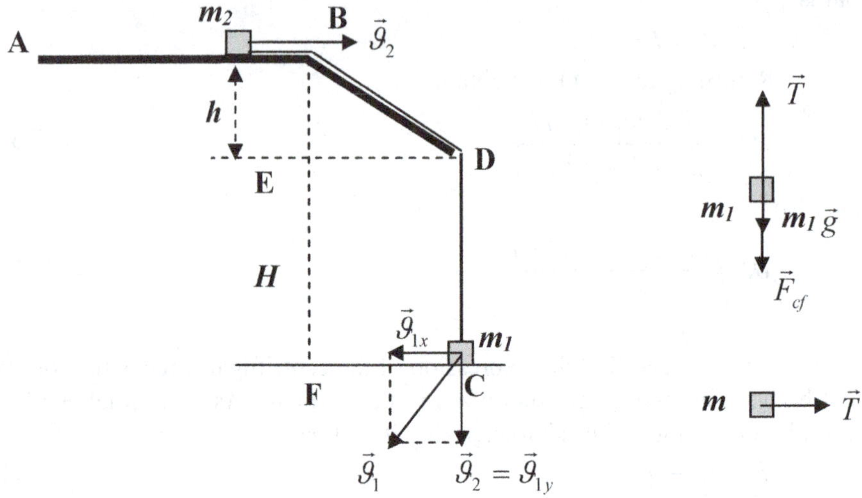

Figure 77

78. The relative velocity of the two bodies is

$$\vartheta_r = \vartheta_M - \vartheta_m \quad (78.1)$$

This is the velocity of the body of mass *m* when it begins climbing on the body of mass *M*. In order to reach point *B* at least, the following condition must be observed

$$\vartheta_r^2 \geq 2 \cdot g \cdot h \quad (78.2)$$

and in order to stop at point A

$$\vartheta_r^2 \leq 2 \cdot g \cdot (h + \mu \cdot l) \quad (78.3)$$

If we take into account the expression (78.1), we obtain

$$\vartheta_M - \vartheta_{m_1} \geq \sqrt{2 \cdot g \cdot h} \quad (78.4)$$

and

$$\vartheta_M - \vartheta_{m_2} \leq \sqrt{2 \cdot g \cdot (h + l \cdot \mu)} \quad (78.5)$$

then

$$\vartheta_{m_1} \leq \vartheta_M - \sqrt{2 \cdot g \cdot h} \quad (78.6)$$

$$\vartheta_{m_2} \geq \vartheta_M - \sqrt{2 \cdot g \cdot (h + l \cdot \mu)} \quad (78.7)$$

$$\vartheta_m \in \left[\vartheta_M - \sqrt{2 \cdot g \cdot (h + l \cdot \mu)}\ ;\ \vartheta_M - \sqrt{2 \cdot g \cdot h}\right]$$

By applying the law of conservation of momentum for the system of bodies of masses *m* and *M*, in the two extreme cases, and by taking into account the expressions (78.6) and (78.7), we obtain

$$\vartheta_{f_1} = \vartheta_M - \frac{m}{M+m} \cdot \sqrt{2 \cdot g \cdot h} \tag{78.8}$$

and

$$\vartheta_{f_2} = \vartheta_M - \frac{m}{M+m} \cdot \sqrt{2 \cdot g \cdot (h + l \cdot \mu)} \tag{78.9}$$

79. Consider ϑ_{13} as the velocity of the bodies of mass m_1 and m_3 just after the collision. Thus

$$\vartheta_{13} = \frac{m_1}{(m_1 + m_3)} \cdot \vartheta \tag{79.1}$$

As the body of mass m_2 keeps its initial velocity, it will start to move relative to the other two, and then it passes to the top of m_3. Consider μ as the coefficient of friction between them; then, the work of the frictional force exerted until the moment when these two are perfectly superposed will be

$$W = -F_{fm} \cdot l \tag{79.2}$$

where

$$F_{fm} = \frac{1}{2} \cdot \mu \cdot m_2 \cdot g \tag{79.3}$$

Therefore

$$W = -\frac{1}{2} \cdot \mu \cdot m_2 \cdot g \cdot l \tag{79.4}$$

The process of passing from the motion with various velocities to the motion of the three bodies with the common velocity is considered an inelastic collision.

The change in kinetic energy following this process will be

$$\Delta KE = -\frac{1}{2} \cdot \frac{m_2 \cdot (m_1 + m_3)}{m_1 + m_2 + m_3} \cdot (\vartheta - \vartheta_{13})^2 \tag{79.5}$$

where ϑ is the initial velocity of the body of mass m_2.

If we take into account (79.1), it follows that

$$\Delta KE = -\frac{1}{2} \cdot \frac{m_2 \cdot (m_1 + m_3)}{m_1 + m_2 + m_3} \cdot \frac{m_3^2 \cdot \vartheta^2}{(m_1 + m_2)^2} \tag{79.6}$$

but

$$W = \Delta KE \tag{79.7}$$

Therefore

$$-\frac{1}{2}\cdot\mu\cdot m_2\cdot g\cdot l = -\frac{\vartheta^2}{2}\cdot\frac{m_2\cdot(m_1+m_3)}{m_1+m_2+m_3}\cdot\frac{m_3^2}{(m_1+m_3)^2} \tag{79.8}$$

then we can get μ as

$$\mu = \frac{(m_1+m_2)}{m_1+m_2+m_3}\cdot\frac{m_3^2}{(m_1+m_3)^2}\cdot\frac{\vartheta^2}{g\cdot l} \tag{79.9}$$

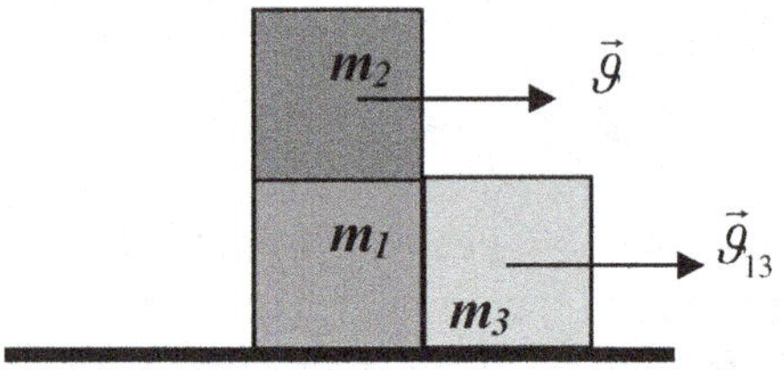

Figure 79

80. By applying conservation of momentum in the direction perpendicular to the rod, we can find the velocity imparted to body 2

$$m\cdot\vartheta\cdot\sin\alpha = 2\cdot m\cdot\vartheta' \tag{80.1}$$

then we can get ϑ' as

$$\vartheta' = \frac{\vartheta}{2}\cdot\sin\alpha \tag{80.2}$$

By determining the distance covered between points A and B

$$s = \frac{1}{2}\cdot\pi\cdot l \tag{80.3}$$

and by applying motion considerations, we deduce the following expression for the coefficient of friction:

$$\mu = \frac{\vartheta^2\cdot\sin^2\alpha}{4\cdot\pi\cdot l\cdot g} \tag{80.4}$$

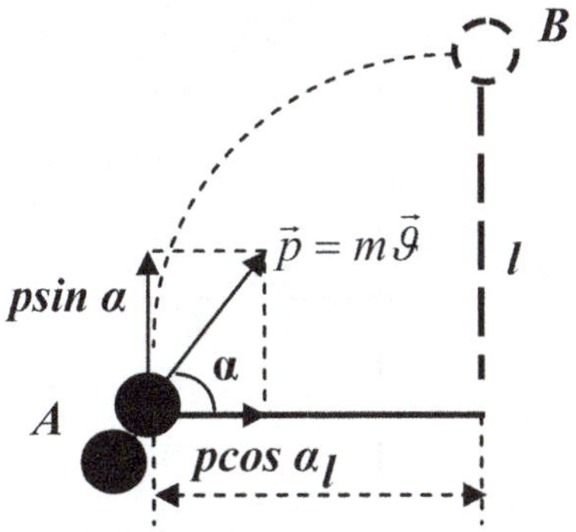

Figure 80

81. Momentum is conserved in the explosion, therefore the angles made by the initial velocities observed from the shell's system of reference with the horizontal are the same. The time difference between the moments when the parts of a shell reach the ground does not to depend on the height where the explosion take place, we will obtain

$$\Delta t(\alpha) = 2\frac{\vartheta_0 \sin\alpha}{g} \tag{81.1}$$

it becomes maximum when α=90° (the parts of the shell start going vertically), hence

$$\Delta t = 2\frac{\vartheta_0}{g} \tag{81.2}$$

$$Q = \left(\frac{1}{2}\right)\frac{\frac{m^2}{4}}{\frac{m}{2}+\frac{m}{2}}(2\vartheta_0)^2 \tag{81.3}$$

which means that

$$Q = \frac{1}{2}m\vartheta_0^2 \tag{81.4}$$

If we take into account the expression (81.2), we are able to write

$$Q = \frac{1}{8}mg^2\Delta t^2 \tag{81.5}$$

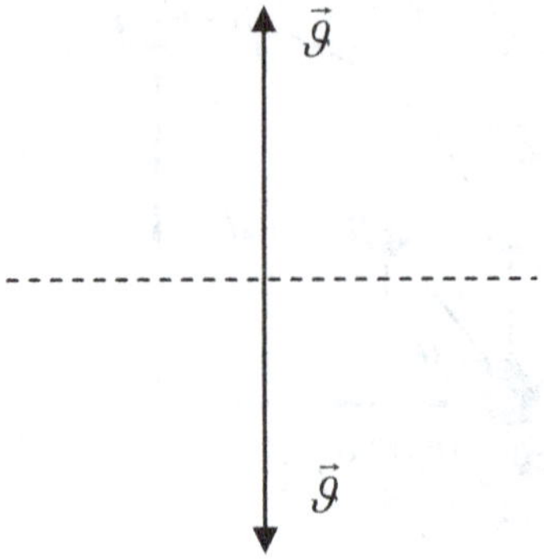

Figure 81

82. The loss of kinetic energy of the system of bodies of mass m_1 and m_2 following their interaction is expressed by the sum of the change in the potential energy of the first body and the released heat.

Thus

$$\frac{1}{2}\cdot\frac{m_1\cdot m_2}{m_1+m_2}\cdot(\vartheta_1-\vartheta_2)^2=Q+m_1\cdot g\cdot\frac{a}{3} \qquad (82.1)$$

Therefore

$$Q=\frac{1}{2}\cdot\frac{m_1\cdot m_2}{m_1+m_2}\cdot(\vartheta_1-\vartheta_2)^2-m_1\cdot g\cdot\frac{a}{3} \qquad (82.2)$$

83. If we apply the law of conservation of energy, we can write

$$\frac{m_1\vartheta_1^2}{2}+\frac{m_2\vartheta_2^2}{2}=\frac{1}{2}\cdot(m_1+m_2)\cdot\frac{(\vartheta_1+\vartheta_2)^2}{4}+m_1\cdot g\cdot\frac{a}{3}. \qquad (83.1)$$

then we obtain a as

$$a=\frac{3}{2\cdot m_1\cdot g}\left[m_1\cdot\vartheta_1^2+m_2\vartheta_2^2-\frac{(m_1+m_2)\cdot(\vartheta_i+\vartheta_2)^2}{4}\right] \qquad (83.2)$$

but in this situation $m_1=m_2$ so it results

$$a=\frac{3}{4g}(\vartheta_1-\vartheta_2)^2 \qquad (83.3)$$

84. If we apply the law of conservation of energy, we can find the velocity of the ball before it collides with the body, in terms of the length l of the string, the angle α and the gravitational acceleration:

$$\vartheta=\sqrt{2\cdot g\cdot l\cdot\cos\alpha}, \qquad (84.1)$$

and its horizontal component will be

$$\vartheta' = \vartheta \cdot \cos\alpha \qquad (84.2)$$

If m is the mass of the ball (see Figure 84) and M is the mass of the body, we can express the velocity imparted to M (if we take into account that the collision is inelastic):

$$\vartheta'' = \frac{m}{(M+m)} \cdot \vartheta' \qquad (84.3)$$

and the distance covered by it until its stops will be

$$s = \frac{\vartheta''^2}{2 \cdot \mu \cdot g} \qquad (84.4)$$

If L is the distance between point O' and the point where the left end of the body will stop, we can write

$$L = l \cdot \sin\alpha + s \qquad (84.5)$$

and by imposing the condition

$$L = 2 \cdot l \qquad (84.6)$$

and making the calculations, we obtain

$$\frac{m}{M} = \frac{\sqrt{(2-\sin\alpha)\cdot\mu}}{\cos\alpha \cdot \sqrt{\cos\alpha - \sqrt{(2-\sin\alpha)\cdot\mu}}} \qquad (84.7)$$

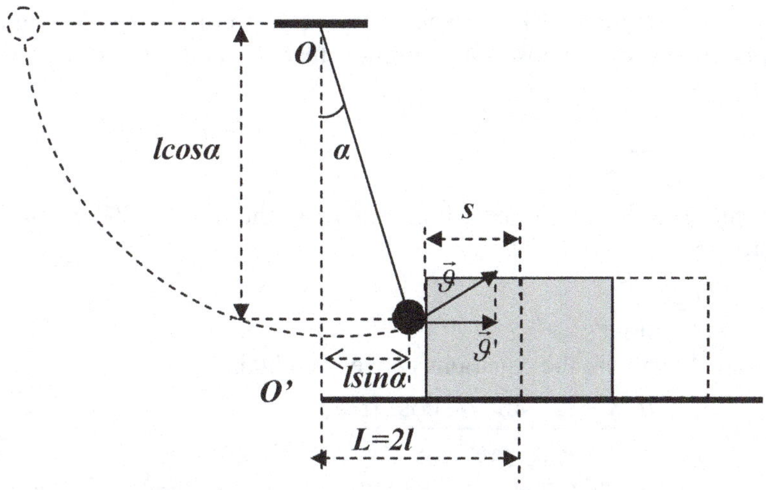

Figure 84

85. On segment AB (see Figure 85) we observe

$$\vartheta_1 = \sqrt{2 \cdot g \cdot (H-h)}, \qquad (85.1)$$

and the initial velocity of the body when it begins to descend on the board is

$$\vartheta'_1 = \vartheta_1 \cdot \sin\alpha. \quad (85.2)$$

At point *C* before reaching the floor, the velocity will be

$$\vartheta_2 = \sqrt{\vartheta'^2_1 + 2 \cdot g \cdot h}, \quad (85.3)$$

and after reaching it, the velocity is

$$\vartheta'_2 = \vartheta_2 \cdot \cos\alpha. \quad (85.4)$$

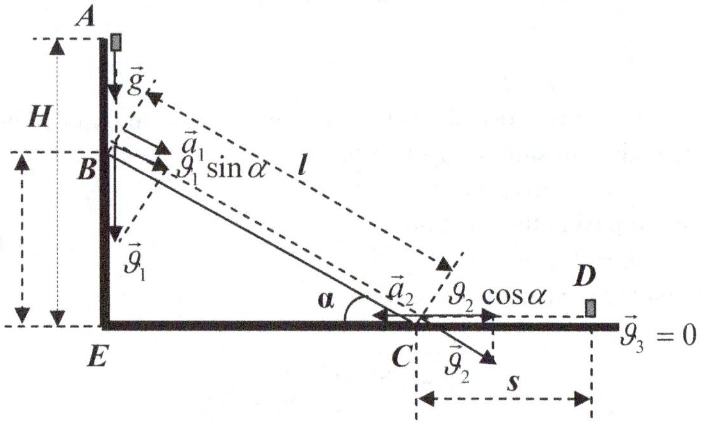

Figure 85

On segment *CD*, if we apply the equation of velocity as a function of displacement and impose the condition that the body stops at point *D*, we obtain

$$s = \frac{\vartheta_2'^2}{2 \cdot \mu \cdot g}, \quad (85.5)$$

and the length of the board depends on the height $BE=h$ through the expression

$$l = \frac{h}{\sin\alpha}. \quad (85.6)$$

By solving the equations above, we obtain

$$l = \frac{\mu \cdot s - H \cdot \sin^2\alpha \cdot \cos^2\alpha}{\sin\alpha \cdot \cos^4\alpha}. \quad (85.7)$$

86. Consider that t_1 is the time necessary for the first ball to reach the ground and t_2 is the time necessary for it to rise to the half of the height it was thrown from, and t' is the time necessary for the second ball to reach the half of the height from where it was released.

We can observe that

$$t_1 + t_2 = \tau + t' \quad (86.1)$$

By applying the equations of motion on portions *AC* and *CB* (see Figure 86), for the first ball we obtain

$$h = \frac{1}{2} g \cdot t_1^2 \qquad (86.2)$$

then

$$t_1 = \sqrt{\frac{2 \cdot h}{g}} \qquad (86.3)$$

and

$$\frac{h}{2} = \vartheta \cdot t_2 - \frac{1}{2} \cdot g \cdot t_2^2 \qquad (86.4)$$

where

$$\vartheta = \sqrt{2 \cdot g \cdot h} \qquad (86.5)$$

which means

$$\frac{h}{2} = \left(\sqrt{2 \cdot g \cdot h}\right) \cdot t_2 - \frac{1}{2} \cdot g \cdot t_2^2 \qquad (86.6)$$

from where

$$t_2 = \left(\sqrt{\frac{h}{g}}\right) \cdot \left(\sqrt{2} - 1\right) \qquad (86.7)$$

By applying the equation of motion on portion *AB* for the second ball, we obtain

$$t' = \sqrt{\frac{h}{g}} \qquad (86.8)$$

By substituting the expressions (86.3), (86.7) and (86.8) into the expression (86.1), we obtain

$$\tau = 2\left(\sqrt{2} - 1\right)\sqrt{\frac{h}{g}} = 0.82\,\text{s} \qquad (86.9)$$

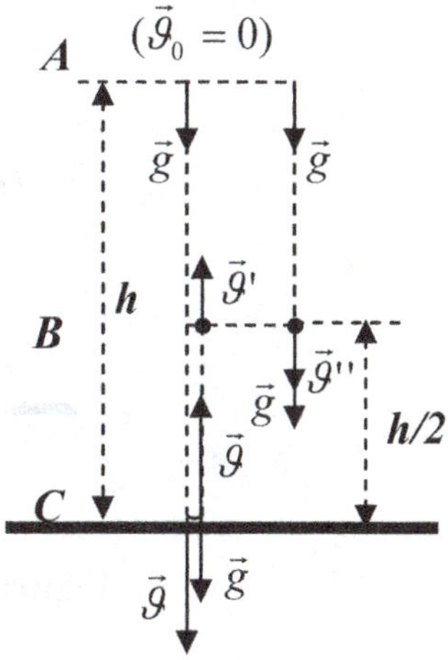

Figure 86

87. If we apply the equation of velocity as a function of displacement on segment *AB* (see Figure 87), we can easily find the velocity of the dumbbell just before hitting the ground

$$\vartheta_0 = \sqrt{2 \cdot g \cdot H} \tag{87.1}$$

this is the velocity with which the body undergoing the elastic collision starts the circular motion.

The dumbbell reaches the vertical position; by applying the law of conservation of energy, we obtain

$$\frac{m \cdot \vartheta_0^2}{2} = \frac{m \cdot \vartheta^2}{2} + m \cdot g \cdot l \tag{87.2}$$

For the dumbbell to lose its contact with the ground, the normal force acted vertically on it by the ground must be zero, therefore

$$\vec{N} = 0 \Rightarrow \vec{F}_{cf} + 2m\vec{g} = 0,$$

therefore

$$F_{cf} = 2 \cdot m \cdot g \tag{87.3}$$

where

$$F_{cf} = \frac{m \cdot \vartheta^2}{l} \tag{87.4}$$

If we make the calculations, we obtain

$$l = \frac{H}{2}$$

and therefore l=2m.

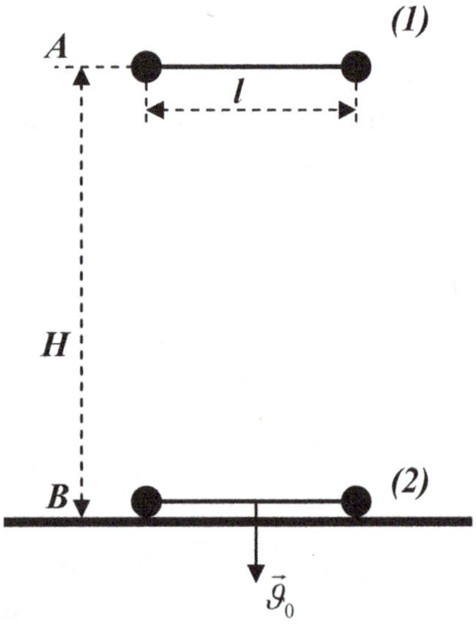

Figure 87 (a)

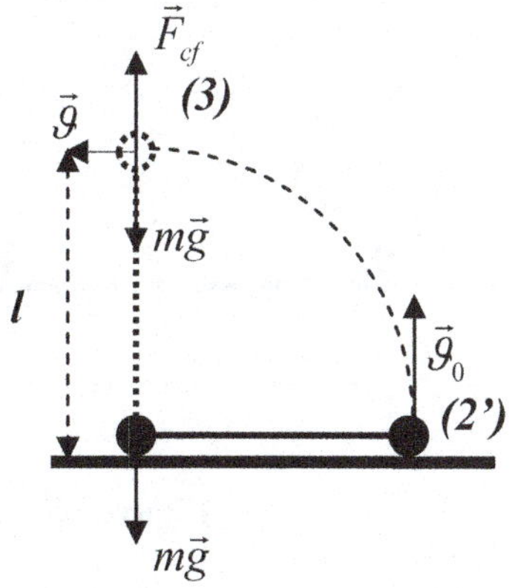

Figure 87 (b)

88. We will impose the condition that before the collision, the ball is at the bottom of the cart.

Therefore

$$\sin 2\alpha = \frac{s \cdot g}{\vartheta_0^2} \qquad (88.1)$$

where α is the angle which the ball makes with the horizontal initially, and ϑ_0 is the initial velocity (see Figure 88).

On the other hand

$$W = \frac{m \cdot \vartheta_0^2}{2} \qquad (88.2)$$

Since the horizontal component of the ball's momentum will be the only one to impart motion to the cart, which is at rest initially, we are able to find its velocity from the expression

$$\vartheta = \frac{2 \cdot m}{M + m} \cdot \vartheta_0 \cdot \cos\alpha \qquad (88.3)$$

By taking into account the expressions (88.1) and (88.2), we can find

$$\vartheta = \frac{2 \cdot \sqrt{m \cdot W}}{M + m} \cdot \sqrt{1 \pm \sqrt{\left(1 - \frac{m \cdot s \cdot g}{2 \cdot W}\right)\left(1 + \frac{m \cdot s \cdot g}{2 \cdot W}\right)}} \qquad (88.4)$$

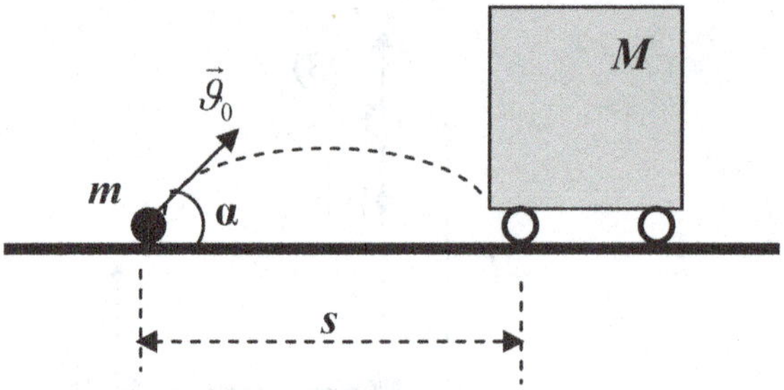

Figure 88

89. Since the first ball continues to move after collision, covering a straight line trajectory (in the vertical, of course), we deduce that its velocity after collision is zero, which implies not only that the second ball has the same mass, but also that the same velocity will be imparted to the second one, which the first ball had before collision (see Figure 89).

Taking into account the observations above and the enunciation of the problem, we deduce that the kinetic energy initially imparted to the first ball is transformed in a sum of potential energies.

Hence:

$$m \cdot \frac{\vartheta^2}{2} = m \cdot g \cdot 2 \cdot l + m \cdot g \cdot L \qquad (89.1)$$

then we get ϑ as

$$\vartheta = \sqrt{2 \cdot g \cdot (2 \cdot l + L)} \qquad (89.2)$$

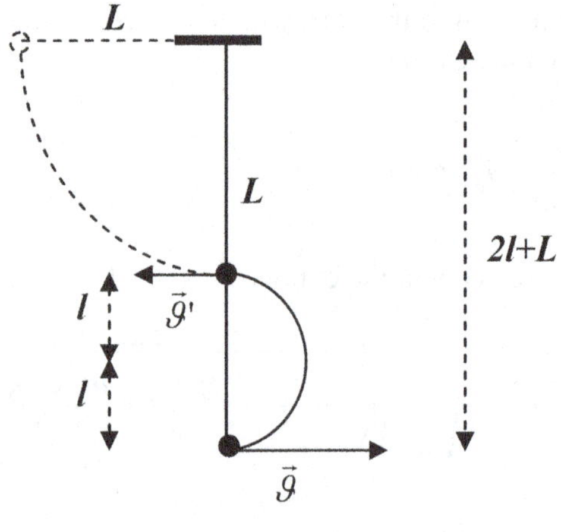

Figure 89

90. In order for the first body to be able to return to the same point covering the same path, we must impose the condition that the velocity before the impact with the inclined plane must be perpendicular to it.

Since the launching conditions of the second body are identical with the first one, we deduce that after the inelastic collision the descent on the plane takes place without an initial velocity.

Consider h as the height where the bodies collide with the plane, then the time necessary for the second body to descend from this point will be

$$t_2 = \frac{1}{\sin\alpha} \cdot \sqrt{\frac{2 \cdot h}{g}} \tag{90.1}$$

On the other hand, the time necessary for the other body to return to the same point will be given by the expression:

$$t_1 = \frac{\vartheta_0 \cdot \sin\beta + \sqrt{\vartheta_0^2 \cdot \sin^2\beta - 2 \cdot g \cdot h}}{g} \tag{90.2}$$

where ϑ_0 is the velocity with which the bodies were thrown from the bottom. This velocity in terms of the height *is*

$$\vartheta_0 = \frac{cas\alpha}{\cos\beta} \cdot \sqrt{\frac{h \cdot g}{2}} \tag{90.3}$$

By imposing the condition

$$t_1 = t_2 \tag{90.4}$$

and by solving the three equations above, we obtain

$$\tan\beta = \frac{1 + \sin^2\alpha}{\sin\alpha \cdot \cos\alpha} \tag{90.5}$$

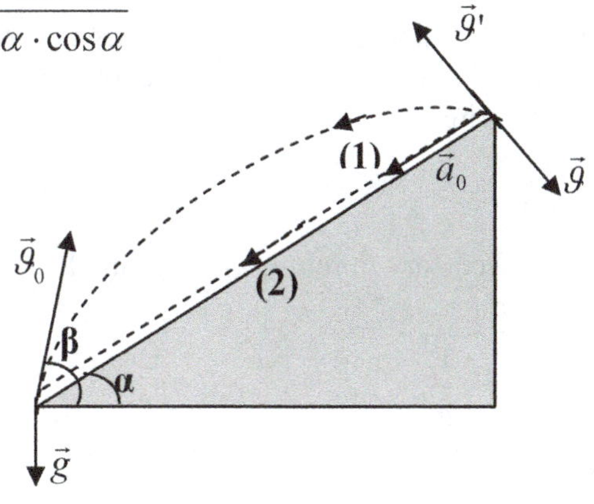

Figure 90.R

91. Since both balls move horizontally after the collision, the total momentum in the vertical will be zero, therefore the magnitudes of the velocities before the collision will be equal

$$\vartheta_1 = \vartheta_2 \tag{91.1}$$

but $\vartheta_1 = \sqrt{2g(h-h_1)}$, $\vartheta_1 = \sqrt{gh}$ (91.2)

and $\vartheta_2 = \sqrt{2g(h-h_1)}$, $\vartheta_2 = \sqrt{gh}$ (91.3)

By taking into account the facts that both the energy and the momentum in the horizontal are conserved during the collision process, we will obtain

$$\vartheta'_1 = \vartheta'_2 = \sqrt{gh} = \vartheta \tag{91.4}$$

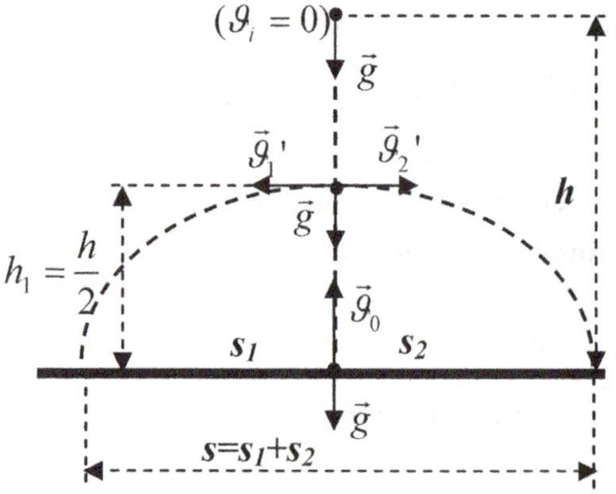

Figure 91

Consider that s_1 and s_2 are the distances covered by each ball until reaching the ground. Then, by taking into account the equation of motion in the vertical we can write

$$\frac{h}{2} = g\frac{t^2}{2}, \tag{91.5}$$

where t is the time necessary to return to the ground.

We will obtain

$$s_1 = s_2 = \vartheta\sqrt{h\frac{1}{g}}. \tag{91.6}$$

Hence

$$s = 2 \cdot h. \tag{91.7}$$

92. If we take into account that the acceleration of the bodies of masses m and M is

$$a = \frac{M - m}{M + m} g \qquad (92.1)$$

we deduce that the body of mass m will reach point B with the velocity

$$\vartheta = \sqrt{gH \frac{M - m}{M + m}} \qquad (92.2)$$

Since the time intervals necessary to cover the distances AB and BC (which are equal) are the same, we deduce that at point B the velocity of the body of mass m is cancelled; therefore the velocity of the body of mass M is also cancelled. Since the collision is perfectly elastic, we deduce that the velocity with which the collided body of mass m_o which is initially at rest will be exactly the one of the bodies of mass m and M. That is,

$$m_0 = m + M \qquad (92.3)$$

In order for the string by which this body is hung to re-stretch after the body's collision, both bodies will have to cover equal distances, therefore

$$\vartheta\tau - \frac{1}{2} g\tau^2 = \frac{1}{2} g\tau^2, \qquad (92.4)$$

where τ is the time interval required. Therefore, by taking into account (92.2), we obtain

$$\tau = \sqrt{\left(\frac{H}{g}\right) \frac{M - m}{M + m}} = 0.31 s. \qquad (92.5)$$

93. For the trajectory to be straight line on side BC the ball will have to reach point B with a velocity that makes the angle α below the horizontal (this way, the elastic collision that would exclude the possibility for the trajectory to become straight line is avoided – otherwise the ball would "bounce" on side BC).

Hence:

$$\tan \alpha = \frac{\vartheta_y}{\vartheta \cdot \cos \beta} \qquad (93.1)$$

and

$$\vartheta_y = \sqrt{\vartheta^2 \cdot \sin^2 \beta - 2 \cdot g \cdot h}. \qquad (93.2)$$

By making the calculations, we will obtain

$$\vartheta = \frac{\sqrt{2 \cdot g \cdot h}}{\sqrt{\sin^2 \beta - \cos^2 \beta \cdot \tan^2 \alpha}} \qquad (93.3)$$

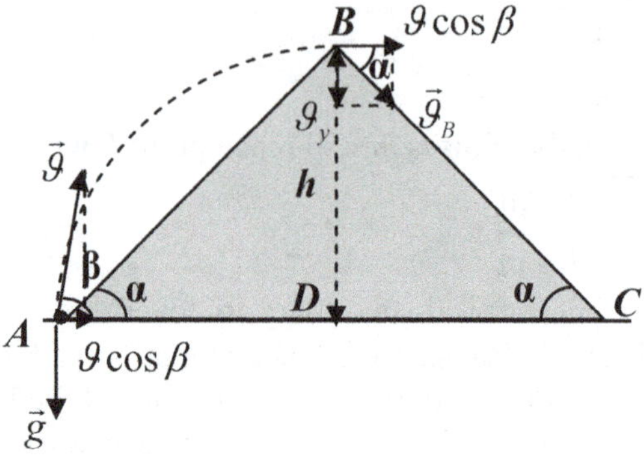

Figure 93

94. By analyzing Figure 94, we notice that

$$d = \frac{R}{2} \tag{94.1}$$

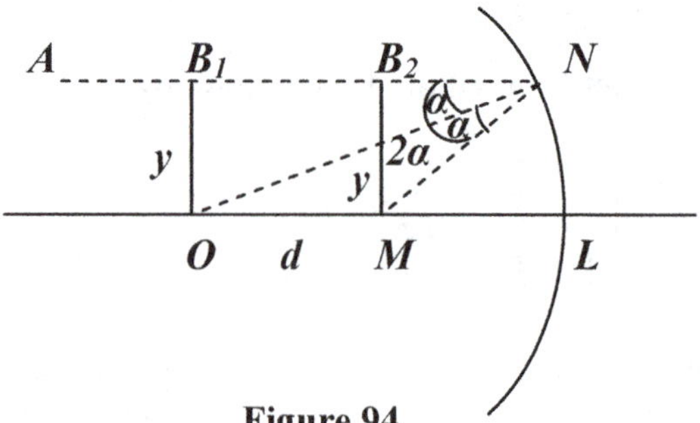

Figure 94

95. Before the squirrel clings to the wheel (at point *B*), we only notice the circular motion of the wheel around point O, while just afterwards we can also notice the squirrel's circular motion. Supposing that the clinging phenomenon takes place within a very short time interval, the angular momentum will be conserved relative to point O. (Angular momentum is conserved relative to point O before and after the squirrel clings to the wheel at point B.)Therefore

$$L_0 = L_1$$

$$M\vartheta_0 \cdot R = (M+m)\vartheta \cdot R$$

that is,

$$M\vartheta_0 = (M+m)\cdot \vartheta. \tag{95.1}$$

Since the motion takes place until the moment when the squirrel reaches point *A*, we may consider that at the end it gains the potential energy

$$PE = m \cdot g \cdot h \tag{95.2}$$

where

$$h = R \cdot (1 + \sin\alpha) \tag{95.3}$$

therefore

$$PE = m \cdot g \cdot R \cdot (1 + \sin\alpha) \tag{95.4}$$

Also because of the total loss of kinetic energy of the entire system (wheel and squirrel), we can write

$$m \cdot g \cdot R \cdot (1 + \sin\alpha) = \frac{M + m}{2} \cdot \vartheta^2 \tag{95.5}$$

On the other hand, if we take into account the frequency and the peripheral velocity in the circular motion, for the situation before the squirrel clings to the wheel we will obtain

$$\nu_0 = \frac{\vartheta_0}{2\pi R} \tag{95.6}$$

By making the calculations, we obtain

$$\nu_0 = \frac{1}{\pi \cdot M}\sqrt{\frac{m}{2} \cdot (M + m) \cdot \frac{g}{R} \cdot (1 + \sin\alpha)} \cong 0.70 Hz \tag{95.7}$$

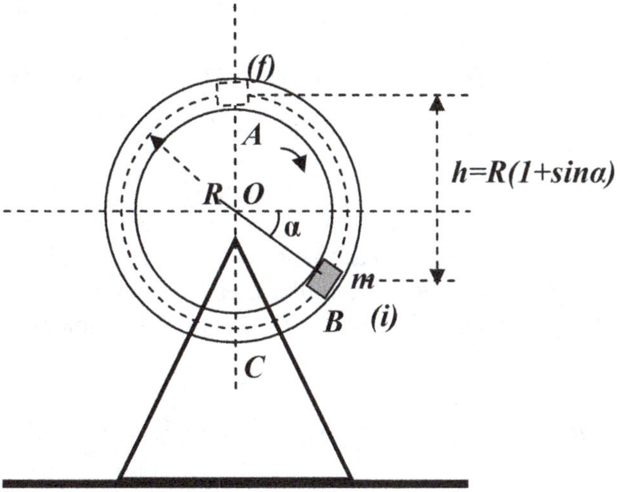

Figure 95

96. If we apply the law of conservation of energy for the displacement of the left rod from the inclined position to the vertical position (see Figure 96) (before colliding with the other rod), we can write

$$\frac{m \cdot \vartheta^2{}_m}{2} + \frac{M \cdot \vartheta^2{}_M}{2} = m \cdot g \cdot l \cdot (1 - \cos\alpha) + 2 \cdot M \cdot g \cdot l \cdot (1 - \cos\alpha)$$
(96.1)

the relation between the two velocities is

$$2\vartheta_m = \vartheta_M . \quad (96.2)$$

Supposing that the two collisions are independent, we can write the expressions of the four velocities just after the collision

$$\vartheta_{m_1} = \vartheta_{m_2} = \frac{1}{2} \cdot \vartheta_m \quad (96.3)$$

$$\vartheta_{M_1} = 0 \quad (96.4)$$

$$\vartheta_{M_2} = \vartheta_M \quad (96.5)$$

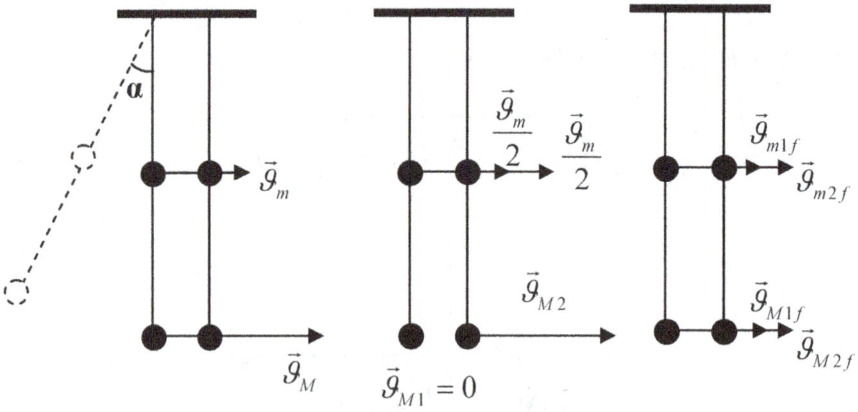

Figure 96

But if we take into account that every two bodies belonging to one of the (rigid) rods undergoes a circular motion around the supporting point, then by applying the law of conservation of angular momentum for each rod we can write

$$m \cdot \vartheta_{m1} \cdot l + 0 = l \cdot m \cdot \vartheta_{mf1} + 2 \cdot M \cdot \vartheta_{Mf1} \cdot l \quad (96.6)$$

and

$$l \cdot m \cdot \vartheta_{m2} + 2 \cdot l \cdot M \cdot \vartheta_M = l \cdot m \cdot \vartheta_{mf2} + 2 \cdot l \cdot M \cdot \vartheta_{Mf2} \quad (96.7)$$

where $\vartheta_{mf1,2}$ is the velocity of the body of mass m belonging to the first and to the second rod, respectively, and $\vartheta_{Mf1,2}$ is the velocity of the body of mass M belonging to the first and to the second rod, respectively.

The relations between the two pairs of velocities will be

$$2 \cdot \vartheta_{mf_1} = \vartheta_{Mf_1} \tag{96.8}$$

and

$$2 \cdot \vartheta_{mf_2} = \vartheta_{Mf_2} \tag{96.9}$$

while the expressions of the angular velocities for each separate rod can be written as follows

$$\omega_1 = \frac{\vartheta_{mf1}}{l} \tag{96.10}$$

$$\omega_2 = \frac{\vartheta_{mf2}}{l} \tag{96.11}$$

By solving the equations above, we obtain the two results we were looking for

$$\omega_1 = \frac{m}{m + 4 \cdot M} \sqrt{\frac{g}{2 \cdot l} \frac{(m + 2 \cdot M)}{(m + 4 \cdot M)} \cdot (1 - \cos\alpha)} \tag{96.12}$$

$$\omega_2 = \frac{m + 8 \cdot M}{m + 4 \cdot M} \sqrt{\frac{g}{2 \cdot l} \frac{(m + 2 \cdot M)}{(m + 4 \cdot M)} \cdot (1 - \cos\alpha)} \tag{96.13}$$

97. a) According to Figure 97, the body of mass m_3 will cover the following distance

$$s = \sqrt{l^2 - d^2} \tag{97.1}$$

Hence

$$t = \frac{\sqrt{l^2 - d^2}}{\vartheta} \tag{97.2}$$

b) The component of the velocity of the body of mass m_3 on the Ox axis (perpendicular to the string) will remain unchanged even after the string becomes tight, while the momentum of the third body ($p_{3y} = m_3 \vartheta \cos\alpha$) will cause m_1 and m_2 to rotate around their center of mass through the string, at the same time, translate motion along its length

By decomposing $m_3 \vartheta \cos\alpha$ as shown in figure 97a, and by taking into account the law of conservation of angular momentum of a body relative to a certain point during the process in the absence of a momentum of some external forces, we will be able to write

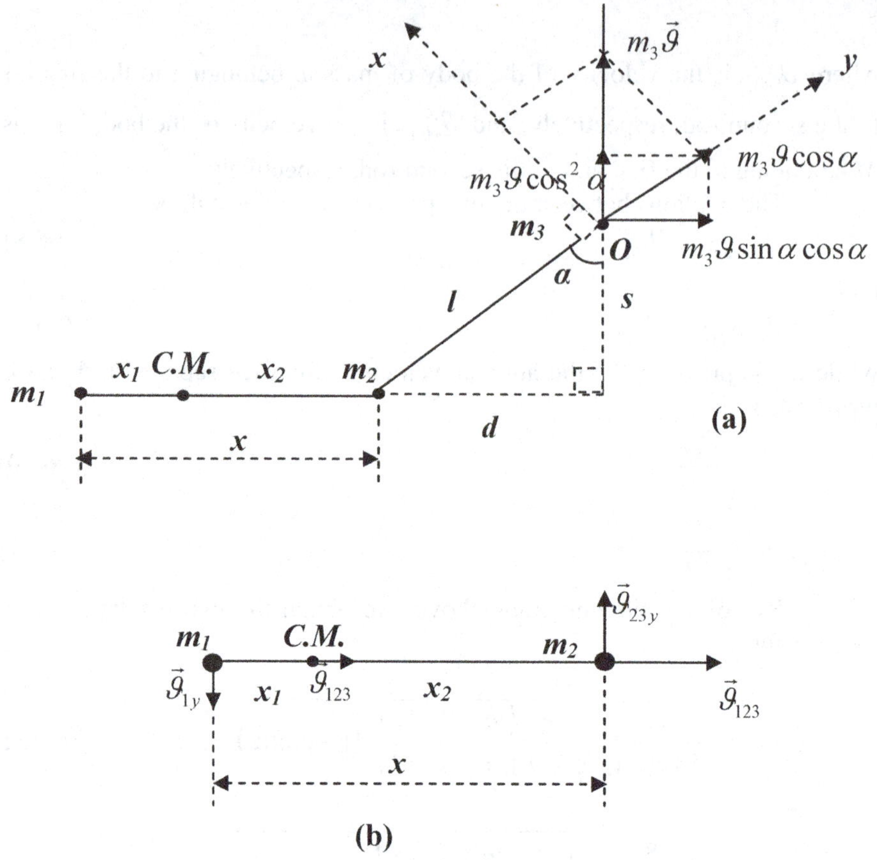

Figure 97

$$L_{3i} = L_{1f} + L_{2f} + L_{3f}, \tag{97.3}$$

where

L_{3i}= the angular momentum of the body of mass m_3 relative to the center of mass before the string becomes tight, and L_{1f}, L_{2f} and L_{3f} are the angular momenta of the three bodies relative to the same point after the string becomes tight.

Returning to the expression (97.3), we obtain

$$x_2 \cdot m_3 \cdot \vartheta \cdot \cos^2\alpha = (m_3 + m_2) \cdot \vartheta_{23r} \cdot x_2 + m_1 \cdot \vartheta_{1r} \cdot x_1 \tag{97.4}$$

where x_1 and x_2 are the distances between the bodies of mass m_1, m_2 and the center of these masses, therefore the distances to the point around which the bodies will rotate;

ϑ_{23r} will represent the rotational speed common to the two masses m_2 and m_3, and ϑ_{1r} will be the rotational velocity characterizing the body of mass m_1.

Consider x as the length of the rod; then, we can write

$$x_1 = \frac{m_2}{m_1 + m_2} \cdot x \qquad (97.5)$$

$$x_2 = \frac{m_1}{m_1 + m_2} \cdot x. \qquad (97.6)$$

If we return to (97.4) and if we take into account (97.5) and (97.6), we obtain

$$m_3 \cdot \vartheta \cdot \cos^2 \alpha = (m_3 + m_2) \cdot \vartheta_{23r} + m_2 \cdot \vartheta_{1r}. \qquad (97.4')$$

On the other hand, as both bodies of masses m_1 and m_2 have the same angular velocity, we will be able to write

$$\frac{\vartheta_{23r}}{x_2} = \frac{\vartheta_{1r}}{x_1}. \qquad (97.7)$$

If we take into account (97.5) and (97.6), it follows that

$$\frac{\vartheta_{23r}}{m_1} = \frac{\vartheta_{1r}}{m_2}. \qquad (97.8)$$

which means that

$$\vartheta_{23r} = \vartheta_{1r} \cdot \frac{m_1}{m_2}. \qquad (97.9)$$

If we return to (97.4) and take into account (97.9), it follows that

$$m_3 \vartheta \cos^2 \alpha = \vartheta_{1r} \left[\frac{m_1}{m_2} (m_3 + m_2) + m_2 \right] \qquad (97.10)$$

that is,

$$\vartheta_{1r} = \frac{m_2 \cdot m_3}{m_1 \cdot (m_3 + m_2) + m_2^2} \cdot \vartheta \cdot \cos^2 \alpha \qquad (97.11)$$

and

$$\vartheta_{23r} = \frac{m_1 \cdot m_3}{m_1 \cdot (m_3 + m_2) + m_2^2} \cdot \vartheta \cdot \cos^2 \alpha \qquad (97.12)$$

If we take into account the absence of external forces when the string becomes tight, we can apply the law of conservation of momentum to the system consisting of the three bodies along the rod:

$$m_3 \cdot \vartheta \cdot \sin \alpha \cdot \cos \alpha = \vartheta_{123} \cdot (m_1 + m_2 + m_3) \qquad (97.13)$$

where ϑ_{123} is the common velocity of the three bodies just after the string becomes tight along the rod.

Consider ϑ_1 and ϑ_2 as the velocities of the bodies of masses m_1 and m_2 just after the string becomes tight.

In this case, we are able to write

$$\vartheta_1 = \sqrt{\vartheta_{1r}^2 + \vartheta_{123}^2} \quad (97.14)$$

and

$$\vartheta_2 = \sqrt{\vartheta_{23r}^2 + \vartheta_{123}^2}. \quad (97.15)$$

If we take into account the previous expressions, we obtain for each body

$$\vartheta_1 = m_3 \vartheta \cos\alpha \sqrt{\frac{m_2^2 \cos^2\alpha}{\left[m_1(m_3+m_2)+m_2^2\right]^2} + \frac{\sin^2\alpha}{(m_1+m_2+m_3)^2}} \quad (97.16)$$

$$\vartheta_2 = m_3 \vartheta \cos\alpha \sqrt{\frac{m_1^2 \cos^2\alpha}{\left[m_1(m_3+m_2)+m_2^2\right]^2} + \frac{\sin^2\alpha}{(m_1+m_2+m_3)^2}} \quad (97.17)$$

where $\sin\alpha = \frac{d}{l}$

and $\cos\alpha = \frac{\sqrt{l^2 - d^2}}{l}$

98. Consider *AB* to be the bottom of the prism, corresponding to the face that is in contact with the inclined plane (see Figure 98).The line drawn from the center of gravity of the prism to its bottom is perpendicular at point *C*. In order for the prism not to overturn, the vertical line drawn from the center of gravity of the prism should intersect side *AB* at point *B* at most. Assuming that side *OB* is perpendicular to the horizontal (at the limit) and that *OC* is perpendicular to *AB*, we deduce that

$$\beta = 2\alpha \quad (98.1)$$

Consider n to be the number of sides we are looking for, then

$$\beta = \frac{2\pi}{n} \quad (98.2)$$

from 1.1 and 1.2 we obtain n as

$$n = \left[\frac{\pi}{\alpha}\right] \tag{98.3}$$

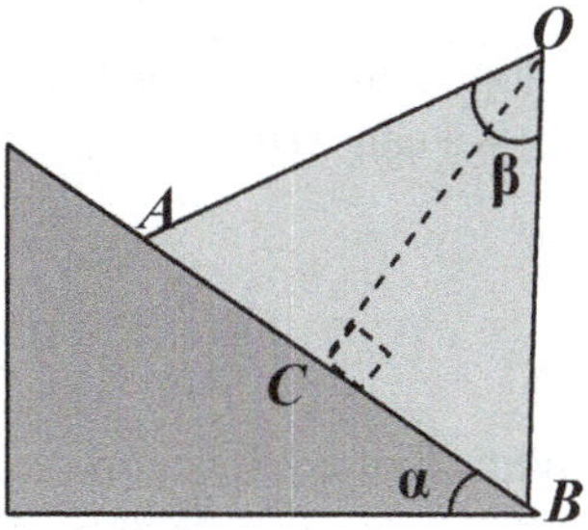

Figure 98

99. At the moment when the pendulum is in horizontal position (see Figure 99), the body of mass *m* will have the vertical velocity

$$\vartheta = \sqrt{2 \cdot g \cdot l} \tag{99.1}$$

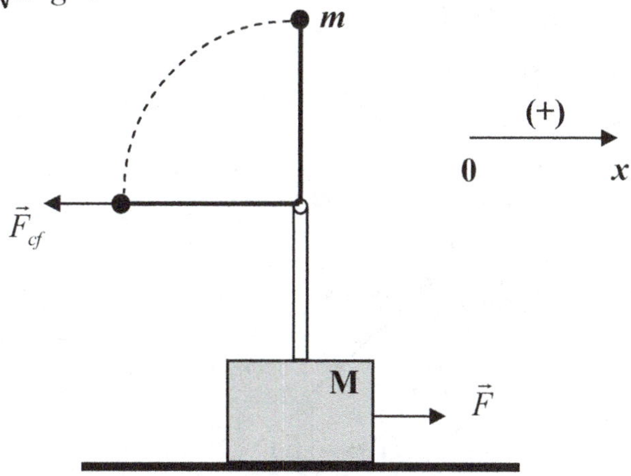

Figure 99

Therefore, the centrifugal force acting on it in this direction and in the direction opposite the external force *F* will be

$$F_{cf} = 2 \cdot m \cdot g \tag{99.2}$$

The resultant force acting on the entire system is

$$R = F - F_{cf} \tag{99.3}$$

then we obtain

$$a = \frac{F - 2 \cdot m \cdot g}{M + m} = 2\ \frac{\mathrm{m}}{\mathrm{s}^2} \tag{99.4}$$

100. From the condition of instantaneous equilibrium imposed on the body of mass m along the rod, we can write

$$T = m \cdot g \cdot \cos\alpha - F_{cf} \tag{100.1}$$

where

$$F_{cf} = 2mg(1 - \cos\alpha) \tag{100.2}$$

By imposing the condition of equilibrium on the body of mass M, we can write

$$N = Mg + T\cos\alpha \tag{100.3}$$

$$F_f = T \cdot \sin\alpha \tag{100.4}$$

and

$$F_f = \mu \cdot N \tag{100.5}$$

Therefore

$$\mu = \frac{m(3 \cdot \cos\alpha - 2) \cdot \sin\alpha}{M + m(3 \cdot \cos\alpha - 2) \cdot \cos\alpha} \tag{100.6}$$

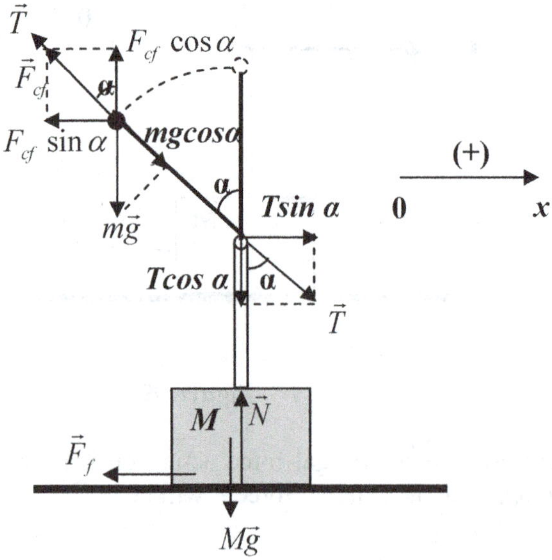

Figure 100

101. Regarding the body of mass m we can write

$$T = m \cdot g \cdot \cos\beta + F_{cf} \quad (101.1)$$

where

$$F_{cf} = 2 \cdot m \cdot g \cdot (\cos\beta - \cos\alpha) \quad (101.2)$$

and for the body of mass M

$$ox: F = F_f + T \cdot \sin\beta \quad (101.3)$$

$$oy: N = M \cdot g + T \cdot \cos\beta \quad (101.4)$$

with

$$F_f = \mu \cdot N \quad (101.5)$$

By solving the expressions above for F, we obtain

$$F = \mu \cdot M \cdot g + m \cdot g \cdot (3 \cdot \cos\beta - 2 \cdot \cos\alpha) \cdot (\mu \cdot \cos\beta + \sin\beta) \quad (101.6)$$

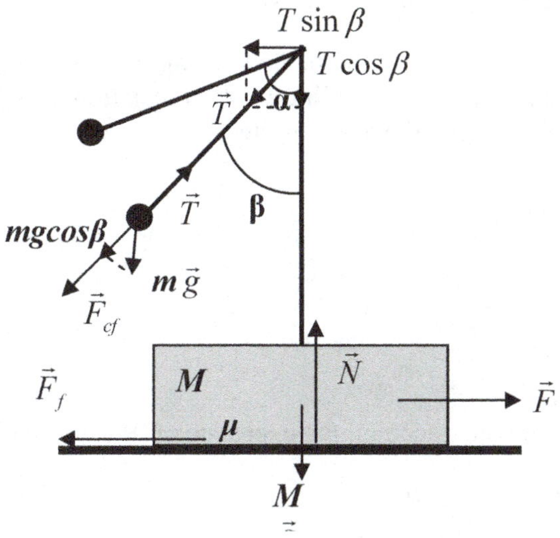

Figure 101

102. We can write the following expressions concerning one of the rings:

$$N = T \cdot \cos\alpha \quad (102.1)$$

$$F_f = T \cdot \sin\alpha, \quad (102.2)$$

and

$$F_f = \mu \cdot N. \quad (102.3)$$

By solving the equations, we obtain

$$\mu = \tan\alpha \tag{102.4}$$

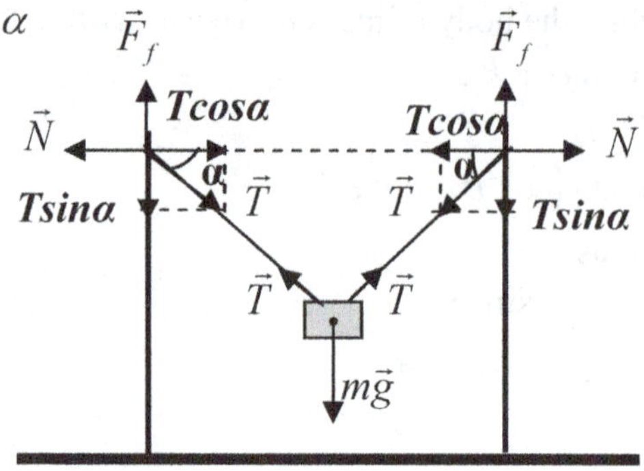

Figure 102

103. Consider l as the length of the rod. By applying the condition of rotational equilibrium about point A (see Figure 103), we obtain

$$F \cdot \sin\alpha \cdot l = \frac{1}{2} m \cdot g \cdot l \cdot \cos\alpha, \tag{103.1}$$

where F is the force with which the body of mass M is sustained.

By applying the condition of translational equilibrium in the horizontal and the vertical, we can write

$$F = F_f \tag{103.2}$$

$$N = M \cdot g \tag{103.3}$$

and

$$F_f = \mu \cdot N. \tag{103.4}$$

Therefore

$$F = \mu \cdot M \cdot g. \tag{103.5}$$

If we take into account the expression (103.1), we obtain

$$\cot\alpha = 2 \cdot \frac{M}{m} \cdot \mu = 4 \tag{103.6}$$

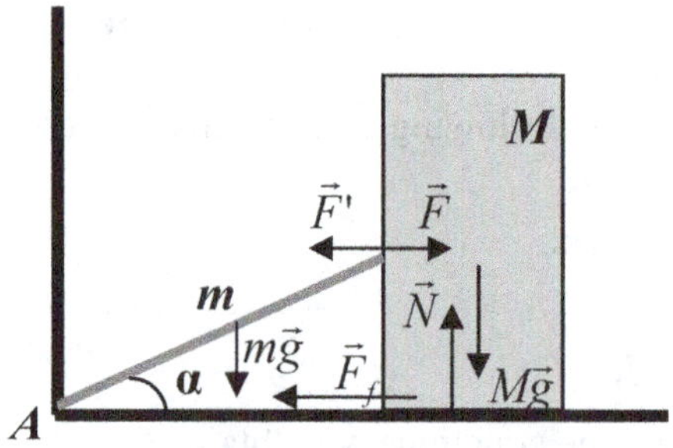

Figure 103

104. For the rods to stay in equilibrium as explained in the problem, they must be placed as shown in Figure 104. That is, the forces exerted by the ends of the rods on the floor must cancel each other

$$F_1 = F_2 \tag{104.1}$$

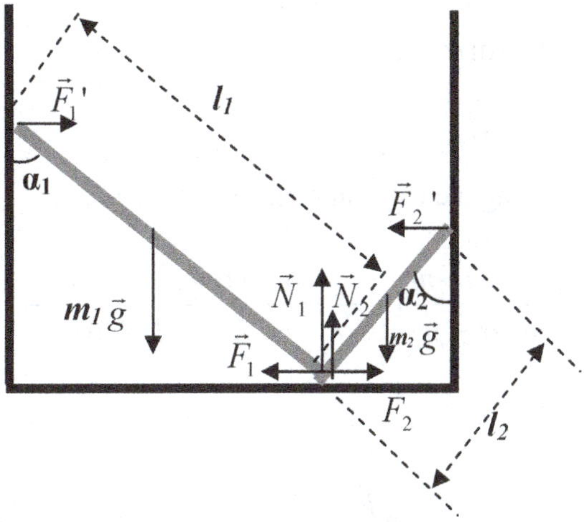

Figure 104

Then we can apply the condition of rotational equilibrium to the rods about the points of contact with the walls.

$$N_1 \cdot l_1 \cdot \sin\alpha_1 = F_1 \cdot l_1 \cdot \cos\alpha_1 + m_1 \cdot g \cdot \frac{l_1}{2} \cdot \sin\alpha_1 \tag{104.2}$$

$$N_2 \cdot l_2 \cdot \sin\alpha_2 = F_2 \cdot l_2 \cdot \cos\alpha_2 + m_2 \cdot g \cdot \frac{l_2}{2} \cdot \sin\alpha_2 \tag{104.3}$$

and

$$N_1 = m_1 \cdot g \tag{104.4}$$

$$N_2 = m_2 \cdot g \tag{104.5}$$

Since the rods have the same density, we can write

$$\frac{m_1}{l_1} = \frac{m_2}{l_2} \tag{104.6}$$

By solving the equations above, we obtain the relationship asked

$$\frac{\cot\alpha_2}{\cot\alpha_1} = \frac{l_2}{l_1} \tag{104.7}$$

105. By applying the condition of rotational equilibrium to the rod (about point A) (see Figure 105a), it follows that

$$M \cdot g \cdot (\cos\alpha) \cdot s + m \cdot g \cdot l \cdot \frac{1}{2}\cos\alpha = F \cdot l \qquad (105.1)$$

Applying the condition of translational equilibrium to the body of mass m_l we can write the following expressions

$$Oy : N = m_1 \cdot g + F \cdot \cos\alpha \qquad (105.2)$$

$$Ox : F \cdot \sin\alpha = F_f \qquad (105.3)$$

and

$$F_f = \mu \cdot N \qquad (105.4)$$

By making the calculations, we obtain

$$s = \left(\frac{\mu \cdot m_1}{\sin\alpha - \mu \cdot \cos\alpha} - \frac{m \cdot \cos\alpha}{2} \right) \cdot \frac{l}{M \cdot \cos\alpha} = 1.6\ \text{m} \qquad (105.5)$$

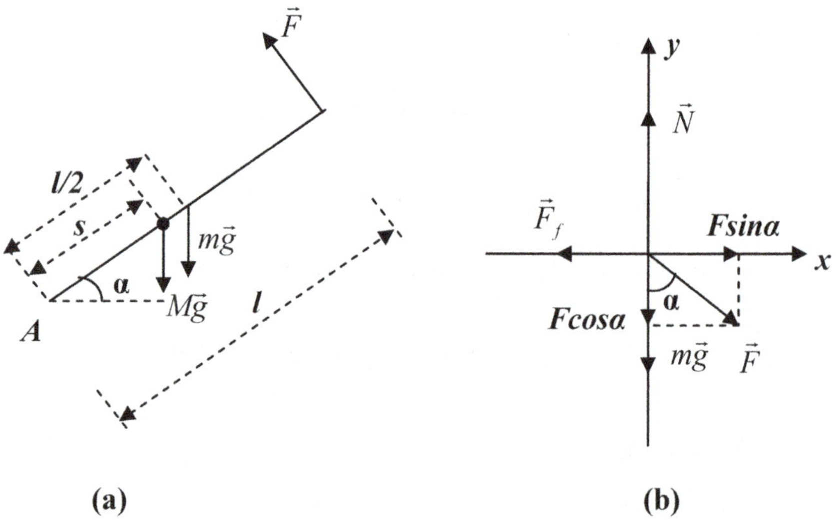

Figure 105

106. If we take into account the expression of the acceleration during ascension, we can write

$$a = \frac{\rho_0 - \rho}{\rho} \cdot g \qquad (106.1)$$

If ϑ is its velocity as it leaves water, then we can write

$$\vartheta = a \cdot t_1. \qquad (106.2)$$

where t_1 is the rising time in water.

and

$$\vartheta = g \cdot t_2 \qquad (106.3)$$

where t_2 is the rising time out of water

then

$$t_2 \cdot g = t_1 \cdot a \qquad (106.4)$$

by taking into account (106.1), we can write

$$t_2 = t_1 \cdot \frac{\rho_0 - \rho}{\rho} \qquad (106.5)$$

we know that

$$t_2 = k \cdot t_1 \qquad (106.6)$$

Therefore

$$\rho = \rho_0 \cdot \frac{1}{(k+1)} \qquad (106.7)$$

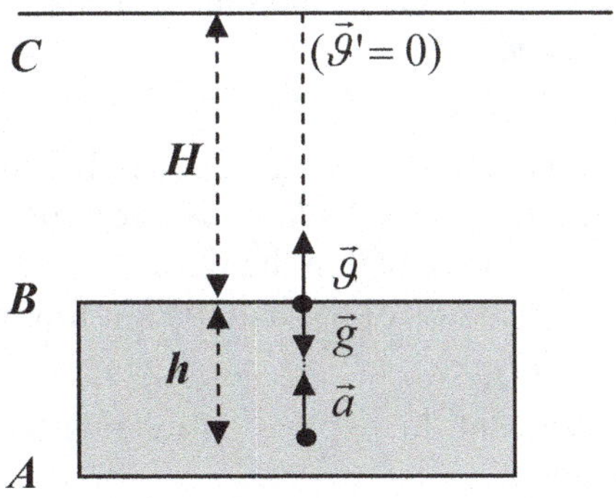

Figure 106

107. During the motion of the entire chamber with a constant acceleration, the liquid will exert a force on the ball in the direction of the acceleration, and the magnitude of this force is equal to the force of inertia of the liquid replaced by it. Therefore, we will be able to write

$$F_i = m_l \cdot a \qquad (107.1)$$

$$F_i = m_b \cdot a' \qquad (107.2)$$

where the two masses can be written as

$$m_l = \rho_l \cdot V \tag{107.2'}$$

$$m_b = \rho \cdot V \tag{107.2''}$$

Consider l as the length of the chamber.

Then, the equations of motion for the chamber and for the ball relative to the fixed reference point will be

$$f \cdot l = \frac{1}{2} \cdot a \cdot t^2 \tag{107.3}$$

$$(1+f) \cdot l = \frac{1}{2} \cdot a' \cdot t^2 \tag{107.4}$$

By solving the equations above, we obtain

$$\rho_l = \frac{1+f}{f} \cdot \rho \tag{107.5}$$

108. Consider b as the distance covered horizontally by the ball before entering into the water and L-b as the horizontal distance it covers in the water. Then, the equations of motion can be written

$$b = \vartheta_0 \cdot t \tag{108.1}$$

$$t = \sqrt{2 \cdot \frac{h}{g}} \tag{108.2}$$

where t is the time necessary for the motion of the ball in the air

On the other hand

$$L - b = \vartheta_0 \cdot t' \tag{108.3}$$

where t' is the time interval during which the ball is inside the water.

In order to find t', we calculate the acceleration in the vertical that characterizes the motion of the ball in the water (see Figure 108).

Consider m as the mass of the ball, then it follows that

$$m \cdot a = F_A - m \cdot g \tag{108.4}$$

and, if we take into account the expression relating the densities, by making the calculations we obtain

$$a = (n-1) \cdot g \tag{108.5}$$

then, the expression of the time interval t' becomes

$$t' = \frac{2}{n-1} \cdot \sqrt{\frac{2 \cdot h}{g}} \tag{108.6}$$

By substituting the expression (108.6) into (108.3), we obtain

$$L - b = \vartheta_0 \cdot \frac{2}{n-1} \cdot \sqrt{\frac{2 \cdot h}{g}} \tag{108.7}$$

By taking into account (108.1) and (108.2), we obtain

$$\vartheta = \frac{n-1}{n+1} \cdot L \cdot \sqrt{\frac{g}{2 \cdot h}} \quad (108.8)$$

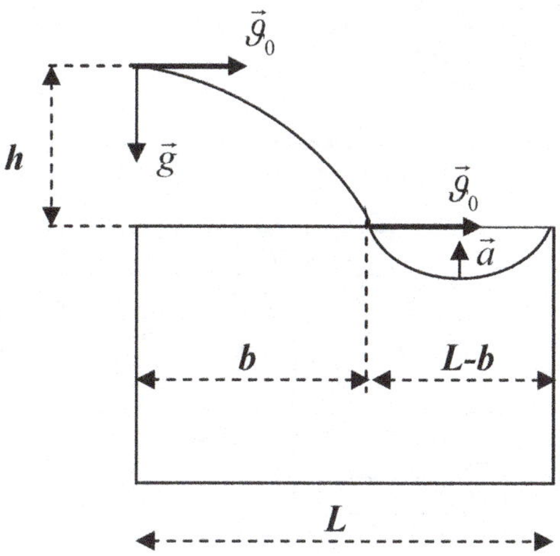

Figure 108

109. For the string to have a relaxed length, the water spurting out of the right branch must exert on the cover (vertically upwards) a force equal to its weight:

$$F = M \cdot g \quad (109.1)$$

On the other hand

$$F = p \cdot S' \quad (109.2)$$

where p is the pressure of the jet at the height h relative to the upper part of the U-shaped pipe, and S' is its cross-sectional area.

By applying the equation of continuity, we can find the velocity of the water going out of the pipe (ϑ):

$$Q = S \cdot \vartheta \quad (109.3)$$

and on the other hand

$$Q = S' \cdot \vartheta' \quad (109.3')$$

where ϑ' is the velocity of water at the level of the cover.

If we apply Bernoulli's equation at points A and B, we can write

$$\frac{1}{2} \cdot \rho \cdot \vartheta'^2 = \frac{1}{2} \cdot \rho \cdot \vartheta^2 - \rho \cdot g \cdot h \quad (109.4)$$

and

$$p = \frac{\rho \cdot \vartheta'^2}{2} \quad (109.5)$$

By making the calculations, we obtain

$$M = \frac{\rho \cdot Q \cdot \sqrt{Q^2 - 2 \cdot g \cdot h \cdot S^2}}{2 \cdot S \cdot g} \quad (109.6)$$

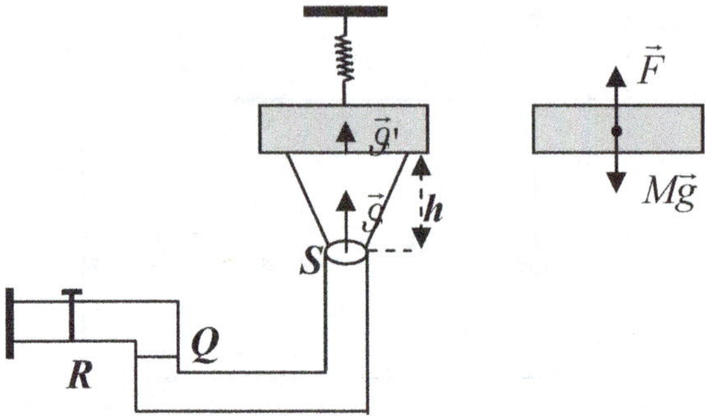

Figure 109

110. In order to remove the necessity of the presence of the string to keep the container stationary, the frictional force must be equal to the component of the weight, which is parallel to the incline:

$$F_f = M \cdot g \cdot \sin\alpha \quad (110.1)$$

where

$$F_f = \mu \cdot N \quad (110.2)$$

The normal pressing force N is the sum of the component of the weight, which is perpendicular to the incline and the force exerted by the liquid spurting out through the orifice of cross-sectional area S_2, as a result of the pressure produced by the pressing force on the piston of cross-sectional area S_1, exerted by the spring. Therefore

$$N = M \cdot g \cdot \cos\alpha + F \quad (110.3)$$

and, on the other hand

$$\frac{T}{S_1} = \frac{F}{S_2} \quad (110.4)$$

If we make the calculations, we obtain

$$T = \frac{S_1}{S_2} \cdot \frac{M \cdot g}{\mu} \cdot (\sin\alpha - \mu \cdot \cos\alpha) \approx 16N. \qquad (110.5)$$

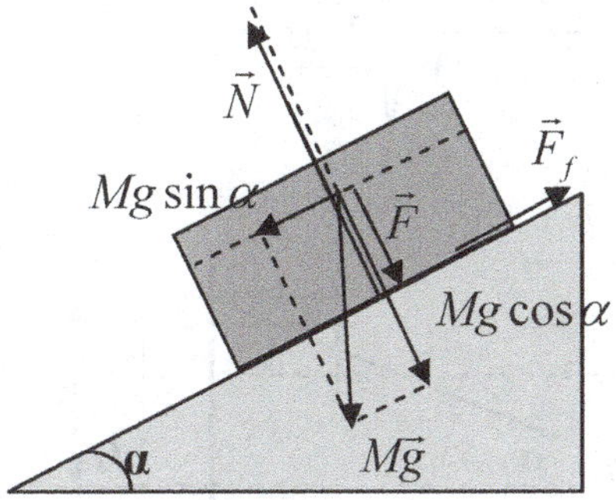

Figure 110

111. At the moment the brake is applied, the liquid will rise on the right wall of the container and its free surface will make an angle α with the horizontal.

Consider b as the difference between the maximum level reached by the liquid on the wall and the level of the orifice. Then, the difference between the two levels at which the liquid reaches on the two walls will be

$$y = 2 \cdot (b + H - h). \qquad (111.1)$$

Then, the water will "spurt out" horizontally through the orifice, having the following velocity with respect to the ground

$$\vartheta_0 = \vartheta + \sqrt{2 \cdot g \cdot b} \qquad (111.2)$$

and will cover a parabolic path until it reaches the ground; therefore

$$H = \frac{1}{2} \cdot g \cdot t^2 \qquad (111.3)$$

$$s = \vartheta_0 \cdot t \qquad (111.4)$$

$$s = \vartheta_0 \cdot \sqrt{\frac{2 \cdot H}{g}} \qquad (111.5)$$

that is,

$$s = (\vartheta + \sqrt{2 \cdot g \cdot b}) \cdot \sqrt{\frac{2 \cdot H}{g}} \qquad (111.6)$$

Since the cart must stop within a shorter distance which is at most equal to the "range" of the water (s), we can write about its motion that

$$a = \frac{\vartheta^2}{2 \cdot s} \tag{111.7}$$

$$a = \frac{\vartheta^2}{2 \cdot (\vartheta + \sqrt{2 \cdot g \cdot b}) \cdot \sqrt{\frac{2 \cdot H}{g}}}. \tag{111.8}$$

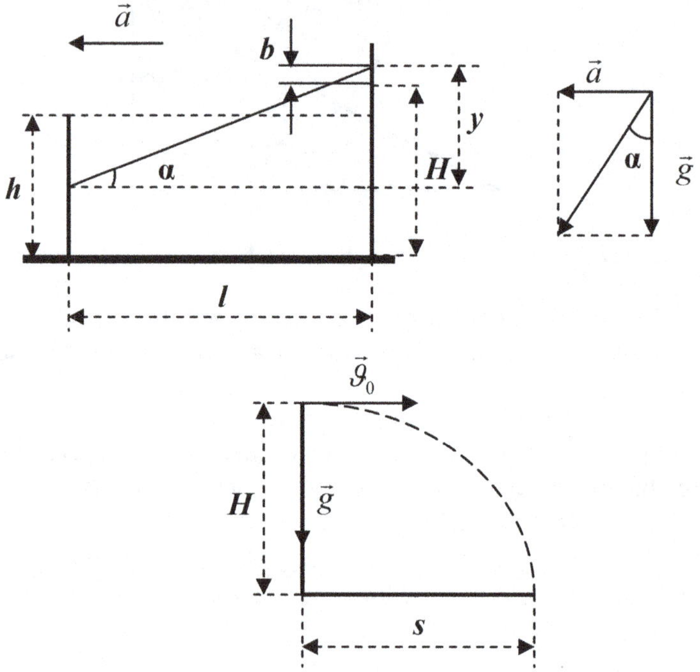

Figure 111

On the other hand, if we take into account the slope of the free surface of the water during braking, we obtain

$$\tan\alpha = \frac{2 \cdot (b + H - h)}{l} \tag{111.9}$$

and

$$\tan\alpha = \frac{a}{g} \tag{111.10}$$

that is,

$$2 \cdot (b + H - h) \cdot g = a \cdot l \tag{111.11}$$

then

$$2 \cdot b \cdot g = a \cdot l + 2 \cdot h \cdot g - 2 \cdot H \cdot g \tag{111.12}$$

By replacing this expression in (111.8), we obtain

$$a=\frac{\vartheta^2}{2\cdot\left[\vartheta+\sqrt{a\cdot l+2\cdot g\cdot(h-H)}\right]}\cdot\sqrt{\frac{g}{2\cdot H}}. \qquad (111.13)$$

If we make the calculations, we obtain:

$$h=\frac{1}{2\cdot g}\cdot\left[\left(\frac{\vartheta^2}{2\cdot a}\cdot\sqrt{\frac{g}{2\cdot H}}-\vartheta\right)^2-a\cdot l\right]+H \qquad (111.14)$$

112. Consider F as the force with which the water is pushed outside (see Figure 112). When a quantity M' of water remains in the container its height is y and the vertical section of its volume will have the longer side as l'.

Starting from the expression

$$p=\frac{F}{S}. \qquad (112.1)$$

it follows that

$$F=\rho\cdot g\cdot y\cdot S \qquad (112.2)$$

If we take into account the third law of Newton, we notice that this force is exactly the force that will impart acceleration to the system horizontally. Therefore,

$$F=(m+M')\cdot a_2 \qquad (112.3)$$

where M' is the mass of the liquid still remaining in the container.

On the other hand, we can write

$$\frac{M}{\frac{1}{2}\cdot(L+l)\cdot H}=\frac{M'}{\frac{1}{2}\cdot(l+l')\cdot y} \qquad (112.4)$$

and if we take into account the following ratio

$$\frac{L-l}{H}=\frac{l'-l}{y} \qquad (112.5)$$

we find out that

$$M'=M\frac{2\cdot H\cdot l+(L-l)\cdot y}{H^2(L+l)}\cdot y \qquad (112.6)$$

then from the expressions 112.2, 112.3, and 112.6 we can get

$$a_2=\frac{\rho\cdot g\cdot S\cdot y}{m+M\cdot\frac{2\cdot H\cdot l+(L-l)\cdot y}{H^2\cdot(L+l)}\cdot y} \qquad (112.7)$$

and

$$a_1 = \frac{\rho \cdot g \cdot S \cdot H}{m + M} \tag{112.8}$$

From here, we obtain

$$\frac{a_1}{a_2} = \frac{1}{f} \cdot \frac{m + M \cdot \dfrac{2 \cdot l + f \cdot (L - l)}{L + l}}{M + m} \tag{112.9}$$

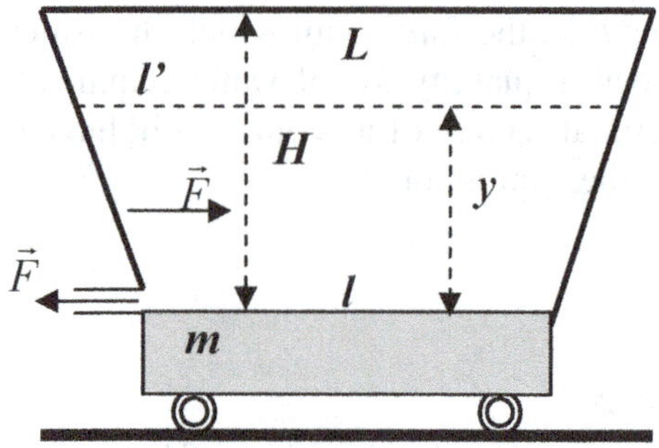

Figure 112

113. When the orifice is opened, the liquid will start to leave the container (horizontally), having the following pressure

$$p = \rho \cdot g \cdot (H - h) \tag{113.1}$$

and the force exerted on it will be

$$F = p \cdot S \tag{113.2}$$

where

$$S = \frac{l \cdot H}{n} \tag{113.3}$$

In this situation, the same force F will be exerted on the container by the liquid leaving the container through the orifice according to the third law of Newton. By applying on the container the condition of rotational equilibrium (see Figure 113), we can write

$$F \cdot h = m \cdot g \cdot \frac{l}{2} \tag{113.4}$$

where m is the mass of the liquid. If we take into account the previous expressions, we can write

$$\rho \cdot g \cdot (H - h) \cdot l \cdot h \cdot \frac{H}{n} = \rho \cdot l^2 \cdot H \cdot g \cdot \frac{l}{2} \tag{113.5}$$

then we obtain

$$2 \cdot h^2 - 2 \cdot H \cdot h + n \cdot l^2 = 0 \tag{113.6}$$

By solving the equation (113.6), it follows that

$$h_{1,2} = \frac{H}{2} \pm \frac{\sqrt{H^2 - 2 \cdot n \cdot l^2}}{2} \tag{113.7}$$

We accept both solutions, since the overturning of the container is possible in both cases.

The valid condition for the problem is

$$H \geq l \cdot \sqrt{2n} \tag{113.8}$$

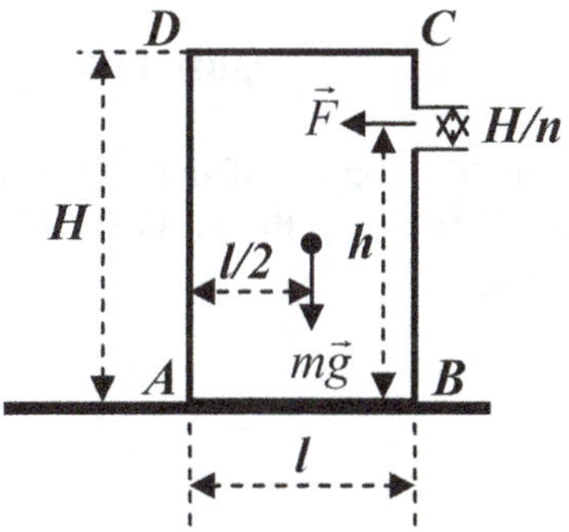

Figure 113

114.

$$ox: l = \vartheta \cdot t \tag{114.1}$$

$$oy: h - h_x = \frac{1}{2} \cdot g \cdot t^2 \tag{114.2}$$

and

$$\vartheta = \sqrt{2 \cdot g \cdot (H - h_x - h)} \tag{114.3}$$

By solving the equations, we obtain

$$h_x = \frac{H - \sqrt{(H - 2 \cdot h)^2 + l^2}}{2}. \tag{114.4}$$

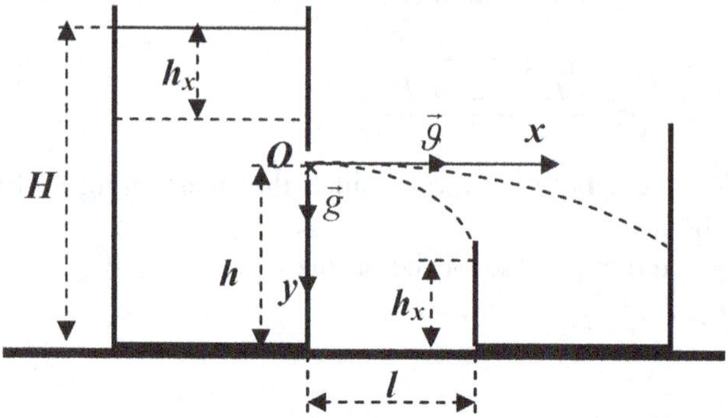

Figure 114

115. Consider l as the length of the spring in relaxed state. Then, l_1 and l_2 will be the distances between the bodies of mass $m_{1,2}$, and their center of mass, then we can write:

$$l_1 = \frac{m_2}{m_1 + m_2} \cdot l \tag{115.1}$$

and

$$l_2 = \frac{m_1}{m_1 + m_2} \cdot l \tag{115.2}$$

Since the center of mass remains stationary during the motion, we can consider that the bodies oscillate at the ends of the springs of length l_1 and l_2, respectively.

Therefore, we can write for the first body

$$T = 2 \cdot \pi \cdot \sqrt{\frac{m_1}{k_1}} \tag{115.3}$$

On the other hand, if we take into account that for any spring the following expression is valid:

$$k \cdot l = E \cdot S \tag{115.4}$$

where E is Young's modulus and S the surface of the cross-sectional area, then we can write the following about the portion of the spring with l_1:

$$k_1 \cdot l_1 = E \cdot S \tag{115.5}$$

then

$$k_1 = k \cdot \frac{l}{l_1} \tag{115.6}$$

and, if we take into account (115.1), it follows that

$$k_1 = k \cdot \frac{m_1 + m_2}{m_2}. \tag{115.7}$$

By getting back to the expression (115.3), we obtain

$$T = 2 \cdot \pi \cdot \sqrt{\frac{m_1 \cdot m_2}{m_1 + m_2} \cdot \frac{1}{k}} = 2.37s \tag{115.8}$$

If we start over the discussion about the body of mass m_2, we obtain the same results.

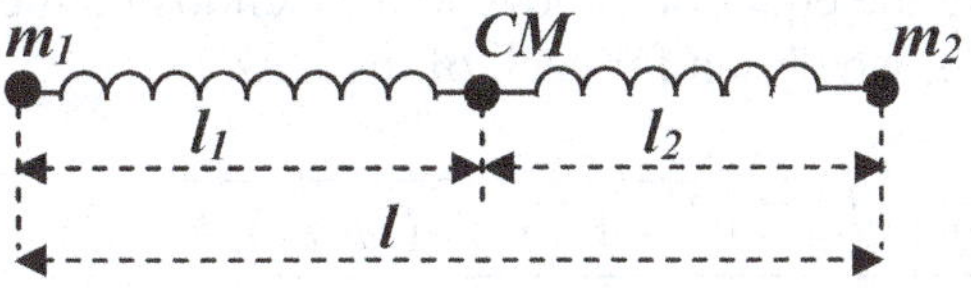

Figure 115

116. Consider the mechanical system consisting of body *A* (see Figure 116) and the assembly of two springs which are under the influences of gravitational and elastic forces.

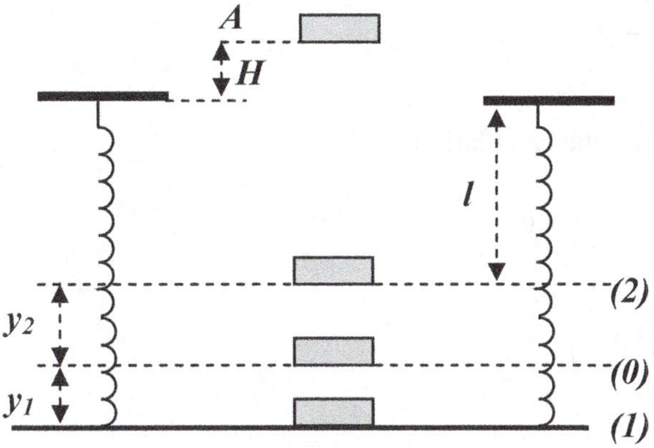

Figure 116

Therefore, since the energy is conserved, we can write

$$E_{(0)} = E_{(1)} = E_{(2)} \tag{116.1}$$

where $E_{(0)}$ is the energy of the system before the object was released to fall, the energy $E_{(1)}$ is the one in the situation where the spring undergoes a maximum extension and $E_{(2)}$ is the energy it had when it underwent the maximum compression.

If we take into account (116.1), we can write

$$m \cdot g \cdot (H + l + y_1) = 2 \cdot \frac{k}{2} \cdot y_1^2 \qquad (116.2)$$

and

$$m \cdot g \cdot (H + l - y_2) = 2 \cdot \frac{k}{2} \cdot y_2^2 \qquad (116.3)$$

where H is the height required in the problem, y_1 is the maximum extension and y_2 is the maximum compression, m is the mass of the body and k is the spring constant of each spring.

By solving the equations above and by choosing the solutions that are physically possible, we obtain for each of them as

$$y_1 = \frac{m \cdot g + \sqrt{m^2 \cdot g^2 + 4 \cdot m \cdot g \cdot (H + l) \cdot k}}{2 \cdot k} \qquad (116.4)$$

$$y_2 = \frac{-m \cdot g + \sqrt{m^2 \cdot g^2 + 4 \cdot m \cdot g \cdot (H + l) \cdot k}}{2 \cdot k} \qquad (116.5)$$

By applying the condition in the text:

$$\frac{y_1}{y_2} = 2 \qquad (116.6)$$

we obtain after the calculations

$$H = \frac{2 \cdot m \cdot g}{k} - l \qquad (116.7)$$

since

$$\frac{m \cdot g}{2 \cdot k} = \frac{l}{2} \qquad (116.8)$$

the height is $\quad H = l \qquad (116.9)$

117. Consider α as the angle (see Figure 117a) made by the string in the case motion continues with constant acceleration and the oscillatory motion stops at the equilibrium position. Then, the maximum angle that the string can make with the horizontal will be 2α, therefore we can write

$$\sin 2\alpha = \frac{h}{l} \qquad (117.1)$$

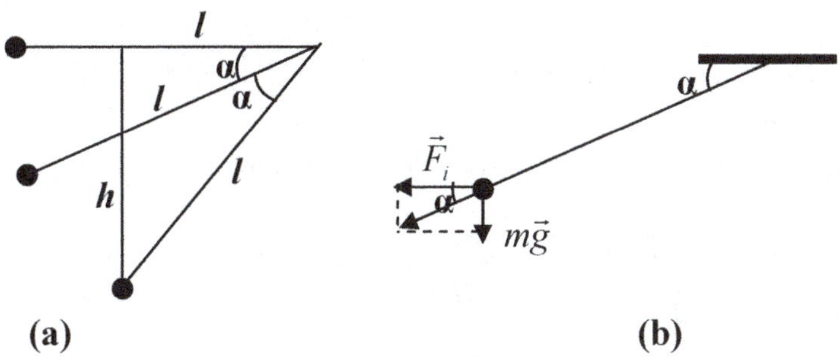

Figure 117

We can write the following expression for the equilibrium position, according to Figure 117b:

$$\cot\alpha = \frac{F_i}{m \cdot g} \quad (117.2)$$

then

$$\cot\alpha = \frac{a}{g} \quad (117.3)$$

By solving the equations (117.1) and (117.3), we obtain

$$a = g \cdot \frac{l + \sqrt{l^2 - h^2}}{h} = 24.48 \frac{m}{s^2} \quad (117.4)$$

118. In the situation when the system is stationary, the condition of translational equilibrium referring to body 2 can be written as follows

$$T + F_A = M \cdot g \quad (118.1)$$

where M is its mass.

From here, it follows that

$$m + \frac{\rho_0}{\rho} \cdot (1 - f) \cdot M = M \quad (118.2)$$

where m is the mass of body 1.

If we change the system's equilibrium position by sinking the body of mass M into the liquid, to a depth of y, we notice that the force of Archimedes (F_A) increases, which will take the system to the state of equilibrium:

$$\Delta F_A = y \cdot S \cdot \rho_0 \cdot g \quad (118.3)$$

On the other hand, we can write

$$\Delta F_A = (m + M) \cdot a \quad (118.4)$$

By taking into account the expression of the period

$$T = 2 \cdot \pi \cdot \frac{1}{\omega} \tag{118.5}$$

the expression for acceleration is

$$a = \omega^2 \cdot y \tag{118.6}$$

and by solving the equations above with the givens in the problem, we will obtain

$$T = 2 \cdot \pi \cdot \sqrt{\frac{h}{g} \cdot \frac{1+n}{1-n} \cdot (1-f)} \tag{118.7}$$

119. Since the amplitude represents the maximum displacement to which an oscillating particle can reach relative to the equilibrium position, we will be able to write

$$A = \frac{\Delta l}{2} - y \tag{119.1}$$

where Δl is the extension of the string at the moment the balls collide, and y is the extension occurred in the situation when the string is hung from the middle with the stationary balls attached to its ends (see Figure 119). Therefore

$$y = \frac{m \cdot g}{2 \cdot k} \tag{119.2}$$

and the expression of the extension Δl will be given by the expression

$$\frac{\Delta l}{2} = \frac{m \cdot g + F_{cf}}{2 \cdot k} \tag{119.3}$$

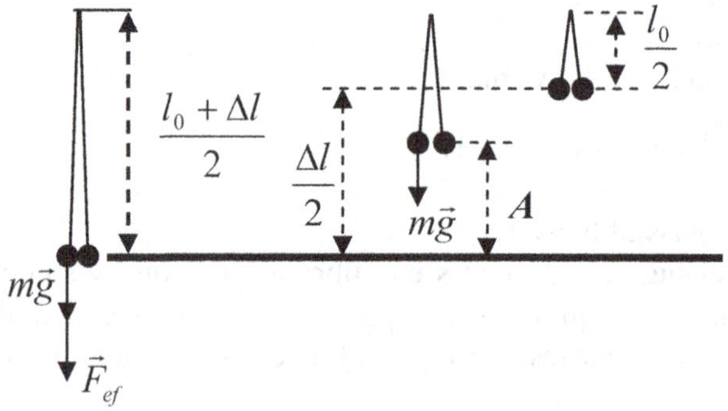

Figure 119

On the other hand, it follows that

$$F_{cf} = \frac{2 \cdot m \cdot \vartheta^2}{l_0 + \Delta l} \tag{119.4}$$

If we apply the law of conservation of energy, we obtain the expression of the velocity just before the collision

$$\frac{m \cdot \vartheta^2}{2} = m \cdot g \cdot \left(h + \frac{l_0}{2} + \frac{\Delta l}{2} \right) - k \cdot \frac{\Delta l^2}{2} \tag{119.5}$$

By solving the equations above, we obtain

$$A = \frac{\sqrt{(3 \cdot m \cdot g - l_0 \cdot k)^2 + 12 \cdot k \cdot m \cdot g \cdot (3 \cdot l_0 + 4 \cdot h)}}{12 \cdot k} - \frac{l_0}{12} - \frac{m \cdot g}{4 \cdot k} \tag{119.6}$$

120. By taking the system out of the position of equilibrium so that the difference between the levels of the liquid on the two arms is $2y$ (see Figure 120), the entire mass of liquid will tend to move so as to return to the equilibrium position. The acceleration imparted to it is due to the presence of elastic forces in the springs, as well as to the weight of the quantity of liquid on the right arm of the tube, above the maximum level on the left arm (at the height $2y$).

Therefore, we can write

$$M \cdot a = 2 \cdot k \cdot y + m \cdot g \tag{120.1}$$

where

$$m = y \cdot M \cdot \frac{1}{L} \tag{120.2}$$

By considering that the motion is harmoniously oscillatory, we can write

$$a = \omega^2 \cdot y \tag{120.3}$$

$$T = 2 \cdot \frac{\pi}{\omega} \tag{120.4}$$

By solving the equations above, we obtain

$$T = 2 \cdot \pi \sqrt{\frac{M \cdot L}{2 \cdot k \cdot L + M \cdot g}} = 1.14s. \tag{120.5}$$

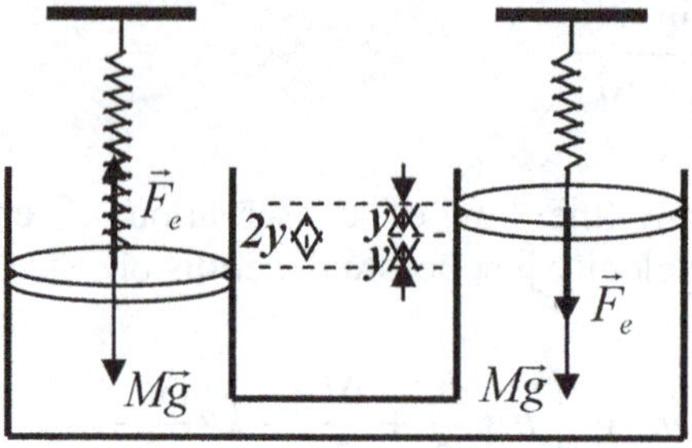

Figure 120

SUMMARY

Made in the USA
Monee, IL
08 January 2025

76352628R00105